THE TIME
of the DIAL

WILLIAM WASSERSTROM

IS THE AUTHOR OF

A *Dial* Miscellany

Heiress of All the Ages

THE TIME

of the DIAL

WILLIAM
WASSERSTROM

Syracuse University Press   1963

Set in Linotype Old Style No. 7 with
display in Monotype Deepdene. Designed
by Freeman Champney. Jacket design by
Freeman Champney and Frank Mahood.

*Manufactured in the United States of America
by the Vail-Ballou Press, Inc., Binghamton, New York*

TO
Rose

Acknowledgments

In writing this book I have been aided by a grant from the American Philosophical Society which enabled me to visit, in search of reminiscence, those persons who wrote for the magazine or knew its publishers; the Yale Collection of American Literature, where *The Dial*'s records are on deposit and from which I have drawn those items of unpublished correspondence cited in my notes; the Worcester Art Museum where The Dial Collection is on exhibit. To Conrad Aiken, Saul Bellow, Van Wyck Brooks, Kenneth Burke, Malcolm Cowley, E. E. Cummings, Granville Hicks, Lincoln Kirstein, Mr. and Mrs. Lewis Mumford, Marianne Moore, Gilbert Seldes, William Carlos Williams, and Dr. and Mrs. J. S. Watson, Jr. I am especially indebted. Conversations with Mr. Aiken, Mr. Bellow, Mr. Hicks, Miss Moore, Mr. and Mrs. Mumford, Mr. Seldes, and, during three years, Dr. Watson, account for some specific information; correspondence, both in the file of the magazine and in my own file, supplies the material on which I have based certain segments of my narrative and argument.

I am grateful, too, to Andrew Lytle, for permission to present here material which appeared in different form in *The Sewanee Review*.

Contents

THE TIME
of the DIAL

Introduction

"WHEN Margaret Fuller and Ralph Waldo Emerson edited their DIAL," said Scofield Thayer in January, 1921, describing the accomplishment of his *Dial* during its first year under his banner, "they met with little encouragement from that alien thing, the American public." And after "four thin transcendental years, THE DIAL cashed in." In Chicago in 1880 it reappeared and continued there for thirty-eight years but "did not put on flesh." Then in "the summer of 1918, Germany having created a diversion, the then publisher . . . [beat] a strategic retreat to . . . New York" where "politics were . . . dove into." Before long, postwar reconstruction lagged, readers fell away, and again "THE DIAL took for her health a somersault," came up on "more or less renovated feet, clad in reassuringly genteel tights," and "smiled stiffly at the world." Directed now by Thayer and James Sibley Watson, Jr., two wealthy young amateurs who were unwilling to "follow The Atlantic Monthly and confine themselves to skipping rope," *The Dial* by 1921 had acquired ten thousand readers. At mid-decade the number had tripled; *The Dial* had become the prime national monthly magazine of art, the one paper in which "exponents of both the accepted and the unaccepted," according to Thayer, were provided with "an agreeable carpet whereon they would fitly and cheek by jowl in their different ways perform." And at the start of its second year, said the editor, tracing this record of old transactions in former versions of his new journal, the management had grown accustomed to receiving only "tiresome letters from foreign and domestic pundits who say we are the best shot at a civilized journal yet fired in English."

One reason for this success and praise was that Watson and Thayer had devised their journal so cunningly that it would itself serve as a symbol of the kind of art they hoped to uncover and display. They did not create this program, but inherited it from a variety of older persons whose ideas, as we shall see, were adapted to this new kind of literary journalism. Their method was to publish, as if at random, the best available work in the new psychology, the new history, the new anthropology, the new philosophy, the new poetry, criticism, painting, and sculpture. Their aim, however, was to create a magazine which displayed the value of imagination in an age of science, the uses of art in the realm of ideas, the nature of spirit in the family of man. Although this was not a new undertaking, earlier magazines and other editors had lacked cash or taste or luck. Thayer and Watson, well endowed with money and mind, contrived to establish their journal as the chief ally of those men of letters who continued to hope that civilization might be saved after all—not by democracy but by art. This view of art as the best way to perceive and reveal radical truth, their belief that art alone can help men to perfect society, I have called the "prophetic imagination."

By designing their journal to embody and to foster this idea, Thayer and Watson assumed a unique role in a society bored by the jargon of American virtue incarnate in Woodrow Wilson and habitual in his address. If men could discover in art a new scheme of values based on a new system of signs and symbols drawn from the human imagination itself, and if the American people could be enticed to remodel their institutions according to this new image, the nation might finally achieve a true destiny. Turning from the politics to the arts of utopia, Thayer and Watson hoped to recover what Lewis Mumford was soon to call *The Golden Day.* Turning out *The Dial,* they evoked an earlier day when an American magazine first manifested the idea of special vocation in American letters, when a native journal deliberately sought to portray the peculiar genius of the American mind.

In order to write about the magazine itself, therefore, I have tried to treat a particular array of ideas and group of persons. These ideas, derived from the materials of social and intellectual history, from historic works by leading writers, furnish matter for special study in each section. Each chapter describes a peculiar segment of the presiding pattern of thought which is itself the subject of this book. To present a comprehensive account of all literary problems and events in the American 1920's is not, however, my aim. My purpose is to represent the chief manifestations and effects, from 1910 until 1960, of the prophetic imagination. To show in what ways *The Dial* is central to this mode of thought in American literary life is a main element in my work as a whole. In support of my analysis of its origins and influence, I have tried to include, either in the text or the notes, as complete a list of sources and references as is currently available. The text is designed to be a straightforward rendering of my argument. The notes, which contain matter from a substantial array of sources, are supposed not only to document but also to amplify. To those who consider my habits of prose or my argument itself nonchalant, allusive rather than exact, I recommend a closer study of the notes in order to test the sturdiness of the substructure.

The superstructure is visible in chapter headings, epigraphs, and text. In composing these, I have sought to identify which aspects of the prophetic mode recur in our culture and to specify which of its notions animate the minds of certain leading figures in American prose and verse. I have not prepared a series of close textual or historical studies of particular works by those writers whose names are invoked, but have introduced them in order to connote some of the ways my subject might be exploited by students of, say, Ezra Pound's career or Henry Miller's. *The Dial,* of course, was not the only journal supported by our writers, nor is its position the only one available in our literature. On the contrary, other little magazines, notably *The Little Review* and *Broom,* enlisted allegiances far more devoted and presented items more daring. But only *The Dial* possessed really high prestige in its own day and possessed a history which fifty years ago, even before its time of greatest celebrity, was unique in American literary journalism. Only *The Dial* transmuted the prophetic mode and adapted it to the uses of modern taste. This is the motif I have undertaken to isolate, stress, and study.

Because *The Dial* was in its own right a work of the creative imagination, an incident in the lives of its publishers, and an event in national history and in the history of ideas, I have sought to combine the virtues of a critic, whose concern is imagination, with the virtues of a biographer and historian, whose sphere is the interplay between private imagination and public life. Determined to place the journal itself in a proper frame, I have applied the modes of textual analysis—the key method of modern literary criticism—

to the study of the magazine as a whole. These techniques, which I suspect have not previously been applied to a work of this kind, have enabled me not only to say why *The Dial* is a representative event of the 1920's but also to describe the uses of a maligned but widely variegated term—organic. The word itself is crucial in the minds of those critics of literature and culture whose work shapes our thought.

Like *The Dial,* this word is central to the life of letters and the study of ideas in our time; like the journal, it evokes certain habitual notions about the nature of culture and the uses of art, notions both classic and current. And like *The Dial,* "organic" evokes an attitude toward art and life which was full blown in the America of the 1920's, an attitude which is today either disregarded or, as in Karl Popper's *The Poverty of Historicism,* disdained. Popper's book was written to discredit a view of history which assumes that prediction is a principal aim of the social sciences and that "this aim is attainable by discovering the 'rhythms' or the 'patterns,' the 'laws' or the 'trends' that underlie the evolution of history." Customarily, Popper argues, historicism is allied with "Utopianism" and bolstered by "the so-called . . . organic theory of social structure—the theory which interprets social groups by analogy with living organisms."

Although this term invariably refers to social theory, it has a much wider range of meanings than Popper implies. Invariably, too, it rests on the belief that nature, created according to some perfect principle of harmony and order, can somehow serve as a model of perfection for all the creations of men's minds. The term organic, however, describes analogy merely and does not, naturally, define what a living organism is. This inevitable failure of definition has led, inevitably, to disagreement over and confusion about the intrinsic nature of art, the proper aim of culture, and the value of the one for the perfection of the other. Indeed, its allure rests on the charm of plausibility. The history of its uses, then, is a record of an almost boundless number of diverse, even conflicting, opinions on the true nature of human life and on the ideal form of human culture.

Associating theory, term, and magazine, I have modified a procedure introduced by another student of history, Raymond Williams, whose *Culture and Society* connects some changes in English industrial and social life with changes in the meanings of key words. I have modified, too, my own earlier method of work: in *Heiress of All the Ages,* I portrayed the range and play of implications inherent in the study of literary plot and social character; I tried to present a kind of social psychology of American art. This present essay treats a single event of culture—*The Dial* —as a manifestation of a specific idea itself defined by a particular word that has a history, both foreign and domestic, of its own. That is to say, I have hoped to make available to American writers, teachers, scholars, and critics that "fresh inquiry into culture" to which Seymour Betsky, in reviewing Williams' book, refers. As one publisher's reader remarked, I have "resolutely *not* written the book that might have been expected." Using "organic" as a base and point of reference, I have sought to describe a certain configuration of thought in our literature, a movement in the life of this nation on which forty years ago *The Dial* imposed a pattern as yet unrecognized even among serious students of letters. Although I have repeated some of the ordinary things that some specialists know, I have placed these within a frame of thought which must itself be isolated and studied if we are to know where we stand in relation to the 1920's and earlier times.

"We are all prophets," Lee Simonson wrote to his friend Van Wyck Brooks, "Puritans like you and Hebrews like Waldo [Frank] and myself." Brooks adds, "All our generation had some such belief as this." However impoverished their belief now seems, however accurate Popper's reasons for condemnation, this idea nonetheless underlay the thought of at least three generations of writers in America. This book records its appearance and weight among historicist prophets of American organic utopia during the last fifty years. This volume and my *Dial* anthology are designed to recall the prophetic function of the organic idea in modern American art, criticism, politics, and character. Neither book has been written in order to say the last word; both may reopen certain lines of thought in our current conversation.

I. *The National Disease:*
EZRA POUND

> It was Tocqueville who first noted two strains in American life—intensive individualism and a positive genius for cooperation. The [Supreme Court] . . . mirrors the struggle—and synthesis. . . . Thus some of the justices have played the role of prophets and others of priests. In each era the prophets have taken the necessary leap into the future, and promoted the nation's growth . . . as an institution of freedom. The priests have conserved the American political tradition— equally important to such destiny.
>
> SAMUEL HOFSTADTER, Justice of the Supreme Court of the State of New York, *Letters to The Times*, September 27, 1959.

"IN THE BEGINNING all the world was America," John Locke wrote, and Arthur Schlesinger, Jr., quoting him, says that today the question is whether or not "all the world will be America again." [1] It is this concern with social order and national purpose which led Vladimir Nabokov in 1957 to choose *Martin Eden* as the most distinguished of Jack London's works. In *Pnin* Nabokov allows his hero, an émigré and an old-fashioned man, to enter an American bookstore in search of *Martin Eden*. This is the book Pnin has chosen as the best imaginable gift for a boy of fourteen. His decision is characteristic, for Assistant Professor Pnin is a specialist in knowledge for which there is no market at all. " 'Eden, Eden, Eden,' the tall dark lady in charge repeated . . . 'Let me see, you don't mean a book on the British statesman? Or do you?' 'I mean . . . a celebrated work by the celebrated American writer Jack London.' " Offered London's *The Son of the Wolf*, he remarks, " 'Strange . . . in Russia, I remember, everybody— little children, full-grown people, doctors, advocates—everybody read and reread him. This is not his best book but . . . I will take it.' " [2] Pnin accepts and presents the wrong book quite as he accepts disorder in a society of which he makes no sense at all and

7

within which his own public failure is itself a parody of our idea of value, of purposeless success. Pnin is foolish to believe that London is London whether the book is *Martin Eden* or *The Son of the Wolf*. Taste in the United States is not capricious but stupid if Americans can scarcely recall the one modern writer whose work represents their myth of special purpose to people elsewhere. Intelligence in Europe is naïve if Europeans expect America to keep its promise, to present the world with its gift—utopia. The modern history of purpose and purposelessness, then, is Nabokov's subject; extravagant parody is his method. And parody, the final stage of a style, dispels piety, enables us to gauge the effects of myth on the American imagination in our time.

I

In 1910 Jack London, the darling of his day, was the best known and highest paid writer in the world. Since that moment his reputation has declined and our wonder and confusion have increased because we are unable to name the reasons why he achieved eminence of any kind. "It is hard to say," Alfred Kazin remarked years ago, seeking reasons for London's prominence; perhaps he was admired "as one of the last Western adventurers, a 'pioneer Socialist' . . . the friend of all those boys who want to run away from home." [3] In *Martin Eden,* neither swashbuckling socialism nor Nietzschean self-glorification is stated or implied; frustration, not fulfillment, is the key idea. Indeed, we recreate London's state of mind and we learn a little about the source of his reputation once we realize that this novel blooms out of the same soil that supported Henry Adams' *Education.* Adams, of course, undertook to show that disorder was the only lesson taught by politics, art, religion, and history. The law of entropy, of dissipation, is the law of life. Thereby he explained the decay of sexual, moral, and social energies visible, to his eye, in all the places on earth but seen most clearly here. London worshiped at shrines established to honor Darwin and Herbert Spencer, Nietzsche and Marx; when Martin Eden discovers that these were men, not gods, he is bereft. Adams smiled at naïvetés of this sort, disposed of the systems with which science solved all problems, and substituted a scheme in which the very denial of method was itself systematic. Charmed by his own intelligence, delighted by his invention of a calculus of history which proved that duplicity is a function of being and irony the style suited to render it, absorbed in his own wit and sustained by his own bitterness, Adams learned to relish defeat and disorder. London's learning was of a different kind but led him to a similar view. He discovered that literary reputation was not earned but was instead conferred by fad or whim. He decided, too, that ignorance and self-interest were greater among the upper classes than among the lower. When he convinced himself that Spencer's system led nowhere, that emergent evolution did not work, he had no resources left. He proceeded to consume his fortune and to sell and destroy himself.

Adams and London do indeed make an odd pair. Adams was nobody's darling, but his book, written in 1906 and in process of revision for a general public in 1912, became a best-seller eight years later. Both men portrayed a situation of the spirit based on their recognition of chaos as the irremediable fact of life. London's work is the more poignant because it referred to matters aside from abstract thought; it incorporated the immediate life of an entire society and dismissed the faiths by which its people lived. Martin Eden, who begins his life affirming universal order and national honor, ends in suicide. And this is an appropriate climax for a novel written as a spontaneous gesture of disgust with the whole progressive idea.

The idea had become a public instrument of politics in 1870 when Samuel Tilden's platform, designed to represent the conscience of an aroused middle class, sought to reanimate that sense of vocation, of high purpose, that classic American idealism which was supposed to define the national spirit. From the beginnings of the colonial experience, America had symbolized nothing less than the immanence of God; this national substance embodied that metaphysical essence. What Hegel had hoped to proclaim for Germany, Emerson and hosts of idealist philosophers in America had established for the United States. After 1859, assimilating Darwin's work, they undertook to support their faith in the survival of those best fit to accomplish God's design for this chosen people. Having selected this land, He had sent His pilgrims to

create a nation destined, in spite of error and lapse, to lead mankind
through successive stages of culture until the perfect community
was established on earth. There, in Poe's city by the sea, Whittier's
snowbound family of man would keep what Melville called Greenwich time—would set its clock according to Christ's chronometer.
Americans would compose that perfect loving race of men and
women, both rural and urban, native and foreign born, which
Whitman "promulg'd" and which Edward Bellamy and other
socialists hoped to administer. Heir of all the ages, as James
imagined, this society blended New and Old World. If during the
first decade of the new century people were uncertain whose crusade to follow, Bryan's or Roosevelt's, Debs' or J. P. Morgan's,
nevertheless they agreed that sooner or later "American law,
American order and American civilization, and the American flag,"
as Senator Albert J. Beveridge stated his imperialist version of the
dream, "will plant themselves in shores hitherto bloody and be-
nighted." [4]

Although the world disbelieved similar aspirations in Germany
and Russia, people everywhere respected the American claim. For
America, everyone's new found land, symbolized the historic
yearning of mankind, not merely tribal greed. By 1912, these
legends had created both the Progressive party and that generation of mugwumps for whom today our historians of reform—
Arthur Link, Eric Goldman, Richard Hofstadter—reserve their
highest praise. London's disgust, however, included the legend, the
movement, the party, and its chief theorist, Herbert Croly. In
1909, Croly's *Promise of American Life*—a book which, according
to Walter Lippmann, "announced the end of the Age of Innocence"—had inspired the mugwump in highest standing, Theodore
Roosevelt, and provided the Progressive movement with a full-
fledged political philosophy. Croly foresaw a government run by
powerful officials, disinterested and professional, in the fashion
set by Thorstein Veblen's business engineers, who would create
that new nationalist state which might enable the American people
to fulfill their "historic mission." These officials could not abuse
their power because they themselves represented a new stage of
evolution, a new model for mankind elsewhere; they assumed
their duties because they were moved by the "feeling of human

brotherhood." All this, grasped at hopefully by many, Adams and London dismissed. And in *Martin Eden* London portrayed his own loss of hope that the forces of redemption would issue from the conscience of the rich.

Neither Adams nor London presents merely another instance of an ingrained gloom in the American imagination, a sympathy for the dismal or malign. Nor can we take their work to represent, in paradigm, a realm of thought which includes Mark Twain's "What Is Man?" or the naturalism of Frank Norris' fiction, Zola's boyish delight in animality and disaster, or even Dreiser's joy in Darwinian games of chance. All agreed that the meaning of life is its meaninglessness. Ordinarily, Dreiser is described as the first major novelist in whom we recognize this "new spirit." But his novelty and power do not derive from his effort to portray disorder itself. Rather, they derive from his decision to show the effects of social and metaphysical turmoil on those persons, of mixed culture, who were most fully exposed to the villainies of urban life. This remained his purpose even after 1912 when he read Jacques Loeb's *The Mechanistic Conception of Life.* There he discovered that human behavior is a matter of physiochemistry, that the human organism is no different in substance from the simplest microorganism. He did not assimilate the new learning; instead, using it to teach an old lesson, he wrote *The Financier* in praise of supermanship, the precise doctrine London had outgrown. In Dreiser's mind, the lobster eating the squid continued to teach men how they might surmount their fate. Only Adams the man of thought and London the man of action, this Brahmin and that wild westerner, the highbrow paleface and the lowbrow redskin, informed the most select of small publics and the largest of international audiences that the fate of America is catastrophe.

William James' *Will to Believe* in 1897 had offered the last gasp of grace. And though Americans cherished their own philosopher, men of thought realized that this work offered an argument no more reliable than the one which it resembled, Pascal's wager, but instead expressed the longings of a sweet and loving man. Twelve years later, Dewey's lecture on Darwin's contribution to philosophy placed squarely on humanity itself all responsibility for cataclysm or triumph, for the acquisition of knowledge and the application of learning. Indeed, from 1900 on, homegrown and foreign scholars, William Graham Sumner as well as Freud, demonstrated that civlization was not made according to God's directive, that the most subtle and the most primitive societies shared common traits and rituals. And no evolutionary principle of any kind whatever, naturalistic in Darwin's biology, idealistic in Herbert Spencer's or C. S. Peirce's philosophy, affirmed peculiar destiny. Franz Boas' *The Mind of Primitive Man* in 1911 "demonstrated conclusively that races and sub-races were mixed and possessed no stability; that no language was . . . superior to another," no people more highly gifted.[5] Oliver Wendell Holmes, too, rejecting the will to believe, maintained that ideas of justice stem from the practice of ordinary men in places remote and near, antique and modern. As in the law, so in philosophy it became increasingly hard for a man to concern himself with metaphysics; in Vienna and in Cambridge, the work of positivists concerned the visible universe alone. In 1912, the year when Spengler in Munich began his study of disintegration, Freud's *Totem and Taboo* offered a synthesis of the new learning. The leading motive which impelled men to establish culture, he said, was fear of nature's force. Ideas about law, order, religion, and art he attributed to oedipal struggle within the primitive tribal horde. Although Freud's extraordinary work frightened people everywhere, it was especially fearful in America where, as Paul Radin said of Boas' accomplishment, each paper, essay, and book destroyed a whole library of national beliefs.

It was of course the work of Thorstein Veblen and Charles Beard that hurt most. Veblen, more implacably forthright than colleagues at home and abroad, dispelled faith in a mystic capitalism that would guide men in the golden land. Instead of faith, this former student of Sumner's at Yale substituted an analysis of the machinery of enslavement. The analogue to Veblen's work appeared in the arts, in the painting of the Eight, members of the ashcan school whose pictures showed life dehumanized not only at Coney Island or the Bowery but at Tiffany's too. During 1908, their painting was seen, by audiences reared to cherish Rosa Bonheur, in New York, Philadelphia, Pittsburgh, Chicago, Toledo, and Indianapolis and given wide publicity as the work of the first

native American school of art.[6] And when in 1913 Beard published
his *Economic History of the Constitution,* American society had
begun to see things more realistically. Informed in the new art,
nevertheless it was shocked to learn that the old architecture of
the Republic was plaster and not marble. The devout in America
were no less distraught than the pious in France who in 1914, reading Gide's *Les Caves du Vatican,* were to discover the false pope
and his plastic saints. Beard was a more effective New Historian
than John Sloan, say, was a new painter or Gide a new novelist.
His style was acerb and not amiable. And if what Beard said was
true, then the "direct, impelling motive" that created the American Constitution was "the economic advantages which the bene-
ficiaries expected would accrue to themselves first, from their
action." "Eden had never been Eden," Max Lerner was to remark
twenty-five years later; the American dream was fake.[7]

Despite the age of reform, despite Herbert Croly's program and
theory, by 1913 American society lacked even a shred of respectable argument in justification of its dream. The men who published
newspapers and sat on boards of trustees, who assumed public
office or held professorial posts could rely no longer on the central
dogma in American life. "From 1912 onwards," Harold J. Laski
remarked in *The American Democracy,* "it was no longer possible
for America to wear the mask of youth or the mask of special
destiny, to conceal the fact that it was part of an ordinary world." [8]

2

This is the situation in which Americans of the older generation
found themselves during the last years before world war. Steeped
in the imagery of chaos, perplexed by the imagination of disaster,
society was unprepared for that unforeseen surge of effort which
occurred. Suddenly, among younger people, an inspired art undertook not merely to inhibit or even to shore up the ruins of culture
but to construct anew. Unfortunately we have not yet located or
diagnosed the conditions that supported this impulse. Our failure
is not dire; we have learned much about the work of these years.
But we are misled in ways which, though supportable, are unnecessary.

The quickest way to illustrate this confusion is to recall, as Richard Chase remarked, that there is no generally accepted name for "the six years or so after 1912 when the character of the modern movement in arts and letters was . . . finally able to break through the conventional surface of American life." [9] And the reason no label has stuck—Chase proposed that this period be named the Resurgence—is that no one has defined its character. Granville Hicks, who adopted the term renaissance, habitual among men of the 1920's, wondered "if the brief upsurge of new talent deserves to be called by that name." His wonder is misleading, however, because he believed that this upsurge represented nothing more than "a strong, though usually undirected, desire for a more decent civilization." "Out of the middle-class revolt at the turn of the century, with its muckraking and its trust-busting, its progressive governors and its single-tax mayors, had come a great hope," a "new insurgency," which in 1912 had no "unity or clarity," only vigor.[10] Kazin, too, preferred the term insurgence, hoped to discover the unity of the movement by naming its books, and agreed with Hicks that its vigor stemmed from "the intellectual ferment that attended Progressivism." Malcolm Cowley is even less cogent. He suggests a kind of cyclism in the economics of mind, a periodicity of boom and bust which maintains considerable prestige in criticism despite its bad reputation in other forms of thought. Our literary history, Cowley says, is a matter of "waves and troughs of waves"; the trough of 1900–10 was followed by the crest of 1912–18 which in turn was succeeded by "a kind of ditchwater," and so on. The same idea is fancier in William Phillips' treatment where it is furnished with the weight of "persistent tradition," a "periodic striving for a unified outlook and . . . inevitable return to a clean slate." [11] Others, F. J. Hoffman among many, search their experience and vocabulary for ways to say "contrivance, experiment and revolt." Forty years of study and speculation are contained, however, in Eric Goldman's glittering summary: "The New Freedom spawned a hundred other . . . escapes from the past—The New Poetry, The New History, The New Democracy, The New Art, The New Woman, the new anything so long as it . . . gave an intoxicating sense of freedom." [12]

If we continue to transmit ideas of this sort we must continue to rely on general theories of ebb and flow, of mere novelty or sheer intoxication. It is of course true that gaiety was the mood of those lyric years when Edna St. Vincent Millay's "Renascence," it is proverbial to say, signaled the arrival of the Resurgent generation. But when we summarize all we know, we discover that we possess a list of attributes, not a definition, of the capital thing. If it is true that the history of American art follows some deep dialectic, some pattern of tumescence and detumescence, then we must wonder why our arts take this pattern. If our inquiry compels us to confront, in the time of Resurgence, a revival of the spirit of Whitman, then we find ourselves studying a specific kind of cyclic renewal. Whatever this cycle may signify, its rhythm led Veblen, Beard, and other sophisticates of the muckrake to annihilate delusions which had sustained their countrymen during a century and a quarter of national life, and led, at that same instant of time, a new "bunch of utopians," as Max Eastman called his friends and associates, to turn to the arts hoping they might learn how to create that storied land of the heart's desire. Outcasts of Eden, they sought to establish a republic of letters which might convey to the nation at large their new vision of Whitman's order. Their subject was apocalypse; their aim was to dispel illusion but to salvage myth; their instrument was art. And their work displays a revival of the prophetic imagination in America.

Revival of Whitman's spirit is the one pervasive thing in a movement which, even at the time Miss Millay's poem appeared, was already a decade old. In 1903 Alfred Stieglitz, a man of prodigious power over taste and style not only in photography but also in American painting, drama, and fiction, opened his Photo-Secession Gallery in order to present works of art that displayed his vision of an "integral society." Stieglitz was certain that American culture would fulfill Whitman's prophecies, would become a "dynamic, organic whole," only when the nation as a whole took its inspiration from a properly accomplished "communal, creative movement" in the arts. To be certain that Stieglitz's program is characteristic not eccentric, we need only recall other manifestations of Whitman's spirit—on the masthead of *Poetry,* in *The Seven Arts,* and at the end of the famed wharf in Provincetown. There another group of utopians supported the efforts of still another prophet, George Cram Cook, to establish a "beloved community of life-givers." Cook's plan was to create a noncommercial theatre, an "oasis of living beauty," where art and utopia would fuse and flourish.[13]

At this point we must interrupt chronology and remark how each of these small groups attached its grand scheme to a classic term that evoked a historic doctrine—organicism. Indeed, both term and doctrine report the aims of prophets not only in the arts but in the fields of history and politics too. In 1910 when A. L. Lowell gave the presidential address to members of the Political Science Association, the shade of Whitman assumed corporeal—organic—form and specific weight. Although Lowell did not refer either to Whitman's person or poems, his address, "The Physiology of Politics," developed a scientific theory of government based on the same metaphor which the men of Whitman's generation had required for their philosophy of culture and art. Referring to the method and discourse of biology, Lowell urged his colleagues to treat human institutions, living society, as a form of discrete, organic matter. Conceived so, the organism of culture could be studied according to a discipline no less rigorous than that employed by cytologists or histologists. Once the ills of culture were diagnosed then surely cures would be found which in time might help to balm the world's ills.[14]

Before long, journals of political science offered preliminary results of this kind of inquiry. The speech itself was published in the *American Political Science Review,* a journal concerned with the pathology of everyday life, with disorders such as child labor and tenement housing. But the most striking public effect of Lowell's theory was its reappearance in the work of the man who served as his successor as president of the association, Woodrow Wilson. Adopting Lowell's metaphor, Wilson realized that it had a history of its own: from Carlyle back through the men of Enlightenment to Shakespeare and into Sophocles, the health of the body politic is a common subject and trope. What was unusual in 1910 was a certainty that physical science provided social science with reliable sanctions and method which enabled men to study and treat organs of government as if these were literally extensions of the human organism itself—a belief that image and idea were

one. The task of political science, Wilson told his colleagues, is
to discover why American life is composed of uncoordinated frag-
ments, "eager, competing interests, the disordered *disjecta membra* of a system which is no system, which does not even suggest
system, but which must somehow be built together into a whole
which shall be something more than the sum of its parts." Only
"organic processes of thought will give you organic processes" of
law, he said; "nothing else will." [15]

Only an organic literary criticism will give you an organic art,
J. E. Spingarn said; no other kind of criticism counts. In 1910,
Spingarn's famed lecture at Columbia on "The New Criticism"
argued that a work of art is a self-contained event of the imagination, a thing in itself that requires the proper kind of study else
it will be taken for something other than itself. He dismissed all
the old rules of rhetoric, all moral judgments of art. It is wrong
to argue, incidentally, as literary historians have been determined to argue, that Spingarn's essays have nothing to do with the
New Criticism, a term "originally used . . . by one of its leading
members, John Crowe Ransom, in his book of that title." This is
Murray Krieger's view, offered in a comprehensive and astute
study of modern movements in literature, *The New Apologists for
Poetry.* Krieger insists that Spingarn's essay is unrelated to Ransom's book except as "every critical school must begin with some
pretension of being 'new.' " [16] Surely there is a palpable and valid
difference of position in Ransom's work and Spingarn's: Ransom's
New Criticism is concerned only with the technical issues of art
and Spingarn's New Criticism includes the problem of relating art
and culture. Despite this distinction, however, both Ransom and
Spingarn are preoccupied by what Krieger calls the "organic
theory of imagination" and traces to Coleridge's "classic formulation." Literary structure is mechanical, Coleridge said, " 'when on
any given material we impress predetermined form, not necessarily
arising out of the properties of the material. . . . The organic
form, on the other hand, is innate: it shapes . . . itself from
within, and the fulness of its development is one and the same with
the perfection of its outward form. Such as the life is, such is the
form.' "

Before long—in the second chapter—we shall learn how

limited is the general view of this intricate matter. Now we are concerned with apparently random appearances, among men of prophetic imagination, of the organic idea. As spokesmen for what
Krieger calls the "Organic Theory of Poetic Creation," American
men of letters from Spingarn and Van Wyck Brooks to T. S. Eliot
share a peculiar respect for the "unique purposes of the poet as
seer." Spingarn is himself unique only because he first suggested
that critics might serve as seers too.* Drawing on Croce's work, on
the example of natural science, he maintained that meaning suf-
fuses form and form contains meaning. Thereby he established
a leading principle in modern literary theory. A critic, confronting
structure in order to comprehend meaning, experiencing the work
itself, determines whether or not the artist fulfilled his own design.
Only so can the act of criticism equal the act of creation, can a
poet receive the kind of serious attention his work requires rather
than the kind of appreciation customary among gentlemen of
letters.[17] Although Mencken was to sneer at "Major" Spingarn's
effort to refurbish old notions about art for art's sake, other critics
—even journalists such as Llewellyn Jones, who reviewed new
books for the *Chicago Evening Post*—defended both Croce and his
disciples. Jones observed that art is not more important than
morals, need not be "pursued to the exclusion of every other interest," but must be recognized as "a region free and autono-
mous." [18] Once this closely reasoned system of technical thought
was established in letters, then it would be possible for American
artists to assume their proper role in society. For Spingarn was
concerned with the interplay between literary and social theory

* Disregard of this American call to prophecy is the one lapse in Eric
Bentley's splendid study of the organic idea in nineteenth-century thought.
Carlyle, Nietzsche, Wagner, Spengler, D. H. Lawrence, and Stefan George are
"Heroic Vitalists," Bentley argues, who created a "religion of metabiology."
But their religion errs because "society is not a vital organism, as Heroic
Vitalists assume. A vital organism and a society are radically distinguished
by the fact that the individual components of a vital organism, namely the
cells, are morphologically as well as functionally differentiated, whereas the
individuals which compose a society are morphologically homogeneous and
only functionally differentiated. . . . As to function—the equation is more
plausible." American literary organicists are, of course, committed to the
plausibilities of function, not to the science of social morphology. *A Century
of Hero-Worship* (Philadelphia and New York, 1944), 257, 260.

and was not preoccupied with technique alone. Like President Wilson and other new scientists of politics, Spingarn urged new poets and new critics to understand their vocations in order to fulfill their mission. "For you," he said later, "America must always be not old but new, something unrealized, something to be created and to be given as an incredible gift to a hundred million men." [19]

From the earliest moments of Resurgence, therefore, the new politics, the new art, and the new criticism shared a common imagery and purpose. And when Woodrow Wilson, whom Granville Hicks called "a more potent force on our generation than any other one person," became president of the United States, he wrote into his 1913 inaugural address most of the ideas introduced in the address presented to colleagues in 1911. He vowed to scrutinize "with candid, fearless eyes" all the "deep, secret things" in industry, economics, and general culture. Then, prescribing cures which would fashion a healthy national organism, he would show his countrymen how to perfect their community and achieve the millennium. Statements of this kind led his contemporaries to see him as a man inspired, "more than just an idealist," Herbert Hoover thinks: "the personification of the heritage of idealism of the American people . . . a born crusader." [20] It is striking that another born crusader, Ezra Pound, at virtually the same moment in time, took on the presidency of the world of letters and urged *his* countrymen to know their subject and to learn the principle of structure in poetry and fiction if they hoped to recover from intellectual, moral, and social "dry-rot."

Before we refer to Pound, however, we must speak for a moment about Carl Becker. Among all the new social scientists of Resurgence, Becker is an exemplary figure. During its heyday, in 1915, he began a career based on the general effort to bolster old ideals with the new learning. His *Beginnings of the American People* established his reputation among associates who had forgotten that Franklin, a man steeped in the life of this world, required no metaphysics in order to affirm his American "sense of destiny and high mission in the world." Not only did this First American personify the dream, so Becker believed, but also he was himself the very personification of the organic idea; "all racial and religious antagonisms, all sectional and intercolonial jealousies, all class prejudice, were . . . comprehended and reconciled in Franklin." [21] By 1920, when Becker published *The United States: An Experiment in Democracy,* his books had made most respectable indeed a version of America quite antithetic to Beard's. It was a shade less well fashioned, perhaps, but beyond a shade less biased. For if Beard's study can be called a history of unnatural special interests, it is suitable to call Becker's work a natural history of American disinterestedness. Although every country is important in its own eyes, nevertheless some nations "have a wide significance for the world at large which gives them a peculiar place in the history of civilization. England, for example, has come to stand for what is roughly called political liberty." And France is recognized as "the source and exemplar of fruitful ideas. The United States . . . in its own eyes and in the eyes of Europe . . . has stood for the idea of democracy. . . . Its history has had the significance of a great social experiment." Becker sought to reinstate that image of America which "John Adams and his associates" had labored to achieve: "a republic founded upon virtue and devoted to the regeneration of the human race." [22] Recognizing this as a *human* desire, arguing that America is the symbol which portrays a historic longing for worldly order, Becker avoided mystique. He preferred not to evoke any forms of mysticism whatever, even though these would have supported his argument. He disregarded, therefore, all the utopians of the nineteenth century, the Shakers, Amanas, Universal Friends, Rappites, Owenites, Wrightists, who, according to their recent historian Everett Webber, saw in America the place "where . . . anything was possible," where they would establish "overnight what the people of Europe had struggled for more than five centuries to obtain." [23] Becker disdained sanctimony and, like his colleagues of political science, urged his compatriots to consider all "the subtler realities" of natural life if they would recreate America as the emblem, the image of redemption in this world.

Convinced that neither despair nor euphoria was a serviceable state of the spirit in government or history, Carl Becker helped to redirect the progressive idea and to establish that climate of opinion on which President Wilson was to rely and which Wilson himself was to coalesce. Becker's major work, *The Heavenly City*

of the Eighteenth Century Philosophers, established the authority
of notions first publicized during the days of Resurgence when
American men of letters, too, undertook to examine the forms in
order to diagnose the maladies of art. His famed essay refers in
detail to eighteenth-century ideas. But one of its main motives was
to show contiguity of thought and consistency of purpose among
American intellectuals—philosophers of Enlightenment as well as
technicians of Resurgence. Having decided that the American idea,
presumably a new thing in history, was in every way orthodox and
cyclic, having observed how closely his colleagues of Resurgence
resembled their predecessors, the men of Enlightenment, and having noticed that the eighteenth-century philosophers themselves
had relied on ideas drawn from a remote medieval European past,
Becker decided to study the idea of American apocalypse in order
to demonstrate that "the new history"—the phrase refers to a
state of the mind, not merely to one of its disciplines—"is an old
story."

Because Becker stressed the connections that linked sacred
and profane doctrine, between the American Constitution and St.
Augustine's *City of God,* his argument seemed to be merely ingenious at that time. Today, the view is familiar. It has been enlarged to include wide movements among intellectuals everywhere.
Arnold Toynbee, for example, traces the origins of a Universal
Republic of Letters to the idea of a Universal Christian Church
and suggests that the one, replacing the other, secularizes but preserves ancient aims. The sociologist Edward Shils remarks that intellectuals have long served as high priests in this church. Among
"The Traditions of Intellectuals," a most persistent motif is revolution, and this rests on what Shils calls the "apocalyptic or millenarian idea." Sacred or profane, the notion represents one of
the oldest human beliefs, the idea that our evil world, "so full of
temptation and corruption, will come to an end one day and will
be replaced by a purer and better world." Originating "in the
apocalyptic outlook of the prophets of the Old Testament," it reappears "in the Christian idea of the Kingdom of God, which early
Christians expected in their own time, and it lingers as a passionately turbulent stream." In Western thought from the eighteenth
century until today, the "millenarian" idea has been associated

with the American idea and embodied in what Albert Salomon calls "messianic bohemianism." [24]

Having connected diverse views drawn from various materials collected by disparate scholars, we are now equipped to say what special motives underlay Resurgence in 1910. At that moment, rebelling against the dogmas of the age of innocence—its social gentility, its "stupefying faith" in a "divinely ordered destiny," and its equally stupefying despair—American intellectuals came of age.[25] Ancient ardor for apocalypse inspired a new generation of messianic bohemians to try once again to fashion still another utopia. Unlike their predecessors in America, the Federalist men of government and literature, they were unwilling to settle for a mere alliance between the political republic and the republic of letters. For the first time in history, men of politics and art spoke a common tongue; this time, therefore, it was possible to insist on nothing less than millennium itself. And in 1912 when Woodrow Wilson was elected president, the national community and the republic of letters fused and became one, united by the organic idea in social science and art.

All these thoughts, aims, and habits of speech animate the mind, work, and life of the man whom T. S. Eliot proposed as the only reliable tutor for utopians who hoped to make the world accord with Whitman's image—Ezra Pound. Invoking Pound we must distinguish the redeemer from the traitor, the messianic bohemian of 1912 from the distraught prophet of 1960. A savior gone sour, he foreswore his nation because he believed it had abandoned him. "Have I a country at all . . . ?" he asked William Carlos Williams in 1920. At the same instant he proclaimed, with bravura, "not that I care a curse for ANY nation as such." Later he said to his teacher Felix Schelling, "You know damn well the country wouldn't feed me. The simple economic fact is that if I had returned to America I shd. have starved, and that to maintain anything like the standard of living, or indeed to live, *in* America from 1918 onwards I shd. have had to quadruple my earnings, i.e. it wd. have been impossible for me to devote *any* time to my REAL work." In response to Schelling's plea that he help reform America and not simply condemn it, he exploded, " 'HELP! Amer-

ica.' God damn it, look at the facts. What I have done right down
to this year. Got *American* authors printed abroad when foetid
American publishing system won't print 'em in America, because
the filthy money won't flow. . . . If there were not a hundred
American writers younger than myself who are grateful to me for
services rendered you might have some grounds for talking about
'HELP!' " [26]

A few years earlier, as Alan Valentine says in a book called
1913: America between Two Worlds, it was commonly held that
poetry would "dominate the next age." This expectation was first
announced in a historic work, John Macy's *The Spirit of American
Literature,* a work which celebrated Whitman's value as the chief
source of inspiration for all writers in the new age. Precisely these
same thoughts had occurred in Pound's mind at least as early as
1909 when he wrote "What I Feel about Walt Whitman." In this
essay he proclaimed that Whitman had "prophesied me": "The
vital part of my message . . . is the same as his." "I have declared my belief in the imminence of an American Risorgimento
. . . an intellectual awakening. This will have its effect not only
in the arts," Pound had written in another pamphlet, *Patria Mia,*
prepared before 1913, "but in life, in politics, in economics." "Letters are a nation's foreign office," and Ezra Pound is chief of state;
he vowed that he would work "with enthusiasm and a propaganda"
for American resurgence.[27] Years later he continued to urge Harriet Monroe to "keep on remindin' 'em that we aint bolcheviks,
but only the terrifyin' voice of civilization, kulchah, refinement,
aesthetic perception." This is of course the voice James had furnished Adam Verver in *The Golden Bowl,* echoed in Pound's warning to Miss Monroe: "The intelligence of the nation [is] more
important than the comfort or life of any one individual or the
bodily life of a whole generation." [28] Like Gertrude Stein, who
hoped to prove that "you could be a good American anywhere in
the world," he chose exile. But he knew that it was "about as
easy for an American to become a Chinaman . . . as for him to
acquire an Englishness, or a Frenchness, or a European-ness that
is more than half a skin deep."

From James he inherited his sense of office. From Ford Madox
Ford he derived his respect for propaganda. From T. E. Hulme he

learned to prize the theory, craft, and form of literature. Until
Pound decided that America had abandoned him and had con-
troverted its own promise, he had sought to exploit his own genius
in order to serve the genius of the nation. "Ezra had a forked red
beard," Ford in 1927 recalled the young man who had appeared
in London during the first decade of this century, "luxuriant hair,
an aggressive lank figure; one long blue single stone earring dan-
gled on his jawbone. He wore a purple hat, a green shirt, a black
velvet coat, vermilion socks . . . sandals . . . and trousers of
green billiard cloth . . . an immense flowing tie . . . hand-
painted by a Japanese Futurist poet." Robed in this elaborate
costume of decadence, Pound was so "aggressively trans-Atlantic,"
Ford said, that "mild Briton as I am, I have found him trying."
He "stupefies himself with the narcotics of reform. In that he
is very American—but what a poet!" [29]

Since 1920, when he ended his career as a propagandist for
America, he has made poems which are true to us in some fashion.
Answering *The Dial*'s inquiry in 1927 concerning his response to
its offer of *The Dial* Award, he wrote to Watson saying that it
was impossible for him to accept an award except for the Cantos
or for his verse as a whole. Thirty-one years later, returning to
Italy, he was asked to name the greatest American poet; after a
brief hesitation, he replied in a strong voice: "Ezra Pound."

The key to his own opinion of his verse is contained in a letter
to Marianne Moore written when she was *The Dial*'s editor. Speaking of Eliot's article on Irving Babbitt, he proposed that Miss
Moore allow him to write a reply which would advocate a form of
Roman polytheism instead of—at this point Pound's letter offers
a string of most vivid epithets—the usual kind of monotheistic
idiocies.[30] But he decided that this subject was better suited to
poetic treatment. The language and gist of this letter give a
clue to Pound's aims. His poetry crams our idiocies down our
throats and, sickened by forced feeding, we expel all the indigest-
ible stuff that attenuates our energies. My figure of speech, which
recalls the image common among men of government and history,
is adapted from another letter in which Pound refused to participate in an anthology edited by William Rose Benét. "I think you
have done too much harm, as asst. edtr. of the *Sat. Rev. Lit.*, from

year to year pouring poison into or onto the enfeebled or adolescent Amurkn mind." "You accept the worst infamies of American imbecility and superstition without a murmur, or without any persistent effort to clean up the mess." "How the deuce do you expect me to swallow all that for the sake of a small sum of money?" [31] But this half-mad homeopath of the arts forces us to swallow his poetry, the specific which will make our blood run clean once more; apocalypse won, we may say, once Americans receive a proper dose of Pound's purgative, *The Cantos.**

"I plead the missionary sperrit: guilty," Pound wrote to the man whom in private he called "that old titterer," Santayana. Beginning in 1910, this spirit invaded all the forms of art, all theories of government; Resurgence occurred when messianic bohemians, animated by the new spirit, brought to an end the age of stupefying faith and of serious disenchantment, the age of London and Adams. By 1922 we read in *Broom,* published by Harold Loeb and edited by Alfred Kreymborg, a letter from one of its readers admiring the new journal because it demonstrated that the new spirit in America "is broad enough to embrace not France only but Europe; not Europe only but the world." Furthermore, the "only way America can save itself and, incidentally, save others, is not . . . by delimiting itself but by extending its field to take in the whole planet." [32] The messianic delusion, H. L. Mencken said as the 1920's came to a close, "is our national disease." [33]

From 1910 until the 1940's, leading historians and theorists of culture, politicians and statesmen, artists, critics—all those priests and poets who sustain the prophetic imagination in America— shared this delusion. But it was Randolph Bourne who was to serve as the avatar of all the enthusiasts and diagnosticians of destiny, of those who sought to study only organic process in art and culture in order that they might root the idea of utopia in some fertile native ground. Leader of the "new fellowship," Bourne hoped to establish among men of letters a "league of youth

* "As there are great specialists and medical discoverities, so there are 'leading writers'; but once a discovery is made, the local practitioner is just as inexcusable as the discoverer himself if he fails to make use of known remedies and known prophylactics." *Literary Essays of Ezra Pound,* edited by T. S. Eliot (New York, 1954), 59.

. . . consciously framed with the purpose of creating, out of the blind chaos of American society, a fine, free, articulate cultural order." [34] Dying young, he left a legacy: *The Dial.*

Before his death, as we shall see, he made himself a spokesman for those men of ideas who experienced what Freud would have called a return of the repressed, a return of that dream which had molded the eighteenth century when new men shaped the new nation and equipped it to assume extraordinary duties in the affairs of the world. No mere ministry of culture, no official post in the Library of Congress suited the talents of men who were determined to remake the world. What they proposed, in Whitman's name, was a theory of organic form with which they hoped to inspire movements in the reform of society and in the salvation of art.

II. Lost, Right and Left:
ALFRED STIEGLITZ

Cairns: [Hegel] would have to exclude America from the development of his system, as he did anyway.
Van Doren: Exclude what?
Cairns: America.
Van Doren: I thought you said a "miracle."
Tate: It is the same thing.

HUNTINGTON CAIRNS, ALLEN TATE, MARK VAN DOREN, *Invitation to Learning*, New York, 1942.

I

"THE IMPACT of the First World War," Richard Chase said, "fragmented and dispersed the Resurgence," and left society with no coherent connections with its past, no certainties of art or culture, merely "the brilliant but unstable performances" of individual men of genius. Victims of this diaspora, we have not yet imagined any homeland at all. We remain pariahs on a lonely planet, suspended men, in William Phillips' phrase, whose last best hope is to maintain "the balance of opposing forces." Before long—in the final chapter—I shall speculate on the reasons why Chase and Phillips, among a group of critics much admired today, are concerned to explain how comfortable we are living in a state of suspended homelessness.

Remarking only that their view is a phenomenon of the 1940's and the 1950's, of the post-utopian era, we must speak first of the 1920's and 1930's when all American intellectuals seized and exploited the leading idea of Resurgence, that utopian vision of perfect homeliness, organicism. Alone among competing ideas, organicism invaded each sphere of thought, each program in politics and art. Despite disillusion, war, prohibition, normalcy, Depression, it seemed to promote an ethic that would reconstitute the body of culture, seemed to present at last a doctrine that guaranteed everyone's apocalypse. Only organicism drew sanctions from empiric philosophy in England and mystic philosophy in Germany, from American myth and Christian symbolism. Only organicism implied

a system, furnished an ideal, supplied an image of culture based
in literary theory. In America its charm was all the more compelling because its applications were infinite in a society that had begun to recover a notion of purpose but had not yet invented a
method. In order to understand the applications of the idea of
organicism in the 1920's and 1930's, we must first understand the
history of the idea itself.

The term is troublesome; its beginnings are murky and its
uses are myriad in the modern history of European and American
thought. "There is a great deal of spadework still to be done on the
origins and development of this idea," we read in an essay called
"Emerson and the Organic Metaphor," spadework especially
promising in Germany "from which it seems to have come to this
country and to Emerson." [1] Indeed, says that most talented student of conjunction between terminology and culture, Raymond
Williams, "Few English words are more difficult than 'organic,'
which has a vast and complicated semantic history." [2] However
indistinct its origins, no matter how complex its history, organicism involves some unique turns of phrase and defines a special
tenor of mind within that cluster of dialects which compose the
American language. We have referred to its first modern applications. Now we must speak of its wider uses during the Resurgence.
It achieved national celebrity in Van Wyck Brooks' program. In
behalf of an organic national community Brooks, who had been
a student of government under A. L. Lowell, published his first
work of prophecy, *America's Coming-of-Age.*[3] But the American
history of this idea is older than either Brooks or any of his
teachers and colleagues understood.* I shall therefore follow its

---

* Although certain critics and literary historians have sought to specify an
exact sequence of influences, in fact most resort to the kind of superficial
summary offered recently by René Wellek: "This organistic formalism has
many antecedents: it started in Germany late in the eighteenth century and
come to England with Coleridge. Through devious channels many of its ideas
entered the theories of French symbolism . . . and . . . from Hegel and
De Sanctis this organistic formalism found impressive formulation in . . .
Benedetto Croce. Coleridge, Croce, and French symbolism are the immediate
antecedents of modern English and American . . . New Criticism . . . [and
of] the positivistic psychology and utilitarian semantics of I. A. Richards."
"The Main Trends of Twentieth Century Literary Criticism," *The Yale Review,* LI (Autumn, 1961), 102–18.

course back and forth, back to the Puritans and forward again to
the utopians of the 1920's, the idealogues of the 1930's. In this way
I propose to set the scene for *The Dial* and to establish its time,
the years between 1920 and 1929, as the period of triumph for
organic style in American art.

Brooks, formulating his program, was aware of only a few
predecessors—Whitman, Lowell, Bernard Berenson, and the Russian Socialist Kropotkin "whom I still love," Brooks' friend Lewis
Mumford says today.[4] Mumford is not one of those young liberals
who "went into the army with Kropotkin under their arms" and
later, as Edmund Wilson remarked in 1927, claimed that "there
was something to be said for Mussolini."[5] Neither was Brooks,
who reserved for himself the task of adapting social theory to
literary theory, of blending Kropotkin and Whitman, socialism
and apocalypse, in order to furnish the argument which would stir
his generation. In his mind as in Henry Adams', organicism was
not a tricky figure of speech. Both men were certain that existence,
being mutable, obeyed laws common to all organisms, laws which
they embodied in a discourse of analogy. Adams, arguing that all
organisms by definition die—"vital energy obeys the law of ther-
mal energy"—proved that the American organism was already half
dead.

But it was Brooks who seized on the creed implicit in all
strands of organic philosophy. This creed, which he shares with two
other modern philosophers of the organic, Martin Buber and Alfred North Whitehead, and which reports the very assumption
that distinguishes romantic organicism from either scientific mechanism or platonic idealism, contends that the universal process of
dynamic change and irrepressible growth is the capital event of
being because it connects all human activities with the whole procedure of nature. To this basic belief Brooks added another
thought. Agreeing that art is itself pure process, he argued that a
society which prizes its artists must perforce embody the unremitting force of creativity itself. He then made that series of pro-
nouncements which enabled him to achieve his first fame. All our
ancient disparities—highbrow and lowbrow, "action, theory, idealism, business"—the artist-seer-prophet-priest casts "into a cruci-
ble" from which, "harmonious and molten," emerges a "fresh dem-

ocratic ideal" based upon "the whole personality" of man, the whole character of culture. Organic American art, Brooks said, properly attended, can nourish civilization.

Nearly twenty-five years later, Bernard DeVoto dismissed these ideas with a phrase, *The Literary Fallacy,* and a book which damned Brooks for believing "that a culture may be understood and judged solely by means of its literature, that literature embodies truly and completely . . . the values . . . of a culture, that . . . life is subordinate to literature." His book is respected still; his phrase occurs in our vocabulary. Even if we overlook inaccuracy, we may not disregard DeVoto's ignorance of those ideas, already historic, which underlay Brooks' work. For Brooks himself was moved to suffuse life and art when, as a student at Harvard in 1904, he discovered the "half-mythical figure" of Bernard Berenson who "in all matters of art . . . had ranged far beyond the limits" evident in his teacher, Charles Eliot Norton. Brooks' own dream of arcadia originated in Berenson's view of art, "his feeling that its function was to build a house for humanity to live in, to serve civilization by humanizing life. He called this life-enhancement." [6] At first Brooks associated Berenson's thought with Italian things, with Mazzini's idea of a harmonious planet in which each people plays a unique role within the entire community of man.[7] Later Brooks preferred to see correlations among Berenson, the architect Louis Sullivan, and the sculptor Horatio Greenough. Greenough, a pilgrim to Italy years before Ruskin arrived, was first to declare that form follows function, thereby offering the phrase and formula that epitomized all organic theories of art.[8]

Greenough, in these words, synthesized ideas drawn not only from his own imagination but also, we may assume, from Emerson's "Thoughts on Art" written for *The Dial* in January, 1841. "We feel in seeing a noble building," Emerson had said, "that it is spiritually organic, that is, had a necessity in nature . . . was one of the possible forms in the Divine mind, and is now only discovered and executed by the artist, not arbitrarily composed by him." [9] Whether or not Greenough responded to Emerson's influence, there is no doubt that Emerson, during those years of his life, composed his mind according to Carlyle's pattern. And Carlyle, like Coleridge, had taken ideas about organic art and culture from German sources, mainly Goethe and Herder, intuitionists whose vision of nature was based in their ideas on the nature of imagination. They derived a metaphysics of harmony, for example, from the physics of sound and then inferred a plan of the world from the structure of music. Unlike Germany, eighteenth-century England presented no one who regarded art as something "organically connected with society," the art historian Kenneth Clark maintains, as "something which springs inevitably from a way of life." "Standard writers of art criticism . . . all described art as something imposed . . . from without," as something mechanical. We are told that Edmund Burke was the last serious thinker who could find the organic in an existing society. And only when Coleridge, Carlyle, and Ruskin had domesticated the work of German masters did the life of art seem to present a model for the moral and cosmic experience of all men. Among all these social prophets of the early nineteenth century, "the key words," according to Raymond Williams, are "mechanical and organic. For what the artist perceives is 'organic,' not 'external,' form. The universal which he reveals is that organic life, Ruskin's 'Typical Beauty,' which is common throughout the universe, and is in fact a form of God." [10]

It is this sequence of European ideas that records a leading train of thought in romantic philosophy, a sequence which results in Greenough's phrase and Emerson's view. Imagining that the world is a "colossal image of the ideal poem," they adopted the European vision. Like Europeans, too, they believed there was in this image an ideal formula for culture: as an artist, guided by personal genius, invents his masterwork, so all men, exploiting similar powers, labor to create their masterpiece, the world. A culture is organic, a work of art—even a figure of speech—is organic precisely because each of its parts interacts with every other part, because it comes into being when its segments in concert and in confluence produce a dynamic whole. American literary men required no flash or leap of fancy in order to see this republic, built of component parts neatly interlocked, ingeniously federal, mirrored in the key principle of organic theory. Indeed, it is tempting to say that Emerson had gone abroad to find an English label and German authority for a thread of thought that led back to those

Federalist men of letters who had founded the *Monthly Anthology* in Boston and the *Port-Folio* in Philadelphia in order to publicize the "parallel between the Federalist logic of political order" and perfect "literary order." [11] Although the term organic does not occur until the nineteenth century, its scheme had appeared during the moment of origins in American critical thought when it explained the process, justified the structure, and certified the value of community in the New World.

Characteristically, the prophetic American imagination first expropriates, then transforms into the discourse of utopia, and finally molds into the legend of mission any proposal of the human intelligence that seems at all suited to its vision of apocalypse. By the middle of the nineteenth century, when organicists had seen how clearly their community incarnated their philosophy, this enterprise was in full swing. They found, however that no one had yet explained one factor—the exact way in which organic art transmits itself, manages to yield itself to the mind—and that explanation of this matter was crucial because their system required precise analysis of the exact relation between writers and readers in order to be dynamic and not purely mechanical. To be properly organic, to possess dynamic life, a work must bring new life to its reader during the very instant when it comes into existence within his mind. Europeans from Coleridge to Ruskin had solved this problem by insisting that somewhere inside the mind there was a special faculty, a moral sense or infallible instinct, which molded human sensibility. This faculty enabled men of genius to create and ordinary men to experience any work of imagination. Among American organicists Poe alone found this an appealing and convincing thought; his associates required a sturdier idea on which to build their ideal community. They substituted in its place a formulation that dates from the earliest time of serious verse in America and can be seen as the special claim of organic art throughout our literary history, the notion of a special sort of transaction, a kind of sacred rite.

American organicism is the first modern movement to seize on the Christian ritual of communion as a paradigm for the secular ritual of art. Subtlety on this point is the more remarkable because today the metaphor itself, communion, reappears among leading students of myth and language who conceive a common origin for the radical motives of religion and art. Although religionists do not dispute these theories, they do distinguish between the kinds of truth rendered in both spheres; they insist on seeing a transcendent or ultimate reality represented in the symbolisms of their faith. Secularists in their turn offer arguments, often no less arcane than those of the religionists, which say that "symbols and myths are an expression of man's unique self-consciousness," inventions of speech that express man's capacity not merely to experience himself as "a being having a world" but also to contrive a way of sharing his experience.[12] Members of each group tend to agree that the language of art, like the work of religion, is "intended to carry on and revive the communication, indeed the communion," which links man to the "perennial sources of life." [13]

Organicists adopted this metaphor in part because it described ideal union between a poet and his public and in part because it offered a theory of communication that completed a great circle of ideas in which cosmic, social, and literary order were interlocked. In this way, too, they joined the twin traditions of American thought, rationalist and Puritan. For their figure of speech was drawn from no alien people or remote philosophy. It came from the American Puritan community itself where a series of covenants—of Church, of Grace, and of the Civil Order—had provided "a kind of organic unity," as Charles Feidelson says, which enabled each member to participate in the prime mystery of Christian belief, the union of divine nature and human nature in Jesus Christ.[14] Election into the church confirmed membership within the community and celebrated a perfect communion between its members and their Savior. In order to describe the things that happen to a poem and its public during the moment of intercourse, organic art adapted and transposed terminology drawn from this crucial Puritan sacrament.

Both terminology and sacrament, in fact, appear first in poems by the Puritan Edward Taylor. Because Taylor did not publish his poems there is no demonstrable connection between the uses of communion in organic theory and the uses of communion in Puritan art. Nevertheless, it is exactly this cluster of attitudes which the poet sought to introduce in his long series of short poems, "Meditations," written during 1711 and 1712. Basing his poetry on key texts from the Bible, Taylor set himself a fearsome task which is as yet quite misunderstood. His best-informed editor says that the "Meditations" reveal Taylor's determination to define "his own notion that the sacrament is a spiritual banquet," its prototype being the Lord's Supper, "in which the participant enjoys a real spiritual and mystical union with the Lord."[15] A remark of this kind, however proverbial, distorts the truly portentous thing. For Taylor's poems do not try to define anything. Problems of definition he treated in prose sermons. The problem he reserved for verse was how to reproduce the most sacred of all experiences his mind could imagine, the mystery of communion itself. It is this effort to communicate the very experience of salvation that makes his poems "distinctively American" and marks "the beginnings of an American . . . literature." What distinguished him in this way was not, as Louis L. Martz thinks, his invention of a special mixture of polite and vulgar language which no British meditative poet would dare to use.[16]

To exploit the language of art in order to manifest ultimate, transcendent reality is the aim of Taylor's "Meditations." Only a poet-priest selected by God to fill two offices, a Puritan baptized and elected into the community of saints by means of the precious sacrament of communion, could hope to communicate in art the mystery of union between man and Christ. Only he might dare to offer his readers poetry designed to link writer and reader in a union scarcely less precious and mysterious, poetry composed in order to harmonize earth, heaven, utopia, apocalypse and thereby to offer sheer salvation itself. And this is to say that he alone was competent to write poems that performed the very ritual which constituted their subject. Reading Taylor's "Meditations," finding ourselves in the act of taking communion, we discover ourselves participating in a ritual which enacts the very heresy all orthodox Puritans were supposed to abominate—the Arminian. The poet has performed an office which the priest is forbidden to practice outside the church. Taylor, like the Jesuit Gerard Hopkins, was enthralled by the grandeur of ambitions that seemed to contradict the logic of piety but to confirm the logic of his poetry. It may well be that he chose to hide rather than print his poems in order to circumvent the charge of heresy. Surely these "Meditations" fulfilled all the requirements of orthodoxy but one, the requirement that salvation be offered only to communicants properly certified: those saved by God's grace not by the poet's grace were qualified to receive the sacrament of communion, were fit to take part in the experience Taylor's art made available to everyone.

Edward Taylor's "Meditations," therefore, prefigure those works of prophetic art which were to offer the kind of communion admired by secular men such as the "Puritan" Van Wyck Brooks who sought salvation in the arts of socialism. Similar motives led a particular group of prophets during the days of transcendentalism to strip organic art from its old theology and transfer its central doctrine from the Christian republic to the republic of letters. The work of transfer was accomplished by those mavericks of the spirit—Theodore Parker and Orestes Brownson, Emerson and Thoreau—who, as R. W. B. Lewis remarks, turned Puritanism upside down. Reared to prize the doctrine of communion, unique symbol of their faith, determined to dilate its meaning, they treated this as an emblem of union in all realms of life and art. Thoreau, for instance, often spoke of devising a sacrament of secular culture which might "bring into being the natural man" whom people everywhere long hoped would prosper here. Brownson, whose sympathies were with the "party of Hope," with those persons who, like the members of another group called Young America, hoped to create a national literature, "pushed and reasoned his way toward his doctrine of communion during the year or so after attending Parker's lectures." By communion, Brownson wrote (in June, 1842), he meant "the doctrine that man lives by communion with man, and through the life derived from Jesus, with God." In his mind the term describes a social gospel of "co-operation, working together," a theology which might resolve "the question of community" in the world.[17]

It was Whitman, however, enlisting himself in a movement which had originated during the 1830's among members of a gentleman's literary club, the Tetractys, who assumed the office of high priest of communal art. In the 1840's and 1850's this movement had developed its own vehicle, the *American Review*, modeled in part on the Emerson-Margaret Fuller *Dial*. By 1858

Whitman described it as "a monthly magazine of a profounder quality than any other," and decided that both the movement and its journal were remarkable because they represented his own views. The first duty of the American poet, he said, was to disregard "the canons of 'mechanical' critics" who quite mistake the nature of dynamic national art. It was in this journal, incidentally, that Greenough had first "broached" his organic theory of structure, a theory consistent with and perhaps the source of Whitman's distinction between mechanical and "progressive." It was mainly in the *American Review* and largely as a result of this accumulation of ideas that organicists at midcentury had revitalized the whole vocabulary or art. In place of a closed circuit mechanism, the world was represented as a dynamic revolutionary oganism in which American poets were called to special mission. They were duty-bound to manifest and communicate to their own people, to the peoples of the world, what Whitman called "democracy, America's destiny," and the progressive "spirit of the age." [18]

2

Almost exactly the same mood and virtually the same doctrines reappear in the theories of organic structure and salvation offered by members of the Resurgent generation. Whatever movement they shaped, left or right or center, whatever hero they worshiped, their work is continuous with the whole history of organicism in America. I stress this fact because critics today habitually treat organic philosophy as a form of politics invented by Brooks and his circle, a form once vital and now dead. A few years ago, for instance, F. W. Dupee in an essay on Brooks referred to that "extravagance . . . commonly generated by the 'organic' conception of society," and wondered how an idea could seem attractive and interesting at one moment, only to be swept a moment later into "obsolescence." [19]

Like DeVoto's misconception, this distorts the facts of letters in our day. When men in all spheres of work rediscovered the organic idea, they believed they had found at last the most serviceable and viable of all systems of culture. In the arts, as we know, it was Brooks who publicized their rediscovery. But it was Stieglitz who served as a teacher to those writers and painters, critics and composers who felt the call. Born in 1864, schooled in New York during the 1870's and in Germany and Italy during the 1880's, returning to the United States to work by 1890, Stieglitz began his career as a pioneer of photography whose dedication to the international life of advanced art was absolute. During those years when the undergraduate Brooks dreamt of Berenson's Arcadia, Stieglitz tried to turn mood and desire into concept and picture. Whereas Brooks touched only the edge of mysticism, Stieglitz was a "mystagogue" of the most compelling kind. In 1903 this oracle placed him in Edward Steichen's former studio where he remained until 1917; there, he said in 1942, "the ice was broken for modern art." Steichen, commuting between New York and Paris, between Stieglitz and Gertrude Stein, brought pictures which Stieglitz exhibited and criticized. Specialists agree that the effects of his criticism are unmistakable in the painting of those American artists— John Marin, Marsden Hartley, Georgia O'Keeffe, Charles Demuth —who came to see and to listen. We know, too, that a large group of writers—Sherwood Anderson and Waldo Frank, James Oppenheim, Henry McBride, Paul Rosenfeld—developed styles in accord with his taste. These are of course the leading figures of Resurgence, the men of art who responded to Brooks' demand that American intellectuals found a school which would lead and inspire the nation.

Brooks shaped their theory and carried their banner, but Stieglitz, their teacher, was himself the chief source of inspiration. Advanced in science and in art, he seemed to invest John Dewey's order with Whitman's ardor. In Sherwood Anderson's impressionable mind, for example, Stieglitz was a "City Plowman," who harmonized Gopher Prairie and Cosmopolis, West and East, Europe and America; in Mumford's most acute intelligence, Stieglitz is identified with "the soil of Manhattan and the pavement of New York." Anyone tapped by Stieglitz was touched by Whitman, and, electrified, vibrated with the spirit of a city, of a nation, which could open itself to everything exotic yet present itself in composite as an American place. As Harold Rugg believed, John Dewey had absorbed the work of research physiologists, neurologists, and endocrinologists in order to create a system which demonstrated, in Stieglitz's words, that "mind is not independent of body" but that the two together compose "one dynamic organic whole. Body and mind are organism not Mechanism."

Stieglitz realized his genius not only as a photographer but also as a theorist who spoke endlessly on one subject alone. Whitman wrote one book and Alfred Stieglitz held a single monologue in which he sang of himself and of all men. "He would talk for hours, for entire days. . . . People came, departed," but on he went in what Waldo Frank calls his "stintless stream of talk, the ever-widening circles of his talk." "He talked me deaf, dumb and blind," says William Carlos Williams, one of those who left. Others stayed. And when they were asked what Stieglitz talked about, they agreed: "He wanted to find out if the pictures he was showing were really alive—what they said to people and what people would become from having seen them. Stieglitz was interested in the *life* of a picture," Harold Clurman decided, and this "included the life of those who made and those who saw them." "To such people he could give life," Paul Rosenfeld adds, "and from them get it in exchange."

Chief spokesman for the total transaction of art, Stieglitz assumed the role of "leader of a communal creative movement, within the march of modern thought." Fulfilling this role, "he undertook to build up an organic statement that shall be different from the sum of the words as a live body is different from the sum of its constituents," said Waldo Frank, whose opinion is notable because it helped to create *The Seven Arts*. Stieglitz was convinced that art, itself the ideal form of civilization, offered a paradigm of order and harmony. Lovingly, therefore, he talked art. He sought to breathe life into the creative spirit in order that it might recreate out of chaos that supreme work of the imagination, America, "a new civilization, a new culture, a new world" where no artist would feel himself alien or would require the kind of irony which shielded Melville and Emily Dickinson, led Mark Twain to his bed, and forced James to renounce his citizenship. Presenting a model life in art, a perfect image of the interconnection between imagination and real life, Stieglitz inspired his disciples to re-establish the dream of an "integral society in which a true person can live . . . in which the whole"—no *disjecta membra*—"gives health to its individual components, even as its individuals . . . give health to the whole." [20]

Although this model and this theory remain viable in our letters, both are today axiomatic in the minds of men responsible for more public works. "The city, as Lewis Mumford says, *is* art," Cleveland Rodgers remarked in 1944. Rodgers, a leading member of the City Planning Commission in New York and an early associate of Robert Moses, treated this as a conceit peculiar to the American imagination. Like Rodgers, the English editors of *The Studio,* an important journal which that year ran a special issue on the arts in America, pointed to many examples of "the great work which can be accomplished for the national well-being by the intelligent and visionary harnessing of art to the life of the people." [21] In 1946 precisely the same idea was on display when the Maxim and Martha Karolik Collection of American paintings, chiefly primitive, was exhibited everywhere.[22] In planning and in painting, therefore, from the Resurgence until now, Stieglitz remains a force.

His influence in literature is more subtle and perhaps less persistent. At first, however, it inspired those men of letters whose first allegiance was to America and who, like leaders of American renaissance in other spheres of thought, hoped to articulate a theory of national life which accounted for the past and promised a future. Ordinarily they are described as chauvinists of American art or as progressives engaged in building Herbert Croly's republic, more or less willing to take war in stride and to accept American entry as a suitable event in the process of national destiny. But a true organicist of art was a patriot whose first allegiance was to the republic of letters, the only place on earth where men would discover the ways to El Dorado. This particular republic of letters, which sought utopia through an organic theory of art, was founded a century earlier, we must recall, by some distinguished English poets, many of whom agreed that America is the best symbol of fulfillment in this world.

In the United States during the second decade of this century, Stieglitz and Brooks were the most persuasive citizens of this republic. As they labored to establish its cult, others were engaged

in similar tasks in the realm of literature itself. New manifestoes
undertook to amend ancient laws; new journals sought to enfran-
chise the latest generation and to establish new spheres of influence. The most accomplished work was done not by politicians of
the avant-garde but by poets who composed individual works that
achieved personal conquests of idiom, syntax, figure, and form.
During the period between 1912 and 1919 there was considerable
intercourse between the two groups—between *The Seven Arts*
group and *The Little Review* group. And in 1919 when *The Dial*
began its career, both groups did in fact become one.

Harriet Monroe's *Poetry* was staunch for controlled novelty
and ordered freedom, and in 1913, one year after this journal
appeared, Alfred Kreymborg brought out *Others* as its replacement. *Poetry* was no longer "a forum wherein competent poets
might speak freely," Kreymborg's friend Williams decided, but
was merely another paper held rigid in "the usual editorial position." [23] Margaret Anderson's *Little Review,* however, managed
to charm everyone, both the wild and the docile new writers, for
the editor possessed a flexible mind which contained in disarray
all the most advanced ideas. She was an inflamed woman who became everybody's special flame: Floyd Dell recalls her "starry-
eyed, unearthly young loveliness," and Gorham Munson refers to
her as the "Goddess of the arts," who created "a magazine that
believes in Life for Art's sake." She was driven by a most American "obsession for enlightening the world," and though this
obsession helped to sharpen her wit, it never unified her journal or
made it self-sustaining.[24] When Ezra Pound resigned his post as
foreign editor, she decided to work for a different sort of apocalypse. She left for France's Institute for the Harmonious Development of Man, where Gurdjieff held court. Gurdjieff, "a seer, a
prophet, a messiah" of a new order composed of mathematics, art,
and the occult, mystified but thrilled Miss Anderson, herself a
mythologist without a myth.[25]

This commitment did not revitalize *The Little Review* but instead led Miss Anderson to lose interest in her journal and its
causes. Despite one great success—publication of Joyce—and
some small accomplishments, the magazine acquired only minor
influence among a public, sturdy and gallant, which responded

more to the editor's personal fire than to her taste. Her only clear overt aim, to present "all the best writers concentrated . . . brought together in an American periodical," pleased contributors who sought a proper forum. But it never provided the magazine itself with a distinct form. At a time when men of letters hoped to create forms of art which displayed the true state of affairs in the spirit, forms which would in turn enable men of affairs to conceive programs of state, forms in which program and poem were one, Miss Anderson's method was inappropriate indeed.

The only program available, Stieglitz's, came to seem all the more portentous. His system had been inherent in his own early journal, *Camera Work,* but it was explicit and even flaunted in every department of two monthly magazines published during 1916 and 1917, *Soil* and *Seven Arts.* These were not magazines of art but were designed to embody the multitudinous life of imagination in America. Every sphere of the national life, every mode of the creative process, was to be represented in a magazine which sought to be neither a political nor a literary paper but the house organ of the whole family of man.* Reproducing in *Soil* the massive work of technology, the power of sport, the explosiveness of poetry, Robert Coady hoped to account for Charlie Chaplin and Wallace Stevens—both the comedian and the letter C.[26]

Before long *Soil,* like so many pioneer little magazines, suspended publication. But *The Seven Arts,* created by men who attended daily sessions at Stieglitz's famous gallery, 291 Fifth Avenue, revived and refurbished Coady's design. "As I recall it," Brooks says in reminiscence, "Waldo Frank was the real creator

---

* "In 1916, Robert Coady, whom [Harold] Loeb and I regarded as an important precursor in the field of popular arts, had published a few numbers of the highly original magazine, *The Soil,* in which selections from Nick Carter's dime novels, scenes from Chaplin's slapstick movies, and photographs of the pugilist Jack Johnson in combat, as well as pictures of new skyscrapers and naked machines, had all been printed together as a medley of native art. 'The true American art,' Coady declared, 'is as yet outside our art world'; it was growing up 'out of the soil,' out of the folkways of our people." Matthew Josephson, *Life Among the Surrealists* (New York, 1962), 190. In *The Dial,* Thayer, who printed sketches of boxing, wrote about boxers, and preferred critical comment on matters of popular culture to mere display of scenes from films, undertook to incorporate Coady's idea of true art within the main arena of American culture.

of *The Seven Arts.*" Frank himself credits James Oppenheim who
in turn recalls meeting Mrs. A. K. Rankine, a lady "who had a
collection of Whistlers and was bored looking at them." Oppenheim convinced her that the pictures must be sold, that she had
been chosen to become the patron of a magazine which he would
introduce and edit. Brooks remarks, fancifully, that this lonely
woman was especially responsive to an appeal of this kind; her
analyst had suggested that a magazine might very well serve as an
"excellent therapeutic measure" in her effort to recover health.
Mrs. Rankine, hoping somehow to achieve a form of personal communion, therefore supplied cash for a venture which sought to end
that loneliness "written all over the faces of the earlier writers
. . . E. A. Robinson and Theodore Dreiser," and to substitute
"a feeling of common cause, the sense of a community of writers
building a new culture." [27] "Although I was in my mid-thirties at
the time," Oppenheim wrote fifteen years after the event, "I was
still shockingly idealistic." "I believed that that lost soul among
nations, America, could be regenerated" by a magazine which
would "evoke and utilize all our native talent, both creative and
critical, give it freedom of expression and so scatter broadcast the
new Americanism." [28] Because Brooks' essay had "struck the note
of the new day," Oppenheim, Frank, and Paul Rosenfeld invited
Brooks to join their staff. This trio was "wild enough to believe
that the artists and critics" could save America, could perform
therapy on the nation and the world.

Sentimental slop, Ezra Pound said. No longer committed to
American renaissance, Pound enjoyed his new role as a leading
international authority on letters. His authority might have been
less formidable, Brooks thinks, had Randolph Bourne "lived long
enough to counterattack." And in truth Bourne, described by his
biographer as "our equivalent for Bertrand Russell," was the most
gifted of those brilliant young men who composed *The Seven Arts*
group.[29] Like Carl Becker at Cornell, Bourne was a "true-blue intellectual," a dedicated "enlightened man" who very early had
decided, beyond slop and invocation, precisely why he prized this
country and its art. "America is already the world-federation in
miniature, the continent where for the first time in history has
been achieved that miracle of hope, the peaceful living side by

side, with character substantially preserved, of the most hetero-
geneous peoples" on earth.[30] Here he saw a cosmopolitan group of
foreign cultures and, like Whitman and Stieglitz, he was certain
that New York was its symbol. In America, no one is melted down
in a pot but is fired in a kiln where personality is confirmed, not
dissipated. America, manifesting what Bourne called transnationality, was destined to fulfill historic prophecies because these
states alone achieved that organic culture for which all civilized
men yearn.

During the last years of his life, Bourne's most important work
appeared in *The Seven Arts* where his program, a dilation of Stieglitz's, was welcomed both at home and abroad. Europeans who had
just finished reading Thomas Hardy's *Dynasts* felt that this journal and its idea came in the nick of time, that its light glowed
strong enough to penetrate the "war-darkness" of 1916 when an
"all-embracing pessimism," Jean Cocteau says, created Vorticism
and Dada among men made wretched by the crisis and collapse of
Western intelligence.[31] At this time, when European letters offered
the solace of hopelessness to underground men everywhere, *The
Seven Arts* made Bourne available in Europe and thereby helped
to establish what Raffaello Piccoli, in *The Dial* for April, 1923,
was to describe as "that Messianic spirit which filled the European
atmosphere at the end of the War. . . . Millennium was the name
of the only land to which it seemed possible and reasonable to
travel." Six years earlier Romain Rolland had welcomed *The
Seven Arts* as the chief herald and emblem of apocalypse. "I re-
joice," he had written to the editors, seeing a magazine in which
"the American spirit may seek to achieve consciousness of its
nature and its goal." And he advised them to seek out their "people's dreams and trials. . . . Aspire to be the Light flushing the
darkness of those murmurous [American] masses," for these compose the community of men which has been "called to recreate the
world." [32]

A year later, however, Bourne himself despaired. In *The Seven
Arts* for August, 1917, he and John Reed in separate essays described "The Collapse of American Strategy" in "This Unpopular
War." Bourne traced collapse to our entry as a wholehearted ally
of the Entente. Although entry itself cost us "the initiative for

peace," American liberals, hoping to salvage the shreds of virtue, "trusted the President to use American participation as an instrument in liberalizing the war aims of all the Allied governments." They hoped that Wilson, remaining disinterested, might succeed in making the world a little better. But the president chose to support autocracy in Italy, France, and England. For this reason, Bourne concluded, "the key to our American strategy has been surrendered" to the only nation that remained true to the liberal idea—Russia. The initiative had passed from Wilson to "the new Russian government," which now assumed the duty of declaring "democratic war-aims." In this spirit the editor wrote a poem which called for an "Isaiah of the factories" who would "ride on the northern winds of Revolution" and "girdle the world." Five years later Albert Jay Nock, anglophile editor of *The Freeman,* saw no way to forestall Oppenheim's Isaiah; the Russian revolution had "liberated 'The Idea' upon the world," Nock said, and it has been "silently spreading over the face of the whole earth, and striking its roots deeper into the unconsciousness of mankind." [33] By 1918 Resurgence had come to an end. And that year, despite Rosenfeld's ceaseless effort to keep him alive with oxygen, Bourne died.

3

American entry into the world war, the death of Randolph Bourne and of John Reed, and later Harding's election and Palmer's raids helped to destroy a magazine and a movement which had almost succeeded in establishing that focal center, that organic school, for which Brooks argued. In 1919 Waldo Frank, who saw in Henry Adams' *Education* "the last word of the pioneer," the end of one version of America and "the apotheosis, the herald of its successor," rallied his associates and told them that the time had come to write books which would dramatize the vision of *The Seven Arts.* Frank then wrote a study of literature, *Our America,* which serves as an epigraph and monument to the work and attitude of Resurgence. Envisioning a union in which "the men who listen to Stieglitz" join forces with those who follow the labor leader Big Bill Haywood, Frank stated a principle which

Lewis Mumford a few years later, in *The Golden Day,* was to call "more drastic than the criticism of the old social revolutionists, and more deeply cultural than all our early attempts to possess the simulacra of culture. It is nothing less than the effort to conceive a new world." "We go forth all to seek America. And in seeking we create her," Frank intoned. "In the quality of our search shall be the nature of the America we create." [34]

The search persisted but was not led by Stieglitz or Brooks, Frank or Mumford. It shifted South to Tennessee where in 1922 the Fugitive group formed about Sidney Hirsch. "Reclining in a sort of oriental luxury among pillows," Hirsch duplicated in Nashville Stieglitz's feat in New York. He "pontificated," to use Allen Tate's word, about "the high eminence of poetry" and, Donald Davidson adds, "elevated into an almost priestly rite the consideration of our verse." [35] Taking their lead from Hirsch, impressed by the example of Eliot, members of the group turned themselves into aesthetes of a latter-day church of art for which they hoped to invent a manual of discipline, a ritual. Very soon they rediscovered the precise principle that had animated the men of Resurgence, the organic principle, which they then rephrased to suit their peculiar notion of past and of place. Tate, claiming that *The Seven Arts* "had little direct influence on us," [36] composed the axiom that unified his group: poetry "requires the support of a tradition based upon a generally diffused belief."

Although Tate and John Crowe Ransom introduced a new vocabulary—tradition, belief, ontology—they preserved some very old and familiar wants. Brooks was determined to discover "the springs of our creative energy" in order that these, once located, might "irrigate the entire subsoil of our national life." [37] Like Brooks, these formalists sought changeless values which would connect the life of art with the moral life of man. At first, absorbed by art, they hoped to isolate imagination from culture in order to study the thing itself; this activity made them famous. But in fact they did not renounce society; on the contrary, they hoped to invent a model life in art so that their lives might serve as a model for the community as a whole. The same springs that fed Brooks nourished Fugitives. Before long they turned themselves into Agrarians and imagined an organic community equipped with an economics, a politics, and an art—an exemplary community which would rejuvenate the South and enable it in turn to revitalize the nation as a whole.

Unlike Faulkner, who introduced similar attitudes in his Yoknapatawpha novels, the Fugitives and Agrarians exploited more public and current ideas, fashioning an organicism of the right. Their movement stirred some notable work but influenced only one major poet, a midwesterner, Hart Crane. Good friend of two leading theorists of literary form and social reaction, Tate and Gorham Munson, this poet hoped to write formal verse in accord with the New Criticism, poems which would serve simply as "communication between man and man." Simultaneously, in his master work, he tried to make an organic poem, "The Bridge," which would display the amplitude and diversity, "the mystical synthesis of 'America.' " Bridge itself would symbolize "our constructive future, our unique identity," he told Munson. And in a separate note to Stieglitz he added, "I feel you as entering very strongly into . . . *The Bridge*." [38] Crane therefore undertook to reconcile Eliot and Whitman, to accommodate the vision of *The Fugitive* to that of *The Seven Arts* in a new poetry which would blend formalism and apocalypse.

By the mid-1920's, a whole series of movements occurred among organicists, right and left, South and North, who imagined schemes which interlaced metaphysical, literary, and social utopia. Perhaps the most famous program of the right is new humanism, "the only critical movement in our land worthy of international interest," according to Gorham Munson. This movement had originated in Paul Elmer More's essays but had acquired celebrity only when Irving Babbitt undertook to fashion a theory of social and literary value based in More's taste for literary and social decorum. By 1928 when Norman Foerster edited *Humanism and America,* the group had its own magazine, *The Bookman,* and many allies. For a time *The Bookman* raised a storm, but when its publisher created *The American Review* in order to support Mussolini, the movement lost organ, adherents, and power.

"They were traditionalists without a tradition," Alfred Kazin says, "Neoclassicists in a plutocracy, reactionaries who found themselves almost alone in their effort to impose standards of order upon a literature for which they had no sympathy." [39] F. J. Hoffman too, in his recent book on the 1920's, agrees that the new humanists were isolated from the life of their day, from the literature and the nation they aspired to lead. But this view is inaccurate. The new humanists undertook to fashion a literary program suited to the taste of those persons who supported the Watch and Ward Society and the Society for the Suppression of Vice. All these groups are identified by their desire to resist, as the *New Republic* said in 1927, "the impact of alien agitations and peoples," to resist what Bourne called organic transnationalization. "There are a great many people in this country," John S. Sumner had explained to readers of *The Dial* in 1921, "who like to bring forward something 'foreign' and hold it forth as an example of the way things should be done over here." [40] Although the new humanists were more judicious than vulgarians of this sort, they promised to import only the "most sedulously cultivated" foreigners: "Homer, Phideas, Plato, Aristotle, Confucius, Buddha, Jesus, Paul, Virgil, Horace, Dante, Shakespeare, Milton, Goethe . . . Matthew Arnold." A "strange assortment of names," Foerster agreed, but it guaranteed "a happy use of foreign culture." And because great art has "always been organic with and supported by the life and vision of a whole people," members of this movement hoped to perfect in America a "humanistic society" in which art (carefully screened) and culture (tidily genteel) are "profoundly integrated." In this way, Irving Babbitt concluded, society at large, molded by "humanistic discipline" and ordered by "humanistic control," would "move towards a communion."

Surely we are wrong to dismiss new humanists as traditionalists without a tradition. Guardians of the classic tradition in organic thought, they contrived a new vocabulary with which they hoped to preserve organicism in its purest form. What they called purity, others recognized as perversion. And when, during the early 1930's, they selected fascism as the form of politics that best fulfilled their ideas on integration, discipline, control, and communion, their movement came to nothing. But because their movement showed how neatly the organic metaphor could fit any program whatever, men of the center became suspicious of a figure of speech so pliant that it could adapt itself to utopias both of the right and left—to John Gould Fletcher's, for example, or Michael Gold's.

To recall the operation of Fletcher's mind is especially useful at this point because it records a lucid history not of pliancy only but of perversion too. In 1923 Fletcher, writing in Van Wyck Brooks' *Freeman,* said that whatever "gods we worship," they must be "gods common to all of us . . . worshipped . . . with the spirit of the mediaeval artist." He warned that Americans must learn this lesson lest they destroy their "last and best opportunity of assuming the spiritual leadership of the world." Presumably Brooks approved Fletcher's thought because it expressed Ruskin's spirit. But in 1934 in the *American Review,* a journal which was named, ironically enough, after the one in which Greenough and Whitman had introduced organicism as the doctrine of art which best guaranteed creation according to the democratic ideal, Fletcher wrote an essay in support of the autocratic ideal. Invoking principles that violate both Ruskin's spirit and Whitman's, he observed that "no god emerges" from Lewis Mumford's *Technics and Civilization.* After more than five hundred pages of talk about utopia and democracy, we still "face humanity crying in the desert for some faith not tainted with the brand of modern progressivism." Fletcher longed for faith not tainted, we must assume, with Whitman's progressive spirit of the age writing, "We must build again, within the framework of the twentieth century mechanical state, the mediaeval state of the guildsmen. . . . In other words, we must tend toward the corporate state of European Fascism" where economic and social life are unified by "one religion, one moral doctrine, binding all." [41] His argument was supplemented by Glenway Wescott's *Fear and Trembling,* written in order to warn his countrymen that they must remake their institutions if they would fulfill their destiny. "Our world is one body," he said, raising old tropes, "one part of it preparing the other's nourishment, the nourished part providing the other's nervous energy in return, one part thinking for others; all the pleasure felt by nerve interlaced with supposedly foreign nerve, all the work done hand in hand." Recalling Coriolanus, about whom Eliot was then preparing a play in verse, he envisioned an "age of government by men who know how to govern," men who would enable the United States to establish a kind of twentieth-century "Pax Americana" which would save the West.[42] In his mind, too, fascism provided the social system best suited to accomplish organic American dreams.

Although American prophets of reaction exploited this metaphor, they preferred to disregard the fact that the metaphor itself, however pliant, did in truth have a history of its own, a history which rendered it quite unsuited to their ends. Deliberate disregard of history is clearest in one of the most familiar, best publicized, and least convincing definitions of the aims and nature of community—Eliot's scheme for a Pax Europa which would achieve, in his adopted land, a version of American utopia. Beginning in 1928 Eliot has written a series of famous books which express straight organic belief: "The problem of the unification of the world and the problem of the unification of the individual, are in the end one and the same problem. . . . The solution of one is the solution of the other." Arguing that a humanism without religion is pointless and that a religion without humanism is savage, he has propagandized for a political philosophy, "founded upon the Christian faith," which would establish a "social-religious-artistic complex." In order to transfigure savagery, he has taken the legend of an organic American community, a legend that stems from the Enlightenment, the age of science, commerce, and Federalism, and redrafted it according to the example of medieval Europe. Determined to undo the work of transfer accomplished by Emerson and the transcendentalists, Eliot offers us communion sanctified by the Universal Christian Republic, not by the republic of letters. In this way he has sought not to pervert or subvert, but merely to controvert history.

Midwestern messiah in Anglican cloth, he has written a continental literature in the American grain. His last official statement of opinion, *Notes Toward the Definition of Culture,* returns to an imagery introduced more than fifty years ago when the new science of politics undertook to compose a functional theory of American government. National culture, Eliot said, is "the resultant of an indefinite number of local cultures," and these in turn manifest the "material organisation" and the "spiritual organism of Eu-

rope." [43] For he and his associates of the right are not simply
zealots who import here and misapply notions developed by Joseph
de Maistre and Charles Maurras. Despite accusations made a few
years ago when Pound received the Bollingen award, Eliot, Pound,
Wescott, and Fletcher have urged good Europeans to think American thoughts if they would be saved.

4

So much for the organicism of the right. A similar mode of
thought came into being when the American Communist party,
underground in 1919, united in 1921 with another group called
Communist Labor, finally emerged during 1923 as the Worker's
Party of America, the official name of the American branch of the
Communist International. This group was represented in V. F.
Calverton's journal, *The Modern Quarterly*, established in 1924.
Its doctrine had been announced by Michael Gold in 1921, the
year when the party merged with Communist Labor. "The old
moods, the old poetry, fiction, painting, philosophies," Gold said,
were accomplished by "proud and baffled solitaries." "We artists
of the people will not face Life and Eternity alone. We will face it
from among the people." [44] This is the "Idea" Albert Jay Nock
had feared. And by 1925 it was incorporated within a serviceable
theory of literature which conceived a proper organic community
as the state where identity and selfhood are not sponsored but are
suppressed in art and politics. This new wisdom must replace old
folly: the "proletarian trend" in art, Calverton said, is "singularly
communistic" because it proclaims the "greatness of the destiny of
the mass." "The individualistic philosophy of the petty bourgeoi-
sie" had reached its peak in 1912 when Wilson was elected president. Americans must replace this with "faith in the common man,
in the mass . . . founded upon a collective instead of an individualistic premise." It is a faith, Calverton concluded, which will liberate "American literature and American life" and will enable the
American proletariat, led by its artists, at last to "remake the modern world." [45] The mystic word is still "America"; the order is still
fraternal; the aim is still apocalypse; and imagery is still organic.

The whole idea, now sovietized, was presented by Gold as "worthy of the religious devotion" of all American workers and artists.

Although Trotsky's *Literature and Revolution,* translated into English during 1925, was the most fully accomplished statement of Marxist literary theory, it did not assert these claims. Indeed, Trotsky argued, "The proletarian regime is temporary and transient," a single moment in an eternal movement toward classlessness. To create a sheer proletarian literature is therefore to mistake the nature of dialectic and of imagination. In Gold's mind, however, and in Joseph Freeman's too, indoctrination was the principal aim of art. Gold's fervor did in fact deprive *New Masses,* introduced in 1926, of support provided by Brooks, Frank, Mumford, Floyd Dell, and Art Young. These contributors to the old *Masses, The Seven Arts,* and the *Liberator,* Lewis Mumford today recalls, had hoped to give Gold's journal a "more popular underpinning than the old *Masses* had—with some of the appeal that *The American Mercury* made. If I remember right they even asked Brooks to be the Editor, and various other liberals and radicals were asked to contribute." By 1928, however, Gold himself had assumed the editorship. Before long "his revolutionary sentiments exposed the communist hands that were backing the enterprise, and drove away earlier sympathizers with the notion of a free-spoken left wing humorous magazine." [46] In 1935, during the heyday of Stalin's power, Joseph Freeman remarked that during the 1920's the *New Masses* group had been "small . . . isolated both from the mass organizations of the workers and from the mass of intellectuals." This was the more distressing because, he remarked in 1936, Gold was a member of "the third generation of revolutionary American writers . . . recapitulating an old experience. The first generation . . . had given us Upton Sinclair and Jack London. . . . The second generation, which produced Floyd Dell and John Reed, arose in the Lyric Year 1912, when the search for new values in life and art seemed to lead logically to the socialist society." In the late 1920's, however, when "the tendencies of the Wilsonian era had . . . run their course," the time was ripe for a new Marxist-American literature. [47]

In order to enhance with myth the charms of world revolution,

Gold and Freeman chose the old rhetoric of organic community and American mission. They chose, too, in place of journalism, the medium in which solidarity was guaranteed and isolation was dispelled. Like Eliot, inspired by visits to English music halls where the most popular artists seemed to manifest the deepest lives of their audiences, Gold realized that his campaign, "agitprop," was most forceful on stage. An organic theory of drama, first publicized by George Cram Cook's Provincetown Players, had been official policy in avant-garde theater since 1915 when Robert Edmund Jones, back home after a year's study with Max Reinhardt at the Deutsches Theater, was commissioned to design Anatole France's *The Man Who Married a Dumb Wife*. Jones had already practiced his craft in Cook's theater. But on this occasion he introduced the "new stagecraft" to considerably larger purposes and audiences. His aim was to create a "balance of speech, gesture, form and light, fluctuating in their continuous interplay but at all times achieving a continuous unity of effect at every moment of a sustained and coherent performance." [48] Drama is not an engine, he said, "running at full speed from overture to final curtain, but a *living organism*." [49] During 1915, too, Claude Bragdon in Chicago gave a series of lectures for the Art Institute where he presented himself, in architecture as well as stage design, as a disciple of Louis Sullivan. Sullivan, we recall, is the man whom Van Wyck Brooks calls "the Boston boy who settled in Chicago and developed the ideas of the old Boston sculptor Greenough." Extending Sullivan's thought, designing Walter Hampden's famed productions of Hamlet first in 1915 and again in 1925, Bragdon sought to unify "costumes, properties . . . lighting," actor and play. Experiencing this spirit of unity, seeing artisan and artist join forces, we observe "the spirit of true brotherhood [in] triumph." This is, he said, "the sum and essence of my aesthetic." * Here then is a

---

* Claude Bragdon, *More Lives than One* (New York, 1938), 229. Applying these ideas to the theater, Bragdon brought into a new field that image of social order which Sullivan, as if in paraphrase of Greenough, had introduced into architecture: "All life is organic. It manifests itself through organs, through structures, through functions," Sullivan had said. Life "acts, organises, grows, develops, unfolds, expands, differentiates, organ after organ, structure after structure, form after form, function after function." *The Roots of Contemporary American Architecture,* edited by Lewis Mumford (New York,

sequence of events which any historian of ideas must cherish. Together, Jones and Bragdon created the "new stagecraft" in accord
with both streams of organic philosophy, European and American.

As a result of their work, by 1926 it was clear to Michael Gold
that drama was the form best suited to engage the full life of an
audience, to organize and point it toward the new order. Planning
to exploit the quintessential idea of organic theory, that year he
started an amateur group which included, among playwrights,
John Howard Lawson and John Dos Passos. Soon a League of
Worker's Theatres materialized; by 1933 the Theatre Union was
established. But by far the most famous and influential of these
is the Group Theatre. There all aspects of classic organic theory
were exploited in behalf of the Marxist movement. Each production, according to its directors Lee Strasberg and Harold Clurman,

1959), 75. Mumford remarks that Bragdon applied these principles of creativity "mainly in his work as stage designer in New York during the nineteen-
twenties and thirties. By reason of his contacts with Louis Sullivan he became
the chief link . . . with the architectural critics of an earlier period." *The
Roots of Contemporary American Architecture,* 422. Van Meter Ames, dis-
regarding the course of events in the American mind itself, traces origins to
Ruskin, whose "honest and imaginative treatment of materials and functions"
expressed a sense of radical decency, "respect for one's fellows" This Ruskin-
ian spirit, "reborn in Louis Sullivan and his Chicago colleagues," led to a
world movement which associated science, technology, and industrialization
in a "new unity of form." Anticipating Dewey's *Art as Experience,* Sullivan's
organicism taught artists how they might instruct men "to make their lives
more creative." In this way, Ames concludes, "American philosophy of art
joins with philosophy of science, with ethics and the philosophy of religion, in
social philosophy." "Aesthetic Values in the East and West," *The Journal of
Aesthetics and Art Criticism,* XIX (Fall, 1960), 3–16. Paul Goodman dis-
agrees with Mumford and Ames on the question of Sullivan's value and
influence, claims that our theory of functionalism does not come from any
American tradition whatever; native notions about "natural growth" are
"desperately sentimental." "Louis Sullivan—Artist in America," *Commentary,*
XXX (October, 1960), 335–39. Taking this position Goodman is, I think,
both wrong and neglectful. Frank Lloyd Wright's Guggenheim Museum, "an
organic building where all is one great space on a single continuous floor,"
attests the vitality and continuity of the tradition, however pernicious its effect.
Indeed, Bragdon's stagecraft and Sullivan's architecture must be included
with Dewey's philosophy, Veblen's economics, Holmes' jurisprudence, Beard's
and Robinson's historiography. In each of these fields, prophets of social reform reached into "the entire social space" around them and selected that
style, cultural organicism, which replaced formalism in American thought.
Morton White, *Social Thought in America: The Revolt Against Formalism*
(Boston, 1957), 12.

was a feat of collaboration not only among members of the group itself but also between the group and its public. The techniques of collectivist drama had been taught to these men by Maria Ouspenskaya, who in 1923 decided to remain in America although her director and her company, Stanislavsky and the Moscow Art Theatre, had left. Clurman's other teacher was Stieglitz, whose sessions he began to attend in 1924. During the late 1920's, he sought to reconcile Stieglitz and Stanislavsky in a theory of art and action which would fuse the organic and the Russian idea. Clurman argued that the first disciples had misunderstood the lesson of the master. Individualists of the old school, they had not realized that Stieglitz hoped to teach artists not to cultivate but to submerge their identity. Only when an artist joins persons of his own kind—not writers and players merely, but spectators too—can he create a "collective organism," the true work of art.[50] In this way Clurman introduced to the Group Theatre what may be called Applied Stieglitz. And in 1933 Clurman's theory and Gold's campaign achieved a historic climax when the audience leaped onto its seats and, with Agate in *Waiting for Lefty,* screamed "STRIKE, STRIKE, STRIKE!!!"

Before we return to the 1920's and *The Dial* we must take a moment to summarize and foreshadow. At the beginning of our century, a new program, designed to achieve perfect civilization in the United States, was formulated by Stieglitz, certified with the stamp of Whitman, codified by Bourne, and offered by Brooks to the world at large. New as it was, we have seen that its elements appear in all forms of utopian thought, Puritan, Federalist, organic, and disclose a semimystical faith in what can be described as the dynamics of imagination. The creed which links each of these in a common tradition and which joins such disparate persons as Edward Taylor, Whitman, Brooks, Eliot, and Michael Gold, is not a matter of politics or theology. All contend that a work of art realizes itself only when an individual incorporates its organic life into his own organism; only then do men experience a new fecundating force that fires them to recreate their lives, personal and national, in harmony with their vision of the wholeness of art.* If we except Eliot on the right and Gold on the left, we can say that all prophets of organic culture were certain that their system provided that moment of American apocalypse when each member of the community, illumined by the genius of art, assumed his role as creator of that final work of perfect genius, America itself, supreme *objet d'art* among nations.

It is this tradition of prophecy, this program for salvation, which engrossed the American imagination in the age of Resurgence. This same tradition supported radical politics in a later day. It would be wrong to pretend that these ideas alone have inspired all men of letters or to claim that these were the only notable views on the proper uses of art in America. Although visionary art today lacks cachet, fifty years ago it was esteemed and powerful. And it would be wrong now to permit our disenchantments to blind us to the modern history of an old idea.

* Daniel Aaron isolates three main motifs of mind and three controlling groups of persons responsible for shaping what he calls the "Spectrum of Rebellion," 1910 to 1919. First, the *Masses* group, served as a twentieth century extension of the American Protestant evangelic radical tradition. Second, the Priests of Young America, an Apostolic Student Movement ("This is a facetious designation but not an inaccurate one") sought to create a literature which would inspire a true social revolution. Led by Brooks, Bourne, Mumford, Oppenheim, Frank, Rosenfeld and, "marginally," Aaron adds, Walter Lippmann, these priests were supported by *The Seven Arts, The Nation, The New Republic* and *The Dial.* The third group, "Literary Experimenters or the Priests of Art," published chiefly in *The Little Review* and *Poetry,* included "artists as widely separated as Pound, John Gould Fletcher, Amy Lowell, Robert Frost, Maxwell Bodenheim, T. S. Eliot." Although many were "America-minded . . . they were less optimistic" than other apostles and evangels, "less confident in the 'promise of American life.' " *Writers on the Left* (New York, 1961), 23–27. Aaron's opinion does indeed accord with my own view of the literary situation in that day. My argument, however, is designed to show how *The Dial* in the 1920's presented a synthesis of movements and voices among these rebellious priests of high art and utopian culture.

III. Beacon of Light:
THE DIAL

I want to be a prophet, if only a minor one.

RANDOLPH BOURNE, "Letters (1913–1916)," *Twice A Year*, 1941.

A review needs a firm centre, a compact group with some similarity of viewpoint or opinion who provide the paper with its character.

MALCOLM BRADBURY, *The London Magazine*, August, 1958.

I

IN 1919, when Sylvia Beach established her bookshop in Paris as a center for American expatriates, the leading genius of national life was not Whitman, whose 1855 edition of *Leaves of Grass* Miss Beach placed on permanent display. Rather it was the gambler Arnold Rothstein who that autumn prepared to entertain a national audience by arranging the outcome of the World Series. Despite Rothstein, despite the transfer abroad of Whitman's spirit, Scofield Thayer and James Sibley Watson, Jr., two young "enthusiasts" of American letters, determined to accomplish what ancient metaphysics, recent politics, current economics, and postwar normalcy had failed to achieve, undertook to connect the ideology and the arts of utopia in a classic journal which by 1919 was nearly defunct. The only "values that had not been betrayed," Lewis Mumford recalls, "were those of art." [1] Thayer and Watson, recognizing the value of pure art and seizing the quintessential idea of organicist thought, decided not to debate or propagandize but simply to replace God and Woodrow Wilson with Eliot and William Carlos Williams, with those men of high art whose genius equipped them to serve the "social body" as its "nerve centre." [2]

Chiefly as a result of their effort, our modern prophets of special destiny have maintained a sense of continuity, of history. All our artists have been able to take for granted a community of associates, a more or less unified and sizable audience, a responsive

society. This achievement is the more notable because Thayer and
Watson, selecting the work of numberless new painters, poets,
novelists, critics, anthropologists, philosophers, and psychologists
who competed for the attention of colleagues and serious laymen,
relied solely on their own tastes. In their view, literary criticism,
impressionistic and casual, political and fervid, psychoanalytic
and inept, was archaic or prejudiced or modish. Thayer and Watson were gifted and well-trained men, and were supported by a
great deal more money than that available to those editors
who published *Tempo, Pagan, The Quill, The Nomad, S4N,
Rhythmus, The Circle, The Forge,* and *Parnassus.* Money enabled them to enlist others and to employ some of the people
who were to contribute much of the most remarkable and diver-
sified writing available today: Gilbert Seldes, Marianne Moore,
Kenneth Burke. Selecting their editors with as much wit as they
chose contributors, Thayer and Watson established a journal beyond the attrition of money. In an age when very young writers
were unable to decide whether or not to take Ben Hecht at his
word, to believe that Hecht and Maxwell Bodenheim would salvage American writing from tricksters like Cummings, *The Dial*
each month offered its work and its criteria of value.

The situation as a whole is best demonstrated in an exchange
of letters which occurred early in 1923, when *The Dial* was beginning to acquire its largest audience and greatest influence. The
following note is written in a child's hand.

> Mr. Dial Editor
>   My Mama told me to ask you what I want to know, so please
> tell me, dear sir. I am 11 years old and my mama lets me cut the
> pages of the Dial each month and I love to look at the funnies,
> next to the poetry.
>   Today I saw some funny potry by Mr. Cummings. It had such
> funny lines and the punktuation and capitellization is so funny. My
> teacher makes me stay after school and my father licks me cause
> I punktuate and capitilize like Mr. Cummings does.
>   I said to my mama now can I write like they do in the Dial
> and she says I ll take your head off if you do what am I sending you
> to school for anyway to write like that.
>   And I said to my mama what does it mean an she said god
> knows cause nobody else does thats sure I've ask lots of Dial
> readers and they dont know no more than I do and at that its

harder to break into print than to break out of jail thats what my
mama said. Please Mr. Dial Editor is it going to be like Cummings
has it then I won't have to go to school any more to learn punktu-
ation and capitellzation. Please answer.

> Your little friend
> Eugene Winton

3153 W. 38th Ave
Denver, Colo.
P.S. My mama says I won't get a reply unless I enclos a stampd
envlup so heres 1.

On February 21, 1923, Kenneth Burke replied, dead-pan, in a letter that could be read by Eugene Wintons of whatever age and degree of seriousness, and must itself be admired whether or not the
original inquiry was honest.

Master Eugene Winton
3153 W. 38th Ave.
Denver, Col.
My dear Master Winton:

I am afraid that we can offer you very little consolation as to the
matter of Mr Cummings' capitalization and punctuation. While
Mr Cummings persisted in spite of spankings, and finally became
a poet thereby, we could not officially council any one else to do
likewise.

You must also remember that if all the world were like Mr
Cummings, Mr Cummings' system of punctuation would lose some
of its effectiveness. It is partially because the rest of us must devote
our time to getting the rules right that Mr Cummings can get effects
out of their violation.

But, going farther than this, I should point out that Mr Cummings does use his violations to a purpose. They are not mistakes;
they are intentional. It used to be the practice, for instance, when
one wanted to emphasize something, to underline it, or in printing
to put it in italics. But we have learned today that much more
emphasis can be gotten by other ways (this old way having been
worn smooth). Look at the advertisements in a magazine, for instance, and see how much is done precisely along the lines which
Mr Cummings uses in his poetry. Yet when you see an ad beginning
with a small letter, do you write to the company in protest?

Wishing you all the success in the world with your school work,
I am

> Faithfully yours,
> Kenneth Burke
> Editorial Department

One other example is perhaps more than enough, an exchange between the photographer Paul Strand and Watson. Reading these four letters we learn as much as we must know in order to understand why *The Dial* succeeded in doing what all the theorists had urged, how it achieved that triumph which, as Merle Armitage says in his book on George Gershwin, made it "the one beacon of light . . . that signalled the emergence of a new America." [3]

> 314 West 83rd Street
> New York City.
> March 1st 1923.

Mr Kenneth Burke
Editorial Department, The Dial
152 West 13th Street, N.Y.C.
My dear Mr Burke:

Thank you for your note and the MSS so promptly returned. Naturally I regret very much that my article should have been completed at just the particular moment when the "extrinsic considerations" you mention, were conditioning factors in its non acceptance for publication.

The latter part of your note, frankly, puzzles me. I recall as well the two very able articles by Paul Rosenfeld which appeared in the Dial, but I fail to see how they "overlap somewhat on the territory" of mine. The essay on Stieglitz dealt exclusively with the subject of his photographs and photography. The other essay on American Painting did have a short critique of the painting of O'Keeffe, but the treatment was assuredly quite different; as different as that of Santayana and Stefan Zweig in their respective essays on Dickens, printed in the Dial. Moreover the editors of the Dial cannot, even though they may not have seen it, be ignorant of the recent important exhibition of O'Keeffe's work which was on view at the Anderson Galleries, from Jan 29th to Feb 12th, and which intervened between the writing of Mr Rosenfeld's article and mine.

Particularly am I puzzled by your feeling that territory has been overlapped when I recall the two above mentioned articles on Dickens; for evidently to write upon the work of an individual someone else has written about, does not in itself constitute overlapping. And further I am astonished when I cannot forget the frequent publication in the Dial, of the work of Zorach, Hartman, Lachaise and the drawings of Cummings, too often absurdly meaningless from the point of view of any development, and which no extrinsic nor any other considerations, seem able to prevent.

> Sincerely yours,
> Paul Strand

March 21, 1923

Paul Strand, Esq.
314 West 83rd Street
New York City
My dear Mr Strand:

Your brief note to me was, until Monday, lost under a pile of things on a desk. I assume you want it answered, although you may very well not. Anyway, I take it you wanted to kill off two birds (Burke and myself) with one shot and were afraid that I might escape through carelessness. Certainly, if Burke deserved killing I did too, for it was at my suggestion that he added the second paragraph to his letter. The first paragraph was the usual editorial lamentation about time and space which means, nine times out of ten, "don't like your article". I hoped that the addition to the letter might suggest the reasons why we needed to consider your article only from the point of view of its intrinsic interest and not worry because it was about somebody who required mention at any cost, or because it represented a sort of opinion which we had not previously given space to. Before explaining what we did not like about your article, I should like to state:

Miss O'Keefe and Mr Stieglitz some time ago very kindly permitted me to have photographs made of several of her paintings. We ran the one that seemed the likeliest for reproduction, with Rosenfeld's article. Thayer wrote me after having seen it, that he felt that it lost so much in reproduction that we should not run any more of them. As this particular one had seemed the likeliest I rather agreed with him about the others. The things we reproduce by Zorach, Cummings, Hartmann, and Lachaise, are at least satisfactory as reproductions. If you know of any line drawings better than the ones we reproduce I wish you would let us know about them as they are very hard to get and we have made it a rule to reproduce four every month. We have never, I think, had more than a sentence about Zorach or Hartmann, McBride once mentioned Cummings' paintings, and one article was devoted to Lachaise. Both Zorach and Cummings do paintings some of which we like, but we have never reproduced any of them because we do not think they reproduce properly. I do not see how Dickens, a subject presumably of perennial interest, has anything to do with the matter, though at that I grudge him the Zweig essay.

Anyway, all I meant to say was that Miss O'Keefe has received as much attention as other painters whom we like equally. Not that she cares, I expect.

Probably you do not feel that your point of view is at all representative of the two ninety one school of thought, but they say that to a Chinaman all Englishmen look alike. That was why I mentioned Rosenfeld's article on Stieglitz.

My principal objection to your article was that you did not say enough about the paintings themselves. Although one of the editors had seen the new exhibit and one had not, both agreed that your article had almost no direct bearing on the paintings. I wish I had your article here to refer to, but, coarsely, this is how I remember it. First you said that Miss O'Keefe expressed the experience of the new woman and did not imitate men in the way that women painters used to do. You said that anyone looking at her pictures felt immediately that here was exclusively the expression of a woman's experience. Well, I want to be shown. No doubt it is hard to analyse the elements which convey this overpowering impression, but I think you should have attempted it. Perhaps you did, but I do not think so and I read the article twice. You may say that these things cannot be analysed or conveyed in words, or that they ought not to be, but if so, why *write* about them? . . . Next you get us ready to see her colour compared with Macdonald-Wright's, but you did not really compare them; you merely contrasted what you averred to be their respective approaches to creation and asserted that Miss O'Keefe's was better. You also mentioned Huntington Wright's theories about colour, saying that Miss O'Keefe had done all that he asked for, but failed to give any definite reasons for this assertion.

I admit that we publish a lot of stuff in *The Dial* which is not criticism in the true sense, but criticism is hard to get and press agent stuff often has poetical or even informative merit. In this case, as I say, the informative part was not absolutely necessary to us. Concentration on actual works of art is difficult, requires great ingenuity and perception, but Miss O'Keefe's paintings deserve it. Mr Stieglitz, for example, once interpreted a drawing of Miss O'Keefe's for me in a very definite style, so I know it can be done. I do not say that simply because an article spoke of the paintings directly we should want to print it.

You see the reason for our first short note. It was superficially polite and saved time.

Sincerely yours,
J. S. Watson, Jr.

During the days when it was difficult indeed to discriminate between, say, Gertrude Stein and Carl Van Vechten, between an innovator and a faddist, Thayer and Watson, Burke and Seldes, Stewart Mitchell, Alyse Gregory, and Marianne Moore, forced to make distinctions of this kind, simultaneously tried to establish the theoretic ground on which these were based. They rejected the kind of criticism encouraged in *The Yale Review* under Wilbur

Cross: "I say that these charming essays reveal . . . the fine response of the best type of American mind to books and life." [4] Watson told Strand that *The Dial* did not want any more of such stuff. Their magazine was not, as Simon Guggenheim described *Broom,* a rich man's hobby,[5] and they never allowed it to become any one savior's private organ.

They paid their money, made their choice, and created the magazine to which we must turn if we would study those amazing years of modern art. It is they far more than the Knopfs or the Liverights who established what Percy Boynton, in 1927 a man of importance, suddenly discovered was available in America: "a best-reader class, large enough to . . . justify publication of good books," reproduction of contemporary pictures, concerts of the most advanced music.[6] By 1946, when Horace Gregory and Marya Zaturenska wrote their *History of American Poetry,* it was clear that *The Dial* had been not merely a magazine, but an "institution" quite like "a college or a university." [7] Trained in this institution (Saul Bellow recalls reading through the whole file) American readers and writers came of age.

2

The issues sketched here will be treated at length during the remainder of this chapter and in the three that follow. Our first concern, however, is the character, the quality, and the history of those two men who in 1919 refashioned this magazine into the most extraordinary but representative journal of our time. Scofield Thayer was thirty-one; Watson was a few years younger. Thayer, born in Worcester, Massachusetts, had attended The Milton Academy at the time when Eliot was a senior pupil there. Indeed, it is startling to discover how closely Thayer's early life parallels Eliot's, how the work of both men is consistent with some motifs in our national life. Although Thayer was a man of ideas, he was especially loyal to a group of distinguished men—Santayana, Randolph Bourne, Freud—whose character and thought helped to shape his own mind and purpose. He had known of Eliot and had known Eliot himself for many years and in a common group of places long before the elder man had published a word of poetry.

Eliot had left Milton in 1906 and Harvard in 1909. He had continued graduate study abroad during 1910 and 1911, then returned
to Harvard until 1914 when he left for Merton College, Oxford.
Whether or not Thayer saw in Eliot an exemplar of the literary
life, preferring Eliot's example to that of his Uncle Ernest who
wrote "Casey at the Bat," he did follow Eliot's path from Milton
to Harvard to Oxford. Before long Thayer's magazine would select
Eliot as the most brilliant of poets, the most characteristic artist
of the new age in American letters. *The Dial* itself would become
famous in the very act of finding a public for the poetry which was
to secure Eliot's reputation. It was in this way that Thayer hoped
to make his mark and to remake the world.

A man of "ice on the surface" and of "molten lava under-
neath," Thayer was "inflammable and satirical . . . sober and
sad"; he alternated "between the tempest and the frozen lake."
Alyse Gregory thought him "slender of build, swift of movement,
always strikingly pale, with coal-black hair, black eyes veiled and
flashing, and lips that curved like those of Lord Byron, he seemed
to many the embodiment of the aesthete with overrefined tastes
and sensibilities." [8] In contrast, Watson seemed to Llewelyn
Powys like one of "those silent, evasive eels . . . that find their
way to the ocean from remote ponds." [9] The pond of origin in this
case was Rochester in western New York. On the way to the ocean,
Watson himself says, he spent six years at Groton School where,
"during lulls of the strenuous life, curiosity about periodicals and
books was not discouraged." Curiosity remained diffuse until he
heard a speech by John Jay Chapman. "Crescit sub pondere vir-
tus," the Chapman motto ("Courage increases under a burden"),
animated the life of this distinguished man quite as Emerson's
image of an American scholar had impelled him to assume the role
of reformer in education and government. Although Watson no
longer remembers what Chapman said, he refers to this as the occasion when, hearing a man fired by modern ideas, his own thought
crystallized.[10] Having already familiarized himself with undergraduate publications at Harvard, he was determined to try for the
Monthly.

Watson early decided, Miss Moore says, to spend little time on
things that did not attract him. In a world where it is customary

for a person to establish himself by shaping his career according to whatever talents he possesses, Watson exploited his enthusiasms and bank account and, he says, "the talents of others" in order to avoid settling on any one career that might be confining. During the early 1920's, in addition to helping with *The Dial,* he proceeded with his plan to take a medical degree and do postgraduate work at New York University. Then in 1927 he left New York and returned to Rochester to produce experimental films with Melville Webber, Remsen Wood, and the composer Alec Wilder. Such distractions kept him from regular hours at *The Dial* office. What he wrote for *The Dial* was generally anonymous or pseudonymous.[11] Because he went to few parties and met few authors, it is not surprising that he should be nearly unknown in literary circles, or that Edmund Wilson should have commented recently that he thought Watson contributed very little else to *The Dial* except money.[12] But in a recent letter Miss Moore insists, "Dr. Watson should be emphasized proportionately as he is retiring. He has no counterpart in performance and attitude." [13]

3

This range of interest, this silent conviction, these subdued talents Watson brought to *The Dial* in 1919 when Thayer, a man of similar tastes but far more flamboyant gifts, proposed that they join forces. Both men shared one special tradition which dates from the time when they wrote for and helped to edit *The Harvard Monthly.* Thayer traced his own lineage to Santayana, who is supposed to have described Thayer as one of the last Puritans, and who was first among earlier generations of Harvard aesthetes. "Aestheticism in some form or other really did rule our minds at Harvard," Van Wyck Brooks says.[14] Its main instrument, the *Monthly,* provided William Vaughn Moody and Bliss Carmen, Wallace Stevens and Robert Morss Lovett, with a system of thought initiated in 1888 when Santayana returned from Germany. The magazine, then two years old, had developed as an organ of the Laodicean Club at Harvard where members met over tea and tokay in order to elect the saints of Laodicea; Santayana had proposed, as his candidate, God. During the 1890's other saints were canonized in both club and *Monthly*—Pater alongside God, Mallarmé, Huysmans. By 1913, when Thayer was a leading member of the editorial board, Santayana too achieved sainthood in a number devoted to essays in appreciation of *Winds of Doctrine.*

Five years later, Thayer turned up in New York as a shadow member of *The Dial's* board, and we realize how far this Laodicean had traveled. As an editor, Thayer found himself supporting Randolph Bourne against John Dewey. This act of friendship and choice, which marks a major event in modern intellectual history, brings us to the moment when Thayer's career begins to influence the lives and careers of artists not only in this country but throughout the world. Before we study the friendship of Thayer and Bourne, however, we must recall in some detail the condition of things in the field of literary journalism during Watson's and Thayer's Harvard and war years when these young men decided to make that field their special work. Hitherto I have touched on this matter only as it concerned the organic idea. Now it is necessary to set the scene and recreate the sequence of events which determined the course adopted by *The Dial.*

According to F. J. Hoffman's, C. Allen's, and C. F. Ulrich's standard history, *The Little Magazine,* more than six hundred journals were published in English from 1912 until 1946. Each of these shared one aim: each was a little magazine obliged to print work in which mass audiences were uninterested, against which serious but careful readers were automatically opposed, and about which trade papers and publishers were undecided or fearful. From 1946 on, almost numberless new organs have appeared and disappeared. Indeed, it is now modish for big institutions of one sort or another, universities and publishers and foundations, to offer subsidies in sponsorship of reviews which lose money but acquire weight. All during our time, however, very few journals, whether grand or tiny, academic or arty, coterie or eclectic, have managed to discover new writers of substantial value or promote advanced writing of radical worth.

Until 1946 little magazines were engaged in what Lionel Trilling, congratulating the *Partisan Review* for having survived its tenth year, described as keeping the roads open when all the ordinary ways were closed. Although some papers chose queer paths, literary journals in general, "from the elegant and brilliant *Dial* to the latest little scrub from the provinces," kept alive a sense of the momentousness and power of literary ideas. We know that in 1919 when Thayer and Watson bought *The Dial*, it was the sense of powerlessness in literary ideas which disheartened most men. Neither Watson nor Thayer was gloomy or gay about the prospects for art in America, but both were certain that a quite new kind of paper might satisfy wants as yet unattended by any existing magazine. When their *Dial* went out of circulation ten years later, it had presented to a large national following all major modern figures in England, on the Continent, and in the United States. It had helped some minors assume majority. And the journal itself, having drawn on the best varieties of literary experience, had preserved just those strains which with proper cultivation would have the most benign effect on the health of the community.

Watson and Thayer did of course rely on the experience of earlier editors and magazines. But the form devised for *The Dial* was their own invention; there were no models for the thing they sought to establish. During those years before 1920, there were of course a number of magazines devoted to poetry. *Poetry* itself had been going since 1912, and by 1919 it had managed to introduce, among others less gifted, Sandburg, Pound, Maxwell Bodenheim, Tagore, Eliot, Marianne Moore, Wallace Stevens, Vachel Lindsay, Amy Lowell, Richard Aldington, H. D., D. H. Lawrence, and Robert Frost. For a time *Poetry* had supported the Imagist movement and in its behalf had presented all available work by members of Pound's circle. In contrast, the old-line magazines such as *Atlantic, Harper's,* and *Scribner's* cultivated William Allen White and Brander Matthews, George Woodberry and Louis Untermeyer. Other magazines, those that had already appeared or were soon to arrive, were either frivolous (*Vanity Fair, Smart Set*) or solemn (*The Yale Review, Sewanee Review*). For the rest, there was a general magazine, the *Literary Digest,* so earnest for culture that it included within its usual eighty pages a three-page section called "Letters and Art." *Reedy's Mirror* in St. Louis had had its moment of splendor in 1914 with Edgar Lee Masters' "Spoon River Anthology"; thereafter, it published materials of chiefly regional value. *The Masses,* from 1911 until its suppression in 1917, had interspersed good verse by Sandburg and other radicals among its pages of socialist prose by Floyd Dell, Max Eastman, John Reed. During 1913–14 Alfred Kreymborg, financed by Albert and Charles Boni, had put together *Glebe* and printed new poets of Pound's choice (Joyce, F. S. Flint, William Carlos Williams). When *Glebe* expired, Kreymborg in 1915 had offered *Others,* printing works of Stevens, Pound, Mina Loy among many whose names are scarcely known today. Until 1919 *Others* appeared spasmodically in an effort, Kreymborg says in his autobiography, to print the work of poets as yet unknown alongside "poets of repute."

At that time criticism was the special province of the fortnightly *Dial.* Fiction, which was nurtured in fairly few journals, became the particular interest of *The Little Review.* Although that magazine printed much poetry too, it distinguished itself by securing a public and American reputation for Joyce. This feat is common knowledge; few people know, however, that the fortnightly *Dial* also made efforts in Joyce's behalf. Everyone knows that Margaret Anderson in 1918 began to print sections of *Ulysses,* but hardly anyone recalls that John Macy and Scofield Thayer, in *The Dial* for 1917 and 1918, wrote essays in celebration of Joyce's art. Mary Colum's *Life and the Dream* and Richard Ellman's *James Joyce* do recount the way Thayer supplied Joyce with money at a crucial moment in Zurich. During the war, Joyce operated a theater in that city and found himself in trouble with those British officials whom he was to introduce into the Night-town episode of *Ulysses.* He wrote to Padraic Colum saying he was in dire need of a thousand dollars. Mrs. Colum called Thayer, who said, "I will give whatever is necessary." "Joyce always said that this sum saved him at the moment." [15] Nothing saved him for long. Thayer's response was characteristic: in his view, argued in public print and supported by private gift, Joyce was a man of art whose genius was worth a king's ransom.

But it was *The Little Review,* stressing experiment in fiction quite as *Poetry, Glebe,* and *Others* stressed experiment in verse, which established Joyce's authority as a novelist. There is in fact a straight line connecting the appearance of *Ulysses* in *The Little Review,* 1918–21, with the appearance of *Work in Progress* in *transition* beginning in 1928. Mainly because of Joyce's influence we find *Broom, Secession, The Double Dealer,* and the *Transatlantic Review* embracing futurisms of every imaginable sort during this period. Publishing writers who, like Joyce, sought new ways to explore strange states of consciousness (Cocteau, Aragon, Dorothy Richardson and Djuna Barnes, Gertrude Stein, Hemingway, Faulkner), these magazines developed an audience for experimental prose.

Regionalism offered one way of modifying these new patterns of literary culture: *The Fugitive,* a southern paper, and *Midland,* a midwestern paper, express two versions of this mode. But there are another pair of directions which have had less publicity and more enduring effect, the "tendenz" magazine and the "critical little magazine." The purpose of "tendenz," say Hoffman, Allen, and Ulrich, was first to recognize, second "to state the forward direction of our thought and culture," and third "to predict or advocate the ultimate ends and aims of our literary aspiration." Studying "tendenz," Hoffman, Allen, and Ulrich contend, we find some important clues to the literature of the 1920's. Not only was this a period marked by the appearance of marvelous single works but also it was a time of general assessment in the life of the mind. In the America of the 1920's, poets undertook to formulate national values and critics undertook to draw these values together.

Although both impulses created the journal which Hoffman, Allen, and Ulrich treat as the emblem of "tendenz," *The Seven Arts,* neither impulse flourished until Thayer and Watson reorganized the paper which was to fuse all main tendencies of mind in that day. Selecting *The Dial* as their vehicle, Watson and Thayer chose a magazine whose own history is unique in American letters. From 1880 until 1916 it had been published in Chicago and edited by Francis F. Browne, who had brought to that city a short-lived monthly of the same name, begun twenty years earlier in Cincinnati by Moncure Daniel Conway. Conway had hoped to introduce in the Middle West a paper similar to the New England magazine published from 1840 till 1844 by Emerson and Margaret Fuller. Their 1840 *Dial* is the "parent of the American little magazine," Hoffman believes. Browne's *Dial,* imitating established journals in Boston and New York, before long was admired as a model of taste in the Middle West. It was majestic and staid. In 1898 *The Dial* absorbed a miscellany of the avant-garde, *The Chap-Book,* itself historic because it introduced in America the tone and mode of all future magazines of experiment. Although it had published new writing by Stephen Crane, Hardy, Yeats, William Vaughn Moody, Henry James (*What Maisie Knew*), its example did not much influence or alter *The Dial* which by 1912 had become a textbook example of gentility in American letters. A dial is after all "the stationary part of a clock or other chronometer," Ezra Pound explained.

Pound's remark had been addressed to Margaret Anderson, formerly a member of the staff of Browne's magazine. There she had been "initiated into the secrets of the printing room" and taught things "indispensable when I began the *Little Review.*" [16] Harriet Monroe, however, had learned from *The Dial* only what not to publish. Since 1892, she had contributed poems to Browne's literary editor, William Morton Payne, who in 1914 called her journal, *Poetry,* "a futile little periodical" because it printed Sandburg's "Chicago." Miss Monroe, outraged, said that Browne was "Incompetent to define the futile," and that his *Dial* stood for all that was wrong in American writing. "It must not be ignored, but fought, if our art is ever to be free." [17] No battle developed because Browne died.

Early in 1917 *The Dial* was overhauled, provided with a new editorial board consisting of Conrad Aiken, Randolph Bourne, Van Wyck Brooks, John Macy, and Padraic Colum, and endowed with a new policy. It announced itself as a "Fortnightly Journal of Literary Criticism, Discussion and Information." That is, it chose to devote its pages to the serious study of literary ideas. This fact is auspicious because it represents the first of a series of decisions which created the journal of the 1920's. In the "Announcement" of January 25, 1917, the editors said that the new *Dial* would carry on a tradition which stemmed from "the original Dial." In the 1840's, "with Emerson among its contributors," it had "reflected the best American radicalism" of its day. Now once again it set itself to "meet the challenge of the new time by reflecting and interpreting" the presiding spirit of the hour, "a spirit freely experimental, skeptical of inherited values, ready to examine old dogmas and to submit afresh its sanctions to the test of experience. If criticism is peculiarly needed, it is because criticism can share almost equally with creative writing the privilege of revealing us to ourselves." In that concluding statement, we hear of course a doctrine which stemmed from Spingarn, would animate *The Seven Arts,* and was to shape the policy of *The Dial* of the 1920's.

By May, 1917, the new spirit of the old journal was obvious indeed. None of its readers could have been offended by the radicalism of Edward E. Hale's reviews of Zane Grey and E. Phillips Oppenheim. In the section called "Casual Comment," there were graceful notes on Barrett Wendell's retirement from Harvard, on the Timid Browser, on the high cost of rare books—the kind of futile chitchat about which Harriet Monroe fumed. Edward Garnett appeared with a purposeless essay on W. H. Hudson, Louis I. Bredvold with a closed-mind piece on Freud's study of Leonardo, J. C. Squire with a London Letter on the doings of Arnold Bennett and Edmund Gosse. But also during this period, January to June, Edward Sapir reviewed Rolland's *Jean Christophe,* and Joseph Jastrow wrote knowledgeably about Jung's first major post-Freudian work, *Analytical Psychology.* Bourne contributed two of his best known essays, studies of Dreiser and Dostoevsky. John Macy, reviewing *Dubliners* and *A Portrait of the Artist as a Young Man,* called the latter book "outspoken, vigorous, original, beautiful." Padraic Colum spoke of the Imagist movement, and Amy Lowell, herself an Imagist of note, treated "Poetry as a Spoken Art." Best of all, Conrad Aiken, in a review of Harriet Monroe's *The New Poetry,* said that the "Monroe Doctrine in Poetry" was far too tame, suffered from "many of the curious inhibitions, for the most part moral, which played havoc with the Victorians." Hoping to balance the tame and the wild, therefore, *The Dial* offered its readers Hamilton Fish Armstrong (currently editor of *Foreign Affairs*), Archibald Henderson, and F. W. Gookin alongside Harold J. Laski, Ludwig Lewisohn, and Carl Becker.

Then in October it printed another announcement. Lamenting the departure of *The Seven Arts,* the editors said that everyone "interested in the cause of literature and art in America will regret that 'The Seven Arts,' which made so valiant a start," has been obliged to suspend publication. But its audience must not despair: *The Dial* would fill unexpired subscriptions. Doubtless this is the event which led Morton D. Zabel in *Literary Opinion in America* to say that *The Seven Arts* merged with *The Dial*. No merger occurred, but in 1917, at the midpoint of its own first year of new life, *The Dial* did indeed choose to expand its policy in accord with tendencies introduced by *The Seven Arts*. It would be an exaggeration to say that *The Dial* adopted wholehog the program formulated by Oppenheim, Brooks, Frank, Rosenfeld, and Bourne. The announcement promised merely that "readers of 'The Seven Arts' will find some of their friends" among *The Dial*'s regular contributors. There was no apocalypse. But there was a distinct effort to fortify that taste for apocalyptic art and criticism which everyone associated with the other magazine.

The clearest sign of new purpose was a change in subtitle. As of January, 1918, the paper described itself as "A Fortnightly Journal of Criticism and Discussion of Literature and the Arts." Shifting its earlier direction, shaping itself to include the aims of "tendenz," it published Van Wyck Brooks' "War's Heritage to Youth." This essay brought *The Seven Arts* to intense life in *The Dial:* "We want to share in the higher life of the world, and we are incapable of doing so because we have no organized higher life of our own." America will be deprived of high culture until its men of letters are properly attended. "For poets and novelists and critics are the pathfinders of society," Brooks continued, intoning the prophecies which were to establish his authority as a major new voice in America. As if in full support of Brooks' idea of visionary art, *The Dial* in February opened with Oppenheim's long hortatory poem, "The Young World." In March, *The Seven Arts* was represented by Rosenfeld, and in April its position was embodied in one of Brooks' best essays, "On Creating a Usable Past." During these months, too, *The Dial* sought to represent the best American radicalism of its day by printing Charles Beard and Thorstein Veblen, John Dewey and Franz Boas. And in tentative fulfillment of the promise in its new subtitle, it began to offer new verse, poems by Edna St. Vincent Millay, Maxwell Bodenheim, and Conrad Aiken.

Then on June 6, 1918, another announcement said that the

magazine would move from Chicago to New York and would be run by a new board of editors: Dewey, Veblen, Bourne, and Scofield Thayer, its shadowy sponsor. Adopting still another form, coming to this new place, the magazine now blended Chicago's brand of prairie liberalism with Harvard aestheticism and fused both with *The Seven Arts'* version of American Resurgence. In this way, at the moment of its departure for New York, its editors and most noted contributors represented all the main movements in the intellectual life of the time: the New History, the New Anthropology, the New Psychology, the New Poetry, the New Criticism. In all departments *The Dial* now was equipped to engage in that postwar examination of the American past which men hoped would enable them to discover the ultimate nature of American life, of being itself.

The journal's purpose, policy, and spirit were best embodied in Randolph Bourne, but Bourne could not bring himself to participate without reserve in its activity. He could scarcely commit himself to its program so long as Dewey sat on its editorial board. In *The Seven Arts* for October, 1917, Bourne had published his "Twilight of Idols," questioning Dewey's honor and the virtue of Dewey's philosophy. "What I come to is a sense of being suddenly left in the lurch," he had written. "The allure of fresh and true ideas, of free speculation, of artistic vigor . . . of intelligence suffused by feeling, and feeling given the fibre and outline of intelligence" cannot exist so long as American intellectuals are led by the thinker who had deserted the cause of pacifism. Even Woodrow Wilson had said privately that the United States could not "fight Germany and maintain the ideal of government that all thinking men share. I shall try it but it will be too much for us." A "ruthless brutality," Wilson was certain, "will enter into the very fibre of our national life." [18] Precisely because Dewey, justifying desertion, had invoked his own philosophy, Bourne was convinced that Dewey's mind was expert in devising systems not values, expert in accommodation merely. This courageous, twisted, satirical ghost of man, as Dos Passos portrays Bourne in *1919,* walked about the city cackling, in paraphrase of Dewey, that war is the health of the state. And Floyd Dell describes how he won Bourne's devotion at "some Village party" when he argued that

Dewey's instrumentalism was a "convenient surrender of principles to force majeure." [19] Not only Dell but Thayer too agreed
with Bourne. Loving the man and foreseeing an inevitable martyrdom, Thayer became the proudest of all Bourne's supporters.

The work of reconstruction, Bourne had said in his famed
essay, can be done only by those "who are thorough malcontents,"
by men who maintain "a bitterness, an intellectual fibre, a verve."
His choice of epithets may have been deliberate, for these define
Thayer's qualities, as Bourne was aware; when he described
Thayer to Alyse Gregory he warned that his acerb friend was ex-
acting. She "must curb any irrelevant witticisms." [20] Thayer, who
had been a dedicated pacifist, could scarcely avoid siding with
Bourne in this controversy, though everyone realized that dishar-
mony, which was wrecking *The Seven Arts,* would ruin the new
Dial too. But Thayer, a solemn man of ideas, was earnest in support of men of action and men of art. During the war he had
planned to establish in Switzerland a mecca for deserters and ob-
jectors, and when the war ended he thought of creating a fund
from which awards of cash would be made to artists who required
leisure in order to work. This is, incidentally, virtually the same
plan that Pound was to conceive, Bel Esprit, and try to initiate in
1921 with a grant to Eliot, then slaving in Lloyds Bank. Thayer
chose a career in which he could more effectively assist in the cause
of high art but, as Robert Morss Lovett says, he "was chiefly interested in *The Dial* as a vehicle for Bourne's writing." [21]

Thayer had been tempted, therefore, to dissociate himself from
The Dial and attach himself to *The Seven Arts.* He had proposed
that its board of editors be reconstituted, that Oppenheim's authority be diminished, and that Mrs. Rankine's money be replaced
with his own. Oppenheim had refused.[22] When Thayer invited Watson to become his partner, Watson suggested that they take over
The Dial. Earlier Lovett had remarked to Thayer "on the anomaly
of putting up money for a paper and letting others have the fun
of running it. Whether he remembered the suggestion or not, he
took up his option." [23] However, it was the desire to drop Dewey
and set up Bourne, to enable his friend to demonstrate that the
elder generation of idols were men whose feet were clay, which
became his chief motive. He believed that only hard men of genius

would save the world, and in 1918 even Van Wyck Brooks seemed too "soft." Thayer, who was accustomed to remark how many proper Americans were good socialists until the chips were down, later changed his opinion of Brooks.

Bourne, aged 32, died in December, 1918. But Thayer and Watson decided to go ahead anyway. They bought *The Dial* and in 1919 reconstituted it according to the principles laid down by Bourne in a series of essays written during his last year of life. Thayer saw himself as the chief heir of Bourne's program, and saw his own image described in the central essay, "Traps for the Unwary": "Do we not want minds with a touch of the apostolic about them," Bourne had asked, "and a certain edge . . . a little surly . . . with an intellectual as well as an artistic conscience, with a certain tentative superciliousness toward Demos and an appalling hatred" for the "bourgeois" and the "sentimental"? [24] Watson too admired Bourne in whose criticism he recognized the great achievement of Resurgence. He did not share his colleague's absorption in this man's life and mind, but writing one of his earliest essays for *The Dial,* he described Bourne as the genius of *The Seven Arts* group. Van Wyck Brooks, Waldo Frank, and James Oppenheim were hortatory, without humor, dull to the uses of satire, but mainly they were too exclusive. They tended to "disregard and despise as un-American very admirable and very American poets like Ezra Pound, Marianne Moore, and William Carlos Williams." Watson, writing under his pseudonym, W. C. Blum, a name contrived to represent his special respect for Williams, praised these poets for writing verse which, though programmatic, was above all authentic poetry—precise, penetrating, sensible. And he believed that Williams in particular must be encouraged, must be published and read, because he is "one of the people who think they know what the United States needs in order to ripen a literature." [25] These are the writers whom Watson favored and whose work, along with Wallace Stevens' and Kenneth Burke's, he made certain each month in editorial horse-trade was published in *The Dial.*

Although Watson and Thayer were motivated by separate aims, both men had come along similar paths and by 1920 both shared a cluster of interconnecting ideas. Nevertheless, friends agreed, "to see Dr. Watson and Scofield Thayer together" evoked wonder at an "astounding association." To a historian there is nothing at all astounding in the partnership of two men who realized, as Matthew Arnold had foreseen, that the barbarians and philistines ruled the world: art alone remained a reliable guide to the moral life. Watson hoped to refashion the American moral imagination; Thayer wished to free artists to do their best work. Together, they agreed with Bourne that there was one way alone to salvage the Resurgence. In a letter written during 1914, Bourne had said that his generation would acquire a "complete social consciousness which would raise the whole world to a Kingdom of Heaven." [26] But in 1917, shortly before he died, he decided, "We shall never be able to perpetuate our ideals except in the form of art and literature." He was convinced, finally, that "the world will never understand our spirit except in terms of art. When shall we learn that 'culture,' like the kingdom of heaven, lies within us, in the heart of our national soul. . . . When shall we learn to be proud?" [27]

A few months before the fortnightly *Dial* had expired, it had printed a eulogy by Oppenheim called "Randolph Bourne." "He rose above his body," that crippled body, and moved among us, an American savior, "prophetic of his race." Watson and Thayer mourned his loss too. Taking on *The Dial*, however, they decided to turn it away from a taste for maudlin moods and incantations. Instead of announcing their support of a single program and movement, they preferred to advance no official cause whatever. They had seen at first hand the disasters of dogma in the conduct of literary affairs. And although they were to make their magazine elaborate, luxurious in form, they were certain that neither the journal nor American art could afford the luxury of commitment to one exclusive vision of salvation. Inheriting a fortnightly paper of "Criticism and Discussion of Literature and the Arts," they established a monthly review in which infighting by the politicians of utopia would be replaced by an impersonal but absorbing inquiry into its "creative and critical arts."

As their critic of painting, Thayer and Watson appointed Henry McBride, a follower of the utopian Robert Coady. As music critic, they chose one of Stieglitz's closest disciples, a member of *The Seven Arts* group, Paul Rosenfeld. As their managing editor, theater critic, and student of general culture, they took their former associate at Harvard, Gilbert Seldes, a man whose father had founded utopian colonies in New Odessa, Oregon and Stelton, New Jersey.* Transforming their magazine into what S. Foster Damon, a man close to their transactions, called a *"Seven Arts* without politics," they undertook to practice what Bourne had preached.[28]

* The first managing editor, Stewart Mitchell, served *The Dial* for a very short time.

IV. *Liberating Dangerous Words:*
WILLIAM CARLOS WILLIAMS

> The story of the *Dial* from 1919 to 1929 is well worth
> a book. On the whole it was the best magazine of the
> arts that we have had in this country. For the young
> American writer of the time, it was marvelous to have
> a magazine that would publish his best work, and pay
> him for it.
>
> Malcolm Cowley, unpublished letter, November
> 29, 1958.

I

Exposing the idea which inspired the leaders of Resurgence, seizing the principle argued by organicists of every persuasion, Thayer
and Watson in 1920 created a magazine whose chief function was
to provide a center, train an audience, and acquire a public for the
arts. Unlike *The Little Review* and its hosts of imitators, *The Dial*
did not try to shock or dazzle. Individual numbers did of course
sparkle, but during its first five years, when Thayer set its style
and established its influence, its pages show only here and there
that vigor and brag which mark each volume of Miss Anderson's
magazine. Thayer's own style was bravura. He addressed his
readers in the kind of rhetoric common among the Mencken group
at the *American Mercury* or the Crowninshield group at *Vanity
Fair,* inflated to suit the exuberance of the time. Elsewhere, both
editor and magazine are restrained indeed, dedicated to the job
of penetrating the center of value.

On the one hand there was restraint and dedication; on the
other, fervor and eloquence: these two moods reflect Thayer's
character, expose his ice and fire. They represent another impulse
too, one that consumed the editor but unified the journal. This impulse is misunderstood even now by those critics who have adopted
the opinions of Van Wyck Brooks or William Carlos Williams,
particularly by Alfred Kazin who believes that "nothing was so
dead in 1920 as the crusading spirit of 1910."[1] Unfortunately,
Kazin mistakes a preoccupation with art for an abandonment of

79

utopia. For two decades, this misconception has shaped our view of the time of *The Dial* when Thayer, fired by apostolic ardor, exhorted his readers to join him in a revolution not of the American political intelligence but of the literary and moral imagination. Rephrasing this impulse to accord with imagery habitual in that day, we recognize Thayer as a leading representative of those men in the 1920's who, animated by the spirit of 1910, saw in art the way to national health. If, as everyone agreed, the arts embody the mind and heart and spirit of man, then clearly the best procedure is to cultivate, as in a laboratory, the phenomenon itself. If we create in America a distinguished art, study its properties, define its quality, exhibit it, and proclaim its virtue, we will inevitably inject it into the world's body. Under Thayer, *The Dial* became a laboratory of the imagination where men of art sought to discover a serum of the soul.

"Thirty thousand readers," the editor announced in November, 1923, and "every new subscriber . . . a participant in the success of *The Dial*—a success which is making artistic history. Join this group of . . . pioneers, and identify yourself with this country's art and letters." America's only "complete magazine of the creative and critical arts," he continued next month, "has accomplished the seemingly impossible" and established itself as the journal which "men and women of intelligence" find indispensable in their lives. "Future Historians of the Art and Literature of America will . . . point to The Dial" as the most distinguished event of the age. "GROW WITH THE DIAL." "THE DIAL is a growing magazine. Let your business *grow with* THE DIAL." Other advertisers imitated Thayer's mode of discourse and, whatever they undertook to sell, shaped their argument to fit the editor's style. Women were instructed to shop at Bertha Holley's store on Forty-ninth Street not because they might find lovely things cheap or magnificent things dear but because they would discover forms of apparel produced in accord with the best principles of form in art.

> The goal of the creative mind everywhere today is to disentangle the quality of beauty from the fact of extravagance, and the quality of economy from the fact of shoddiness.

> For women's dress this goal has been attained by the Bertha Holley interchangeable, accumulative wardrobe, founded upon the artistic

truth of color and line, and achieving for the serge of business the same distinction as for the gold cloth of romance.[2]

These statements advertise far more than clothes or journal. In Thayer's blurb and Miss Holley's, we recognize what Josephine Herbst, speaking of " 'The Dial' and Modern Art," calls that "passionate intellectual search . . . [for] a truly creative attitude to life itself" which impressed everyone who read this new "Miscellany," this cornucopia of the mind.[3] Literary criticism by Eliot and Paul Valéry was supplemented by the social criticism of Bertrand Russell and Harold Laski. Both kinds occurred alongside studies in the plastic arts written by Henry McBride and Paul Rosenfeld. Sherwood Anderson (whose story "I'm a Fool" was published when Watson told Gilbert Seldes, "This can't do us any harm.") Anderson, and Proust were juxtaposed among the poems of Robinson and Millay, Hart Crane and Yeats, Aiken and Marianne Moore. Pound's "Hugh Selwyn Mauberly" was underscored by Wyndham Lewis' portrait of the renowned Ezra. Reproductions in black and white and in color, the plates for which were made by *der Sturm* in Berlin and tipped in by hand, were selected mainly by Thayer, whose taste included the impressionists and postimpressionists, some expressionists, but no cubists. The theater and popular arts were surveyed each month by Seldes, whose taste excluded nothing. He described the place of Krazy Kat in American civilization, compared Chaplin and John Barrymore, reported the new movements in American film and among the Provincetown Players.

Invaded by the color of Franz Marc's horses, the public read McBride on Dada and Rosenfeld on Schoenberg (his style "recalls the silent and atrocious music that goes on in the body during bad . . . hours"). It saw Joyce and Stravinsky through Stuart Davis' eyes. It came to know very well indeed Chagall's image of the world and Picasso's as well, which Thayer called "the chief ornament of our time." Particularly in these departments we observe Thayer's impulse to display and to propagandize. Reproducing painting and sculpture by artists whose work he considered most "intense," *The Dial* introduced Americans to the new art. Publishing McBride's criticism, Thayer encouraged a person of imagination more sturdy than that of his predecessor on *The Sun,* an earlier crusader, James G. Huneker. A specialist in these matters, Oliver Larkin, describes McBride as a man "with a bantering humor and a touch of Mencken's sarcasm . . . [who] assured his *Dial* readers in one of his monthly essays that America was in no imminent danger of catching up with the moderns." [4] Perhaps Mr. Larkin referred to McBride's testy comment on "the New Bedford public librarian who . . . banished *The Dial* from his library because he thinks [its] . . . illustrations constitute a danger for the young." But a remark of this kind is rare not habitual. Although McBride was fluent and knowing ("Gertrude liked . . . very much" the décor "Juan Gris made for the Ballet Russe"), nevertheless he saw himself as a missionary in the American cause. And he told his readers that they need no longer go to Paris to see great pictures or to learn the craft of painting. As early as 1921 he listed the gains since 1910: "We now have . . . an Independent Society of Art, a Montmartre in the shape of Greenwich Village, The New Society of Artists and . . . *The Dial*. All that remains to be wished for is a public."

Neither McBride nor Rosenfeld, however, allowed his zeal to corrupt his taste. McBride, who had served as an assistant to Van Wyck Brooks' father-in-law, John Ward Stimson, in the latter's Artist-Artisan Institute, never divorced art and American culture but tried not to praise the first because he loved the second. Nor did Rosenfeld, who also relied on a vocabulary of love, confuse his affections and his values. In 1922 he visited the Bach Festival in Bethlehem, Pennsylvania, and he returned to say that he had "seen beauty issue forth from common American bodies." Addicted to prose of this kind, unalterably committed to Stieglitz's thought, propagandist for American music, Rosenfeld remained acute in discrimination between the accomplishment of Copland or Sessions and, say, Howard Hanson. In 1928, Pound wrote to Miss Moore congratulating her that Rosenfeld had left her; although he did not wish to hammer a weak and affable and well-intentioned man, he could not resist saying that Rosenfeld never understood *anything*. He added that he had met Rosenfeld once or twice in company with, in the wake of, another writer whom Pound abominated, Sherwood Anderson. [5] Nevertheless, it was Rosenfeld who most fully understood and shared Thayer's aims, his effort to fuse what Robert Penn Warren calls "the democratic mystique" and the "aesthetic mystique." [6]

Elsewhere in the magazine, criticism ranged over the whole field of modern inquiry, studied matters of major interest both then and now, and offered speculation which is notable because we recognize in each essay a foreshadowing of the critic's later sustained work. The anthropologist Alfred Kroeber, reviewing Edward Sapir's new theory of language, predicted that "its ultimate influence will be revolutionizing." Sapir himself, who often wrote poetry and reviews, warned his readers that modern anthropology forced them to recognize how irrational, "primitive," were some of their "warmly cherished" notions. Thayer, fascinated by these new sciences of man, wrote to Freud to ask the classic question: Does psychoanalytic therapy diminish the creative powers of an artist? Freud responded, saying that his experience in this realm of thought, and that of his colleagues, was limited. But those artists who had submitted themselves to treatment had been helped, not hindered. Thayer may have taken this as reassurance of a quite personal kind for he was himself, a few years later, to leave for Vienna to place himself under Freud's care. In any event, he published the correspondence. He also published Santayana's essay, "A Long Way Round to Nirvana," written as an extended review of Freud's *Beyond the Pleasure Principle.* Edmund Wilson, treating related ideas, discovered in Lenormand a dramatist who tried to connect the wound and the bow, and was distressed "a little at admitting that human character can so easily be reduced to a complex."

What was most impressive about the magazine, however, was not the range of its interests or the quality of its taste or the vehemence of its propaganda. At a time when society hoped to retreat within its own frontiers, to abandon its role as a leading member of the international community, Thayer and Watson labored to make their magazine an international organ which would represent and address men everywhere. It offered fiction by Louis Aragon and John Dos Passos, Virginia Woolf and E. M. Forster, Capek, Schnitzler, Unamuno, and Mann—the last of these being virtually unknown here until Kenneth Burke, who had been introduced to Mann by his teacher, Ludwig Lewisohn, at

Ohio State, translated his work for *The Dial*. This roster of contributors caused Glenway Wescott to marvel at what a hall of
fame *The Dial* had become.

For the first time in our history, a national audience was informed in the events of art as these happened in each European
capital. Until 1923, Eliot wrote the London Letter and Pound the
Paris Letter. I resist the impulse to illustrate with batches of quo-
tations their opinions of each other, of Joyce, Frost, Sandburg,
Marianne Moore; of Diaghilev's ballet, Nijinsky, Cocteau. But
their prose, reprinted often, is commonly known and is found elsewhere. One series of reports and exchanges, however, is both un-
matchable and irresistible. Pound, in 1922, ashamed of his countrymen, said that "all men should 'Unite to give praise to Ulysses,' "
a book then banned in America "where every child of seven has
ample opportunity to drink in the details of the Arbuckle case."
Shortly thereafter, John Eglinton, who appears in Joyce's novel as
"Eglintoneyes," the source of silly and prim comment during Dedalus' discussion of Shakespeare, reported in the Dublin Letter
that city's response to the novel. "Just as it was a disappointment
that Sweden—a land, one fancied, with bones of iron and breath
fragrant with the pine—should produce . . . a mere bundle of
nerves like Strindberg . . . so it is a little disconcerting to find
Ireland—the country where, as the world fancied, Faith still lingered in all its bookless artlessness—breathing out no healing airs
from its boglands into European literature, but rather—in this its
most important contribution . . . for some time—a particularly
strong and composite odour from mean streets and brothels."
Compare this to Eliot who, a month earlier (September, 1922),
said that *Ulysses* is "at once the exposure and the burlesque of
that which it is the perfection." Poor Eglinton, forced to admit
that he simply could not understand the novel, even that episode
"in which I have myself taken a humble part."

Eliot at his own request was relieved of his duties as London
correspondent and was replaced by Bloomsbury's Raymond Mortimer. Thayer sent Seldes to Pound with a request for his resignation because he preferred to have a correspondent native to the
country from which the letter was sent. Paul Morand was Pound's
replacement, and instead of the latter's pyrotechnics, Morand sup-

plied *The Dial* with gossip about Paul Claudel and Jacques Mari-
tain, about Gide and the *NRF*. His criticism was sententious but
his chitchat was quick; he specialized in the inside dope. From
six years of gossip I have culled one striking observation, that it
was pleasant to see German artists again in Paris, particularly
Rainer Maria Rilke, "the greatest contemporary German lyric
poet." In May, 1926, nine months before Rilke's death, *The Dial*
published translations of nine segments from his *Lay of the Life
and Death of Cornet Christopher Rilke,* a work not available in
English until 1932.

     Although he lost Eliot and Pound, Thayer did acquire Thomas
Mann whose correspondence begins to appear at about the time
theirs disappeared. "I am delighted," Mann said in his first letter,
"I write this . . . it is translated into the language of Poe, Emerson, and Whitman. And my words will be followed with friendli-
ness and sympathy by a bold and kindly-disposed type of mankind. . . . That is beautiful . . . such bonds and such comrade-
ship." How lovely, too, this "internationalization of art." Mann's
tone was perfect. Each letter managed simultaneouly to teach the
lesson of internationalism and to report the central matters of
German literary life. Describing Spengler as a "frigidly heroic
thinker," Mann felt that this man's "self-conquest and self-
denial" were "gruesome"; soon his readers would see in "Death
in Venice," a story which would itself be published in *The Dial*
for March, 1924, his version of Spengler's quality and effect. But
in general his correspondence records his hope not his fear, his
faith in Germany's humanism. Confronted daily "by corrupt thinking," he said, perhaps we may "preserve our own thought from corruption." For this reason he described his pleasure in the Reisiger
translation of Whitman: it enabled Germans to discover in Whitman a sense of democracy which involved no party politics whatever.

     By 1923, however, the Italian correspondent was convinced
that humanism and democracy were antique. He saw in fascism
and communism "universal principles sufficient to the whole spirit
of man," so coherent and implacable that no nation would resist
imitating either the Italian or the Russian modes of life. The
Russian letter for 1924, written by Alexander Eliasberg, said little

about politics but discriminated between the official poetry of communism, as composed by Mayakovski, and the classic poetry, written wholly in disregard of the theory and practice of revolution.[7] The best verse of this latter sort, he said, is available in the work of one young poet who stems from "the great line of Russian verse descending from Pushkin. He was also known before the war, but it is only in recent years that he became prominent." This poet's syntax and imagery are "of such an unusual and yet quite spontaneous peculiarity that he can often be recognized in a single one of his lines . . . [and] images." The poet is Boris Pasternak.

In this fashion, *The Dial* introduced European writing of the most advanced as well as the most customary kind. Thus, too, Thayer adapted and dilated another major element in Randolph Bourne's thought, the principle of transnationality. Thayer applied this not to politics merely or to American culture alone but to the world in general and to the arts above all. We publish Europeans, he said in an editorial, as confrères who participate "in the Western-civilized-Christian-European-American-tradition." It is a tradition which does not stifle individuality but does stress community: each literature maintains its "independent existence," its "separate, precious character," its uniqueness within the community as a whole. Vowing that *The Dial* would never become "the organ of a clique or group," Thayer turned from "the fumy scene of contemporary politics" in order to fulfill what Eliot was to describe as "The Function of a Literary Review": " 'to maintain the autonomy and disinterestedness of literature, and at the same time to exhibit the relations of literature . . . to all the other activities which, together with literature, are the components of life.' " Thayer approved Eliot's thought but rephrased it to suit his own idea of eloquence: "To distinguish the delicate from the fragile, the exquisite from the unusual, the imaginative from the fanciful, the original from the eccentric; to whip the *crème de la crème* from the milk-pails of the Elysian Fields; to astonish the stupid, to bewilder the clever, to stimulate the intelligent, to satisfy the intellectual, such . . . is the *rôle* of the famous *Dial* of the 'twenties.' "

By mid-decade, therefore, the magazine had fulfilled the ambition of its founders and editor, had achieved an international triumph. Raymond Mortimer said publicly that London envied New York its magazine: "Why not an English edition of *The Dial?*" Praise of this kind, we must realize, represents an extraordinary turnabout in the state of letters, for only fifteen years earlier, the opinion of English critics had been decisive. London had decided matters of worth and reputation in literature. But now Logan Pearsall Smith, writing to introduce a young man, Cyril Connolly by name, destined to make his mark, lamented the lack in England of a "paper like 'The Dial' which can welcome and discover new talent." [8] Ortega y Gasset wrote requesting permission to reprint material in his own magazine. He reminded the editor that he must fix his price low: "You must take account of the great difficulties which may be overcome for conquering and maintaining in this country the affection for" *The Dial's* kind of "subtle and refined literature." [9] Von Hofmannsthal, who served as the correspondent from Vienna, reported that *The Dial* gave him much pleasure as often as he received it. "I feel so homely among its contributors—it gives me a feeling better than any of the European reviews. There is something more generous in it, I think, just the contrary of blasé." [10] Alfred Stieglitz, finally, a man of quite another sort, sent a letter in 1925 when Thayer published *Living Art,* saying that his disagreement with its policy was "of no moment—it is the good will—the kind spirit, that touch . . . me deeply." [11]

Thayer and Watson had succeeded in establishing a sense of colleagueship similar to that linking undergraduates at the university, where earlier they and their associates had undertaken to make *The Harvard Monthly* a magazine at once properly "aesthetic" and stirringly avant-garde. Instead of Harvard's *Advocate,* their neighbor now was Albert Jay Nock's *Freeman.* A short distance away on West Thirteenth Street were *The Menorah Journal* and *Soviet Russia Pictorial.* But it was *The Dial* alone, at luncheons and dinners in its office and in each of its monthly numbers, that dramatized the idea of community. Entrance was granted, Maxwell Bodenheim's no less than Clive Bell's, according to no dogmas or snobberies whatever, constrained by ordinary human limitation but restricted by no meanness or arrogance at all. It is this tone which Europeans especially admired, but even Joe Gould, the notorious philosopher-bum of Greenwich Village, found himself charmed. His lyric—"Who killed *The Dial?*" "I . . . with my inimitable style, I killed *The Dial*"—is often cited as evidence of the editor's preference for the usual rather than the extraordinary kinds of experiment.[12] Gould himself, however, having written a letter saying that he would never submit anything to the editor's splendid mausoleum of European reputations, and having received a winning reply, before long begged to be put on the staff. No other magazine had managed to combine *The Dial*'s homeliness and daring, its peculiar form of decency and disinterestedness, its satire and zeal: Watson and Thayer.

2

Despite *The Dial*'s success abroad, its amazing number of readers at home, its crusade for ideas central to the life of our time, and its publication of new writers and major works, by 1925 it had alienated many of the people whom the editors admired most. Socialists believed that it had falsified the connections between art and life; nationalists were certain it discriminated in favor of foreigners. Gorham Munson, who led *Secession,* complained that *The Dial* lacked homogeneity; that is, it did not agree with Munson's diagnosis of America's social disease or his remedy, the humanism and politics of the right. Hemingway never forgave the editors for their neglect of his early poetry and prose, and, indeed, became a main source of opinion concerning their disregard of younger writers. Once in the 1930's, in the late hours of a party given by Paul Rosenfeld, he telephoned Miss Moore and said that he would send a cab if she would come and tell him why *The Dial* had refused to publish his work. He had heard rumors that she was responsible. Malcolm Cowley, incidentally, in 1924 wrote to Miss Moore complaining about Hemingway's faith in rumor: "He might have hunted me up and found out what I had to say." [13] Hemingway claimed that he submitted poetry and was told that he would never be much of a poet; there remains no memory or record of this transaction. Once or twice he offered a sketch of war. The editors were unable to agree on its merits and they solicited Miss Moore's opinion: "I have read Mr. Hemingway's story with great interest," but as it stands "I would say no." [14] One or two rejections hardly define neglect. Furthermore, from 1924 until 1929, *The Dial* published essays in review of virtually all his work. In 1924, when Hemingway was one of a dozen interesting new writers, it offered an essay by Edmund Wilson, a brisk study of *Three Stories and Ten Poems* and *In Our Time.* The publishing of a signed review by one of the best new critics was no accident; it implied respect for both reviewer and books reviewed. Less important matter was placed in another department called "Briefer Mention," composed of unsigned notices such as the one which described John Crowe Ransom's first book of verse, *Chills and Fever,* as a volume crammed full of "unrewarding dissonances, mountebank persiflage, mock mediaeval minstrelsy, and shreds of elegance." In contrast, Wilson's review said of Hemingway's earliest published work that the "poems are not particularly important but his prose is of the first distinction."

Hart Crane's complaints were even louder than Hemingway's. In 1923 he told Allen Tate, "There is no use in my sending anything more to *The Dial* . . . it is plain that their interest in helping American letters is very incidental. Note the predominance given to translations of the older generations of Germans, etc. . . . They aren't printing the younger crowd of any country." [15] Crane's poetry, which had been published in one of the journal's earliest numbers, continued to appear there throughout the 1920's. The Germans he referred to—Schnitzler, Hauptmann, Von Hofmannsthal, Mann—were scarcely aged in 1923. But complaints persisted and even included the suspicion that the editor paid foreigners more than he paid natives. Everyone was certain that there were two scales of payment, one for the Irish Senator Yeats, another for the Jersey scribbler Williams. They would not believe that "there is absolutely one price and that is two cents a word for prose and ten dollars a page for poetry," Seldes wrote to Williams.[16]

The editor was adamant about maintaining this policy. He rejected the opinion gratuitously offered by George Moore, who laughed at their pretension and said that one contributor is after all worth ten times another.[17] The editor insisted that there was no connection between cash and literary worth. His magazine published the best work available, domestic or foreign, and the state of a writer's reputation was not a matter in which the editor was concerned. There was a certain bravado, of course, in this position. But the editor deliberately took his stand on the highest theoretic ground and hoped thereby to force American writers to extend themselves. Thayer did not condescend to write a letter of thanks to, let us say, Edwin Seaver, but he did describe his gratitude upon receiving *Felix Krull:* "I like the work immensely. I do trust that you are going on with this remarkable story and that we may enjoy the maturity of this gifted youth . . . for which you have here in so many details finely prepared." [18] His behavior involved editorial manners far more than it implied editorial policy.

Thayer was a man of moods; formal and fussy, he allowed no one to violate the privacies of his mind and person or to instruct him in the conduct of *The Dial*'s affairs. Hemingway, Crane, and all the rest did not know, therefore, that he had closed its pages to further contributions from J. Middleton Murry because Murry had written, for *The Yale Review,* an essay in aspersion not in criticism of Cummings' poetry. "Feeling as you do about the work of so important and characteristic a contributor to The Dial as Mr Cummings, I should not think you would care to write further for The Dial." [19] Murry replied in a way that avoided the issue, and there was no further talk between them.

"When Miss Moore was editor of *The Dial*," Kenneth Burke wrote years later in *The Grammar of Motives,* "her ideal number . . . would I think have been one in which all good books got long favorable reviews, all middling books got short favorable reviews, and all books deserving of attack were allowed to go without mention." [20] Nevertheless, a certain habit of disrespect was usual among writers of the younger generation. It appears again in another objection common during the 1920's when people were convinced that *The Dial* never published a new writer. From countless manuscripts placed on the editor's desk, he selected Glenway Wescott who, later moving toward fascism, admitted that he was heretic toward *The Dial* but his heresy was that of a disciple, one anxious for the approval of those who, by example and encouragement, gave him his start.[21] More notable at the moment is *The Dial*'s publication of Louis Zukovsky, today imitated by those Beat poets who see themselves at the farthest frontier of the latest literary movement. And no less striking is its publication of Stanley Kunitz, quite unread until suddenly he received a Pulitzer Prize.[22] Making discoveries is as much a matter of luck as of taste. Far more important is *The Dial*'s campaign for "The Waste Land" at a time when Eliot was down and out in London, its support of Lawrence when he was a pariah at home, and its selection of Conrad Aiken's best criticism to which now Irving Howe traces much of the prestige and effectiveness of contemporary critical thought.

These were the miraculous years of art, as R. P. Blackmur reminds us; from 1920 through 1925, Pound, Eliot, Joyce, Stevens, Proust, Mann, Ortega, and Valéry produced those works of poetry, fiction, and criticism which dignify our modern literature.[23] This was the time when, Blackmur says, Yeats' verse bloomed toward that ripeness peculiar to the poet's last years. Although most of these writers had been taken up by the little magazines before Thayer and Watson refurbished *The Dial,* only one of their number, Joyce, had achieved any recognition in America until this journal campaigned in their behalf. With the addition of a poem by Joyce, Blackmur's list is identical with Thayer's and Watson's. Indeed, announcing in 1925 that Van Wyck Brooks would receive *The Dial* Award, Thayer reminded his readers that the Nobel Prize for literature, conferred on Yeats, had gone to a man who was "virtually unrepresented in pages of other American magazines" and whose "present thoughts," but for *The Dial,* "would be unknown in America."

It made no difference how often Thayer reported his sense of the magazine's achievements or maintained that its victory was not a personal but a national triumph: "Columbia," he said in 1924, "sports upon the digits of one patriotically mottled hand five readable magazines." "Piety to our original editress, the late Marchioness Ossoli, compels us . . . to attribute The Dial . . . to Columbia's index finger. The Nation and The New Republic are, as usual, in the relatively safe middle. The Yale Review occupies, thickly, the thumb. . . . On the little finger . . . Vanity

Fair." No matter how often he described letters from eminent people or notices of commendation from distinguished papers, he was
unable to gain the allegiance of writers who preferred to imagine
themselves somehow lost. Embattled revolutionaries, they pelted
everyone. And they aimed especially at *The Dial* because they saw
it as a monument in brownstone inhabited by Wallace Stevens'
high-toned old Christian lady. They quite forgot that it was this
magazine, publishing Stevens' poem, that dramatized the poet's
own conviction: "Poetry is the supreme fiction, madame." Few
indeed had Stevens' restraint. In 1925, responding to the editor's
request for an essay on William Carlos Williams, Stevens replied
that he was certain "one of the things I ought not to do is review
Williams' book. What Columbus discovered is nothing [com-
pared] to what Williams is looking for. However much I might
like to try to make that out—evolve a mainland from his leaves,
scents and floating bottles and boxes—there is a baby at home." [24]

Unrestrained, consumingly ambitious, worried about unfed
babies at home, all the wild young men sneered at Thayer's journal: "For God's sake," Malcolm Cowley wrote to Kenneth Burke,
"let's brew some stronger liquor." [25] It was William Carlos Williams who spoke for all his disenchanted friends when early in the
1920's he saw in the magazine a reproduction of Chagall's "On
Dit," the study of a Talmudist done in hues of green. He ripped
it out and wrote in the margin: "If there is a loonier pack of nit
wits in the world than you fellows who are making The Dial, they
are not advertising it to the world as you are. This is the brazenest
kind of prostitution, because it is a colossal affectation, the Greenwich Village brand of moral and spiritual and artistic degeneracy.
You are not discovering new worlds, but only helping to ruin the
beauty in this. You ought to be suppressed—and shamed." Gilbert
Seldes, replying for the editors, wrote to say how grateful the staff
was to hear Dr. Williams' opinion: "What The Dial has always
needed has been constructive criticism of this sort." [26]

Williams' reactions, his displeasures and his delights, always
were hair-trigger, and charting these, we record a complete
graph of American thought about *The Dial,* the reasons why it
pleased its European public but perplexed people at home. Not
long after the Chagall incident, Williams read Elie Faure's essay

THE
DIAL

NOVEMBER 1922

VOLUME LXXIII   NUMBER 5

50 cents a copy

Marianne Moore as photographed about 1940.

Stewart Mitchell, first managing editor of *The Dial*.

The Dial's second managing editor, Gilbert Seldes, about 1922.

James Sibley Watson, Jr., who with Thayer began
publishing *The Dial* in 1919. Photo taken in 1929,
the year publication ended.

Dial music critic Paul Rosenfeld, left, observing 1925 eclipse with Scofield Thayer. (Photo by J. S. Watson, Jr.)

The Dial's co-publisher, Scofield Thayer, as he appeared about 1916.

Author Kenneth Burke, about 1923.

on Greek art and a poem by Lawrence, and wrote again, saying these "have come pretty near planting a monkey gland in my thigh I guess by the feeling I now feel." He was beginning to respect the magazine because he had learned how "to pick and choose . . . the things which are, to me, the best. And, must I add to my own shame, these things are usually by some Europeans." [27] When Watson in 1926 offered Williams *The Dial* Award, the poet was enraptured, unbelieving: "surprise and delight have so upset me," that he could scarcely write the note of acceptance.[28] Eventually, he told Miss Moore, now installed as editor, that he wished that he "could communicate the relief given me . . . to twenty others and that we could all together do something with ourselves that would liberate—Dangerous words! Yes, that's it after all: Liberate dangerous words." [29] In 1958 his letter recalls the emotion of that moment; "Receipt of *The Dial's* Award was an epoch making event for me, it put me on my feet." And, he adds, "Make no mistake about it, *The Dial* was an important influence in my generation." "Whatever Scofield Thayer's interest in publishing that periodical may have been it was certainly an original effort geared to the time." [30]

Acclaim comes thirty years late because most American writers, like Williams, were uninformed in Thayer's purpose and policy. "An organized higher life," Brooks had said in the fortnightly *Dial,* "that is what the world demands of us." And this is precisely what people elsewhere admired in the life of organized high art as presented by the monthly *Dial.* Because Thayer never publicized his credo, his American colleagues were unaware that he labored to make *The Dial* the very organ they all demanded, international in bias, apocalyptic in purpose, synoptic in design. This motive is implicit in each monthly number but it is explicit in the twenty-one pages of instructions Thayer left behind when in 1925 he turned over to Marianne Moore the duties of editor. There the role of each employe and the policy of the journal, are codified as if for eternity. His concern was not that of a man unable to deprive himself of authority. Rather he insisted that the form of *The Dial* be maintained. It had been designed by Bruce Rogers, gifted and renowned designer for the Riverside

Press. Rogers had made it a magazine elegant in every detail, one which harmonized "the beauties of type and format and paper." [31] Harmony of detail was stressed in the organization of items for each number, too, and during nearly ten years of monthly publication, *The Dial* never violated Thayer's injunction. "Impressionistic pictures should follow realistic, and landscapes follow figures." "Verse . . . should not be published just before or after an illustration. Verse like illustrations should be used to break up long prose stretches." "Two pieces of fiction, like two pieces of verse by different poets, should not be juxtaposed." [32] In Thayer's mind *The Dial* was itself an organic work of imagination; to describe its intention was to violate its nature.

Thayer's form dramatizes his purpose, as A. R. Orage was aware when he said in his own journal, *The New Age,* published in England, "The American 'Dial' is perhaps the most fully realized of all the promising literary magazines now current in the world." It addressed people everywhere "who really read . . . for their lives: to appeal to the latter class is to be 'of the centre,' for the centre of every movement of life . . . is the most vital." [33] At a time when American artists hoped either to rid themselves of their past or to select only what was "usable," in an age of cabal, Thayer refused to align himself or his magazine in support of random projects. Indeed, he argued that his magazine was the best in the world because it "suspects the extreme left wing in literature of being a little barren, the extreme right wing a little senile." His contributors, steeped in the life of their time, committed to the prejudice for revolution or the prejudice for reaction, dismissed him as a mere playboy of the mind. Thayer saw himself, however, as a crusader, ardent to provide society with forms of art which would enable Americans to discover within themselves the kingdom of heaven. Inspired by this discovery they would establish at least the perfect state of man. Simultaneously, American artists, guaranteed a public and thereby stimulated to fulfill their own personal promise, would create that sublime literature in which the meaning of America would be palpable.

Until now I have tried to explain why and how *The Dial,* despite caveat, complaint, and confusion at home, acquired international fame. Also I have maintained that it presented a synthesis of ideas current among literary men during the first two decades of our century. Another way to say similar things is to recall the labels borrowed from the Hoffman, Allen, and Ulrich volume: combining the aims of "tendenz" with those of the "critical little magazine," *The Dial* imposed its pattern on the American 1920's. Furnishing society with a national magazine of the creative and critical arts, Thayer and Watson enabled artists and critics to collaborate in the formulation and assessment of values in letters and life. Now, however, let us put aside explanation and argument and confront the document itself. Describing its contents from January, 1920 until January, 1923, the moment just after it gave its award to Eliot, we can judge why this journal was in fact a momentous event of national culture. Although it is unnecessary to list every item in each of the thirty-six issues, it is appropriate to take a proper sample of those initial three years.

In 1920, the new monthly *Dial* opened with Randolph Bourne's "An Autobiographic Chapter." Not only was this a telling way to present a magazine dedicated to Bourne's spirit, but also it was an extraordinary chapter in itself. Retitled "Fragment of a Novel" by Van Wyck Brooks, it is one of the major pieces in that posthumous collection, *The History of a Literary Radical,* on which Bourne's influence rests today. In later issues that year, Brooks himself was represented by two chapters taken from a forthcoming work, *The Ordeal of Mark Twain.* Essays by other members of the fortnightly *Dial* and *The Seven Arts,* by Dewey and Laski, Aiken and Oppenheim, were common during those first months. These were associated with critical pieces by Dos Passos and Cowley, Cummings and Eliot, Marsden Hartley and Deems Taylor. An international bent was evident, too, in the appearance of Arthur Symons, Bertrand Russell, Yeats (an open letter to Lady Gregory about "A People's Theatre" in Dublin), Rémy de Gourmont, Julien Benda, Coomaraswamy. In fiction there were Sherwood Anderson ("The Triumph of the Egg"), Waldo Frank, Kenneth Burke, Manuel Komroff as well as Schnitzler, George Moore, Proust ("Saint Loup: A Portrait"). And in poetry, Bodenheim, Aiken, Sandburg ("Jazz Fantasia"), Witter Bynner, Cummings, Miss Moore, Miss Millay, H. D., Miss Lowell, Williams, Hart Crane, Pound ("Hugh Selwyn Mauberly" and "Fourth

Canto"), Yeats, and Osbert Sitwell are printed in substantial amounts. In the visual arts we find Demuth, Cézanne, Robert Edmund Jones, Marin, Pascin, Kahlil Gibran, Lachaise, Gropper, Lipchitz, Stuart Davis, Gauguin, Vlaminck. Aside from these, there are some special items: "Kiri No Meijiyama, A Noh-Drama in Japanese Syllabics" by S. Foster Damon, Ford Madox Ford's reminiscences, and Joseph Conrad's prefaces to *An Outcast of the Islands, Lord Jim,* and *Nostromo.* In one way or another, in extended essay or brief mention, some three hundred separate titles and authors from Sholom Aleichem to Henry Adams are noted or reviewed during the twelve months, January to December, 1920. Furthermore, *The Dial* offered each month its regular comments by McBride, Rosenfeld, and Seldes on that month's round of affairs in art, music, film, drama, and vaudeville.

In 1921 some new names occur alongside the familiar ones on Thayer's list of favored critics: Ralph Barton Perry (reviewing Santayana's *Character and Opinion in the United States*), Santayana himself, Croce, and Jean Cocteau. A remarkable essay by Rosenfeld on Stieglitz's technique requires special mention because it represents the sole occasion when *The Dial* recognized photography as a fit method of performing the lofty ritual of art.* More impressive, however, is the inclusion of fiction by Mann ("Loulou"), May Sinclair, and Giraudoux, and the publication of a one-act play by Andreyev ("He, The One Who Gets Slapped"). Lawrence is suddenly a featured poet. And in addition to the customary number of pages given over to other favored poets, there are verses by E. A. Robinson, Mina Loy, Richard Hughes, Joseph Campbell, Babette Deutsch, and Thomas Hardy. In the visual arts, there is a sudden interest in William and Marguerite Zorach and in Wyndham Lewis. Weber, de Chirico, Zadkine, and Georgia O'Keeffe appear for the first time.

In 1922, Hermann Hesse and the psychologist of behaviorism, John B. Watson, the historian James Harvey Robinson, Roger Fry, von Hofmannsthal, Spingarn, Edmund Wilson are among the

---

* "It is not alone the fact that he has expressed us, and so communicated the impulse to create, that moves us so," Rosenfeld said of Stieglitz. Rather, his genius is in demonstrating how "all others of his time, who so desire, can help free themselves for the life of the spirit, the life of art."

new contributors. The roster included, of course, critics whom *The Dial*'s audience had come to expect: Pound, Eliot, Burke, Russell, Croce, Santayana. But in fiction and poetry there were some novelties, chief of which were Ivan Bunin's "The Gentlemen from San Francisco," Wallace Stevens' "A High-Toned Old Christian Woman" and "The Emperor of Ice-Cream," and Eliot's "The Waste Land." The arts too were distinguished by major pieces and persons: Archipenko, Kuniyoshi, Matisse, Rousseau, Marc, and Brancusi ("The Golden Bird"). From start to finish, indeed, 1922 was the year of triumph for Thayer and *The Dial*.

That January it had opened with the editor's comment on the magazine's choice of Sherwood Anderson for its first award. And it closed with "The Waste Land" and with Edmund Wilson's study of Eliot's poem, the first published essay in what has become a library of criticism treating that historic work. Perhaps because Thayer realized that *The Dial* was now unrivaled, he spoke openly about his purposes. Reflecting on his pleasure in hearing people approve *The Dial's* award to Anderson, he said that he was happy to find a steady growth of readers who "support us practically and morally and with a warming enthusiasm. We think it is because we put into action their own principles and, on their behalf, are asking more of American artists than has been asked, and allowing more." The journal was imbued with one intense idea to which at last society at large had begun to react. Anderson's award had caused people to realize that it was not the magazine alone, not the gift or amount of money, and not "the suitability of Mr Anderson" which really counted. Rather, "the beginning of a new relation between the American creative artist and the American people" was "the essential thing." This thing I have called communion.

However quiet Thayer's pleasure, however conventional his words, his comment reports his belief that Bourne's kingdom was at hand. The one event which seemed to certify this achievement, publication of "The Waste Land," I have reserved for special discussion in the next chapter. There we discover why Thayer decided to present that poem as the prime and prodigious achievement of American prophetic art in our time. Selecting a work that portrays doom and offers salvation, that describes the disasters of the body and prescribes a therapy of the spirit, Thayer hoped to perform the rite, communion, which would enable this nation, redeemed by organic art, to save the world.*

* In 1922, as Matthew Josephson's recent memoir confirms, a vague idea that *The Dial* was "pursuing an educational function" of some interest but of no special militancy seemed, to most members of the literary community, the sole explanation of its aims. Harold Loeb and Josephson decided, therefore, that *Broom* should follow another course, "should become in essence a *tendenz* magazine"! *Life Among the Surrealists* (New York, 1962), 188.

V. "Living Art":
T. S. ELIOT

> Then out of the blue *The Dial* brought out *The Waste-land* and . . . wiped out our world as if an atomic bomb had been dropped upon it.
>
> WILLIAM CARLOS WILLIAMS, *Autobiography*, 1951.

ANYONE who examined *The Dial*'s advertisements might have recognized Thayer's effect on his time, inferred his motive, and given the magazine its due. But if such a testimony seems too subtle or too frivolous, less ingenuity is required to see precisely the same motive in its dedication to the work of a poet better favored than, say, Bertha Holley—T. S. Eliot. Men of the 1920's were accustomed to associate "The Waste Land" and *The Dial,* to see in the one a reflection of the other. Precisely what each reflects has never been clear. Van Wyck Brooks, for example, is certain that *The Dial,* embracing Eliot, achieved a coup of literary politics which instituted that betrayal, both social and literary, he attributes to Eliot and Pound, Tate and Ransom, their imitators and disciples. But Thayer sponsored Eliot's verse and prose for precisely the same reasons which led him in 1925 to publish *Living Art,* a folio of modern painting and sculpture. Both poem and folio manifest Thayer's understanding of the creed central to all organicist thought. Each was published in order to create that moment of mystic fusion, to convey that special serum of the imagination with which Thayer hoped to revive the true American spirit. Taken together, Eliot's poem and Thayer's folio help to clarify an abiding problem in modern literary history.

What Brooks failed to realize is that Eliot impressed all members of *The Dial* group as the very man they had been waiting for, the writer who would help to establish the new American spirit and make it count in the world of art and affairs. The group could not know that Eliot had cut American ties and had elected to make an exclusively European reputation in order to serve as an organicist of international culture. The members of the group, admiring his work, had planned to enhance his career and simultaneously to publicize their journal at home and abroad. Alone among American poets, Thayer thought, Eliot was not victimized by that " 'localism' which . . . takes so much of American writing out of the field of comparison with European letters . . . and requires for American writers a special standard of judgement."[1] Watson found similar virtue in Eliot's criticism and believed that it performed a major service because, "temporarily at least," it rearranged and clarified ideas "in the same surprising way as do for example Freud's theories of sex in childhood." Both Thayer and Watson agreed with Miss Moore, not yet a member of the staff, who wrote their review of *The Sacred Wood* and approved Eliot's own conviction: in a muddled time the best teacher is often the writer who is both a critic and a creative artist. Indeed, each in his own fashion saw in Eliot the apogee of exactly the kind of American man of letters who Brooks' friend, Randolph Bourne, had said must be encouraged if America were ever to fulfill its promise in art and in life.

But it was Thayer, whose life and Eliot's had intersected at certain moments during their early years, at Milton and Harvard and Oxford, who was most profoundly moved by the elder man's genius. For Thayer was committed to the very principle which Eliot was to establish as the leading dogma in modern letters. Although Eliot derived some main ideas from Gourmont and the Symbolists, he applied his thought chiefly to English and American subjects, to those poets who "feel their thought as immediately as the odour of a rose." I have cited a key phrase from a famous essay, "The Metaphysical Poets," written in 1921. Remarks drawn from E. E. Cummings' review in *The Dial* of Eliot's first volume of poems would scarcely present a similar bouquet. Nevertheless, despite Eliot's carefully wrought vocabulary, both he and Cummings share essentially the same notion about the quality prime in art of the first rank—intensity. This quality, best exhibited, according to Cummings, in Eliot's verse and Pound's prose, provokes in the reader a heightened sense of his own being, of human existence as a whole. Only when this occurs does the work of art come fully to life. Cummings, who credits his friend S. Foster Damon for his introduction to the New Poetry, attributes to Scofield Thayer this principle of criticism. He adds that he has no "notion how Thayer evolved the idea that *art* is au fond *intense* (& unart isn't) but feel sure the idea first came to me from him." [2]

This idea is not, however, original with Eliot or T. E. Hulme, Pound or Cummings, or even Thayer, and has a history of its own which began, according to M. H. Abrams in *The Mirror and the Lamp,* when Longinus said that sublimity is "a product of an inspired moment of passion." [3] That aspect of Longinian theory reappears among the Romantics, mainly Keats and Coleridge, whose work led others, notably Poe and Arnold, to adopt intensity itself as a leading idea of value in verse. Abrams does not refer to its next transmutation, to Pater's description of the flaming intensities of art, though this illumined the minds of aesthetes at Oxford and Harvard. Pragmatized and Americanized, it occurs in Bernard Berenson's system as the principle of life-enhancement: "a plunging into a state of being, or state of mind, that makes one feel not only physically alive but morally and spiritually as well; reaching out to the topmost peak of our capacities." [4] Among generations of Harvard aesthetes, therefore, Pater's thought was succeeded by Berenson's art for life's sake. And its translation to modern literary theory was accomplished for Thayer by Henry James: "If one *is* intense (and it's the only thing for an artist to be) one should be economically . . . so." Thayer used James' remark as an epigraph in *The Dial.* In editorial discussion, Marianne Moore recalls, "the word reiterated oftenest" by Thayer as a testing quality "was 'Intensity!' " [5] It is, finally, this private and public history of ideas which is subsumed in Eliot's position, argued during the last twenty years, that verse drama is the ideal form because drama itself and verse rhythm "make for intensity" and in an age of diffusion "an hour and a half of *intense* interest" is precisely what art must recover.

Eliot told an interviewer for *The Paris Review* in 1959, "My poetry has obviously more in common with my distinguished contemporaries in America than with anything written in my generation in England . . . in its emotional springs it comes from America." [6] Eliot is modest. We must include not his poetry merely but his whole achievement as well, not springs alone but program too. From 1922 until 1929 he, Thayer, Williams, Watson, Miss

Moore, and all their distinguished contemporaries in America hoped somehow to perform an organicist ritual of art which would unite poet and audience, player and play, much as "the working-man who went to a music hall and saw Marie Lloyd and joined in the chorus was himself performing part of the work of acting; he was engaged in that collaboration of the audience with the artist which is necessary in all art and most obviously in dramatic art," and in which men "find the artistic expression and dignity of their own lives." Eliot wished to call a halt to the encroachments of that "listless apathy with which the middle and upper classes regard . . . art." If men allow this immoral attitude to shape moral life in modern commercial civilization, we will all "die of boredom." "You will see," he concluded this essay, that "the death of Marie Lloyd has had a depressing effect." In its original form this famous essay served as *The Dial*'s London Letter for December, 1922.

These ideas, then, underlay *The Dial*'s response to Eliot's mind, its decision to support his career. When, out of the blue, "The Waste Land" arrived, Watson was delighted but Thayer was disappointed. He thought it was not so good as Eliot's earlier verse. Watson insisted it was a major work and Thayer, who earlier had decided to present Eliot with the award for 1922, agreed that it should be published, that the occasion itself must be celebrated. Approving the work, unaware of the man's desire to serve as an English not an American prophet, neither Thayer nor Watson questioned Eliot's reason for sending "The Waste Land." Only Conrad Aiken, among Eliot's old, unexpatriated friends, understood his purpose. In *Ushant,* Aiken recalls how he and Eliot, as undergraduates, spoke of laying "siege to one or another of European countries." Aiken remembers another notable fact too: Eliot's warning that he "should never, under any circumstances, in English literary society, discuss his 'first-rate' ideas, lest they be stolen and rushed into print at once." The best procedure was to speak only of one's "second-rate ideas, as the loss of these wouldn't so much matter." [7] This advice was in fact accurate; the shamelessness with which English writers cultivated the habit of piracy is well known. But Eliot, a specialist in literary policy, is also a poet who has stage-managed his career with unique craft; he is the only poet in history, his old friend remarks with wonder, not malice, who has trained three voices in order to play Trilby to his own Svengali. He refers to Eliot's preference for highlights that expose, shadows that suppress images of himself created to dramatize private states of mind and spirit. It is extraordinary, too, that Eliot has had the very good luck to have at each stage the support of Pound, *The Dial, Hound & Horn,* the Establishment in England, and the whole apparatus of letters in America—readings, lectures and reviews, professorships—in his creation both of literature and of *mise en scène.*[8] Harriet Monroe's *Poetry* might publish "Prufrock"; *The Little Review* would do for "The Hippopotamus"; later, *Hound & Horn,* which each quarter adored Eliot anew, was excellent for "Difficulties of a Statesman." But considering the size of *The Dial*'s circulation, the quality of its audience, and the resources and the imagination of its editor, this was the appropriate journal for "The Waste Land" and "The Hollow Men." [9]

The Dial's reasons for accepting the former poem were mixed. Watson prized the work itself, but Thayer was determined to use Eliot's verse as evidence that this work, this magazine, and this national literature now assumed their proper role of leadership in the international community of letters. For Eliot and Thayer proposed to exploit each other. In January, 1922, Eliot had told Pound he had written to Thayer asking what *The Dial* would offer for the poem. In August, the editor, preparing to publish the poem and offer his award to the poet, formed careful plans. "With Liveright I have arranged as follows," Seldes told Watson: "We pay them nothing and we publish the poem without the notes in our November issue. They bring out the book after our date of publication and we send them an order for 350 copies at our usual discount (about 40%) and in connection with our advertising contract with them." These details seem humdrum, but we must realize that in 1922 Eliot was among the least known of young writers, and that Liveright and *The Dial,* prepared to engage considerable amounts of money in order to publish a mere poem, wanted to make certain that it would be properly attended. "We take the entire lot of 350 by January 1st and make financial settlement by that time. (The idea, of course, is that we will push the book mightily in connection with our subscriptions. The book sells for $2. so that if it remains a total loss on our hands we will be paying about $350.) I have suggested that they number all the copies of the first edition, giving a bibliographical value to it, and they have promised to use no publicity mentioning the award until we release it." Turning next to the poem itself, Seldes remarked, "We must assume that Eliot O.K.'s publication in *The Dial* without the notes . . . which are exceedingly interesting and add much to the poem, but don't become interested in them because we simply cannot have them." [10]

These issues settled, the editor next tried to find a critic whose opinion would help readers to decide in the poet's favor. He wanted a man of reputation who would write a favorable notice; serious criticism would come later. He would not settle for an essay which was not worthy of its subject, and early in October Seldes, instructed by the editor, wrote to George Saintsbury about the plan to publish "The Waste Land," which "we consider a notable poem indeed," and about the decision to give Eliot *The Dial* Award. "Because Eliot's poetry is not widely known," Seldes continued, we plan to present "an essay upon his work. We would like this essay to come from you." [11] Saintsbury replied that he was sorry, what they asked him to do was impossible. Watson's first choice was Pound, but he knew that Thayer would not agree. Then he considered Padraic Colum, whom he admired and thought capable of writing "fair criticism" which pleases "the conservatives and 'poetry lovers.' " Earlier Edmund Wilson had offered to supply an essay in criticism of the poem and, pressed for time, Watson finally agreed.

To publish Wilson's essay, the work of another little known American writer, was to compound the gamble. But his study, "The Poetry of Drouth," did not embarrass them at all; its learning was subdued but sure, its exposition was crisp, and its judgment was deft. This essay, therefore, rounded out *The Dial*'s effort to introduce the poet whose "trivialities are more valuable than other people's epics." Although Eliot's "poems seem the products of a constricted emotional experience," Wilson continued, the work of a man who "appears to have drawn rather heavily on books for the heat he could not derive from life," nevertheless

Eliot's "detestation of Sweeney is more precious than Mr Sandburg's sympathy for him." When it was announced the next month "that for the year 1922 *The Dial*'s Award goes to Mr. T. S. Eliot," the editor's delight is unmistakable, the more pleasing too because "the most active and . . . the most influential editor-critic in London found nothing to say" about "The Waste Land" except that it was an "obscure but amusing poem." Thayer suggested that his readers, comparing this with Wilson's essay, later revised for *Axel's Castle,* might "judge of the state of criticism in England." Had Thayer noticed a review by an obscure Southern critic named Ransom, writing in *The Fugitive,* he might have been prouder still. This man disapproved of the poem because it committed all the modern and typically American errors of thought, particularly the absurd idea which says that each age should have its own poetry, and in each age poetry should create its own form.

Thayer himself, satisfied that his magazine had accomplished one main segment of its duty by presenting the work of the greatest living American poet and critic, one who might very well fulfill the American mission, now turned to his second major task.[12] Searching about for some way to dramatize *The Dial*'s role and influence in the plastic arts, he conceived a plan to create a folio and an exhibition. This plan preoccupied his mind from 1922 until 1925. He decided that the folio must be printed in Berlin by the Ganymed Press, noted for its craft in the production of facsimiles. Thayer himself decided which artists should be presented. And although he invited Raymond Mortimer to help select individual pictures, he did not solicit suggestions of any other kind. This folio, called *Living Art,* was composed of thirty prints, ten devoted to sculpture and the remainder to water colors, oils, drawings, engravings, and embodied Thayer's academy of living immortals. Picasso, rose or blue, Matisse, Bonnard, Chagall, Laurencin, Marin, Demuth, Pascin, Lachaise, Meštrović, Maillol—these were his favorites. All the serious abstractionists, Léger and Gris, Braque and Klee, even Brancusi, were excluded. In 1924, after many delays, the folio was published in an edition of five hundred copies, one hundred for review and four hundred for sale at sixty dollars each. It was elaborately advertised in the magazine and in the exhibition prepared to enable prospective buyers, seeing the originals, to compare these with Ganymed's reproductions. The exhibition was held first at the Montross Gallery in New York, then at the Worcester Art Museum where it is on loan today, and later at Smith College. Thayer offered it to museums elsewhere but was refused; some directors said it was too advanced, others said it was too trivial. The folio itself did not have a great success. Eventually its price was reduced, and finally it sold out. Not until 1959 when Louisa Dresser and Daniel Catton Rich at the Worcester Museum recreated and expanded the exhibit, called now "The Dial Collection," was Thayer's contribution properly attended. "In a review in 'Art News' of the year's 'Best,' the exhibit is said to share top place with the Museum of Modern Art's exhibit of Miró." *

Living Art did receive considerable acclaim among critics. This did not especially please Thayer whose purpose was not to astonish

---

* Letter, Rich to Watson, January 21, 1960. Reviewing the exhibition for *The New York Times,* May 4, 1960, Dore Ashton described how "Scofield Thayer . . . amassed what is known as 'The Dial Collection' as a natural counterpart to the magazine and a reservoir for reproductions." In this statement is virtually all that is left among us of Thayer's vision of national redemption: *Living Art* reappears in The Dial Collection. The journal itself Ashton recalls as "a literary and art magazine of the Twenties which not only took a serious view of literature, but also took just as serious a view of painting and sculpture." There is, however, a certain historic residue and resonance in Lincoln Kirstein's achievements and influence, both public and private. Not only did *The Criterion* and *The Dial* serve as examples for his journal, *Hound & Horn,* but also "I did own the DIAL portfolio . . . and this unquestionably influenced me in the founding of the Harvard Society of Contemporary Art. . . . I met Gaston Lachaise, the sculptor, having seen his work in the Dial, and had my portrait done, and got Edward Warburg and George L. K. Morris to have his or theirs done, too." Letter, Kirstein to Wasserstrom, December 3, 1958. Although Thayer's influence on Kirstein is of course notable, even more striking is Thayer's role in the American history of fine art. That this is as yet unrecorded is serious not because Thayer's reputation suffers, but because *Living Art* represents the first attempt to publicize, within society at large, an attitude which E. H. Gombrich discovers in all forms of plastic expression today. Beginning with the impressionist movement, "the artist gives the beholder 'more to do.'" Drawing him into "the magic circle of creation," an artist "allows him to experience something of the thrill of 'making'" which had once been the unique privilege of the creator alone. *Art and Illusion* (New York, 1960), 202.

his colleagues but to rouse the public. His folio is "a paean to an intense individualism," Thomas Craven wrote in a review for *The Dial*—an echo, I am certain, of Thayer's official line. And Thayer himself invited those compatriots who did not find "in either of those twin shrunken Caesars, Calvin C. Coolidge and [Bishop] William T. Manning, that perfect peace after which the heart hankereth," to visit the Montross Gallery where "eyes will thereupon be opened." "Standing amid the singular masterpieces of his own generation, he will be aware . . . that not the Sainte Chapelle herself has lightened and burned more variously, or gleamed with a more subtle and a more intricate charm, or has prevailed with a more true inward poignance." Thayer believed that the pieties of poetry and painting were no less solemn than those ordinarily associated with the worship of God. For he saw himself as a kind of John the Baptist crying in behalf of a Christ of art who would make men whole.

In Eliot's mind, worship of God was only a shade holier than devotion to verse: he saw himself as the Christ of art whose own journal and Thayer's were designed to spread his Word. In *The Criterion* and in *The Dial*, Eliot, inspired by Marie Lloyd, wished to confront the public with dramatic verse, absorb its life within the life of the poem.[13] Thayer, attempting to absorb public life within the life of *The Dial*, hoped to implant in the consciousness of his readers and contributors what Miss Herbst calls a heightened awareness of the "profound urgency" of intense art. In Thayer's mind this choice term was burdened with the entire weight of a Harvard education and with the whole tradition of organicist thought. The term itself represents Thayer's vision of apocalypse: when poem and public, *Dial* and dream fuse, ordinary men are inspired to remake their lives.

Nearly forty years ago Gilbert Seldes, discovering jazz, said that Americans were wrong to imagine that this native music was merely a "spasm of energy before death." On the contrary, jazz is "the normal development of our resources, the expected and wonderful arrival of America at the point of creative intensity." He found in "Runnin' Wild" a masterpiece of the genre. But Watson saw in "The Waste Land" a masterpiece more impressive. And Thayer, assenting to publication of the poem, preparing to present

Eliot with his award, offering the best *Living Art,* hoped to publicize the uniqueness of American writing and the authority of American taste.

Once we agree that *The Dial*'s policies and Eliot's poems were motivated by this semisystematic idea, the idea that only intense art can perform the rite of organic communion, it becames clear why the tone of Eliot's verse especially pleased Thayer's ear. Had the poem appeared in *The Little Review* or *Poetry* unattended by Wilson's essay or *The Dial*'s award, its effect would doubtless have been neither more nor less stunning than its effect in London during October when it came out in the first number of *The Criterion.* Had there been no award, there would have been no essay. Both award and essay, like poem and journal, represent main aspects of Thayer's program; *The Dial*'s crusade in Eliot's behalf is identical in spirit with Thayer's crusade in behalf of American letters. For it is nothing less than the crusading spirit of 1910 that had by 1922 conferred on this journal its peculiar power.

Knowing that Thayer tried to publish only those works of poetry, fiction, painting, and criticism which intensify a man's experience of his own being, we are compelled to treat "The Waste Land" not only as a work of Eliot's art but also as the work which best identifies the inner life of a magazine designed to interlace American art and civilization. By 1925 when Thayer resigned his post, he half-playfully believed that he had enabled this national literature to fulfill its ancient destiny: America now stood first among equals in the republic of letters.

VI. The Mark of a Poet:
MARIANNE MOORE

Poetry is the founding and naming of Being and of the essence of all things. . . . Therefore the essence of language must be understood on the basis of the essence of poetry and not the other way round.

MARTIN HEIDEGGER, *Quarterly Review of Literature,* August, 1959.

Positive theology says what God is; negative theology shows that he is not that which is said of him. God transcends everything that can be said about him, and therefore it must be denied in the moment in which it is said. Symbolic language unites positive and negative theology.

PAUL TILLICH, "The Word of God," *Language: Enquiry into Its Meaning and Function,* 1959.

The Negative. Perhaps the one great motivational principle that man, in his role as the language-using animal, has added to nature.

KENNETH BURKE, *The Quarterly Journal of Speech,* December, 1952.

I

ALTHOUGH by 1925 *The Dial* was read and admired "all over the English-speaking world," as Mary Colum observed in *Life and the Dream,* nevertheless very few people understood what Thayer "was trying to do for art and literature, and what a rare spirit he was. Sad to say, some years later he fell a victim to that dread ailment of the sensitive American, a nervous and mental breakdown." In Mrs. Colum's view, Thayer's collapse occurred because he was "distracted and lonely. Loneliness can seize Americans in a way I have never seen happen in old countries." But her opinion, common among those British writers who admire America yet find it harsh and not genial, confuses loneliness with a more troublesome thing, with that desolation of the mind which occurs among Americans who prophesy utopia and take too seriously the myth of destiny. No man, however gifted, and no work, however triumphant, can achieve millennium. Pursuing this chimera of the American spirit, Thayer, Harvard aesthete become national prophet, sought to turn out each month a flawless journal, hoped to mold every disparate element in American culture into one organic community where men of art were also men of power. Tainted by the national disease, doomed by what Henry James called our complex fate, Thayer resigned.

In an extraordinary coincidence of social history, the man whom he chose as his successor, Van Wyck Brooks, joined him in emotional collapse. Late in 1924 Thayer presented Brooks with the award. Then, early in 1925, he offered him his post, but Brooks refused. Brooks was asked not to publicize the offer, and it remained unknown until 1958 when he informed Gilbert Seldes. Later Brooks said, "I was offered the editorship . . . but I was at the moment at the beginning of a serious nervous breakdown and could not have accepted the offer. Besides I was no longer interested in editing a magazine. Mr. Scofield Thayer asked me at the time not to mention this, but as it is now more than thirty years ago I see no reason for keeping this a secret." [1] Had Brooks taken over *The Dial*, we may assume that modern letters would have had a considerably altered history. The magazine might have been better or worse, but we must guess that Brooks would have labored to establish the American school of art for which he had made a most persuasive case in *Letters and Leadership*. Had Brooks accepted the most influential literary post in New York, he would have been empowered to counter the New Criticism.

Nineteen hundred and twenty-five was indeed a critical year. It was then that men of the right and left, less patient and subdued, became fiercer in support of new programs for national culture. Then, too, younger men, shaping what Samuel Putnam called "The After-War Spirit in Literature," tried "to bring science and literature into contact, and to employ literature as an implement, as an instrument of investigation." [2] They borrowed ideas from all spheres of learning in order to acquire a theory of imagination which would equip men of art with the kind of knowledge available to men of science. Thayer, alert to these new currents, transferred his interest from "the creative arts" to the "critical arts," thereby molding what we must recognize as the second distinct period in the time of *The Dial,* a period which continues in our own time.

The first generation of American critics, Pound and Spingarn and Brooks, had disagreed on matters of taste and methods of study. But each had been an evangelist, concerned to establish here a literary situation out of which a momentous art might occur. By 1925 fastidiousness had replaced evangelism, and a proper critic, Gorham Munson said, was "absorbed in the technical problems of literature." Agreeing that Brooks had "created a . . . certain way of thinking about literature," Munson introduced that objection to Brooks' criticism which has become classic: he has tended more and more to draw "away from the literary document." [3] Although Thayer believed that Brooks was a man of "supreme importance" even if "one fails to accept the whole body of his doctrine," he too realized that Brooks' criticism of novels was less acute than, say, Heywood Broun's analysis of games. "Tactics and strategy, technique and art, compose [Broun's] . . . one passionate interest." Thayer advised experts of literature to take some cues from those experts of sport whose work is "far better . . . than nine-tenths of the criticism of arts and letters. . . . The writer usually knows what he is talking about" and he writes "with his eye on the object."

At mid-decade Thayer stressed the uses of textual criticism. Watson, however, was impressed by the uses of science, the effects of Freud on the study of art. He decided to respond to an essay by Clive Bell, published in his journal, in order to answer some leading vulgar objections to Freudian thought. All artists dream of being great men and "having a good time," Bell said. "Now this, I dare say, is a pretty good account of what housemaids, and Dr Freud presumably, take for art. . . . The housemaid dreams of becoming a great actress and being loved by a handsome earl; Dr Freud dreams of having been born a handsome earl and loving an actress. . . . I have attempted [to explain art to] a roomful of psychologists," he continued. "I told them that if Cézanne was for ever painting apples, that had nothing to do with an insatiable appetite for those handsome . . . fruit. At the word 'apples,' however, my psychologists broke into titters." Tittering louts— these students of a man who "has made himself slightly ridiculous by talking about things of which he knows nothing." [4] Watson's essay remarks that "unconscious processes are important in the making of a work of art," that the study of one must enlarge our knowledge of both. Above all Watson admired Freud's effort to provide data especially useful for such critics as Mr. Bell who still "does not seem to realize how very nearly nothing at all his definition of the artist's problem or job really means, or how little his various books elucidate it. The metaphors 'aesthetic emotion,' 'significant form' . . . are just the sort of uncomfortable lumps which beg for analysis. To show what psychoanalysis might do for them I have only to point to what psychoanalysis has done, in Freud's 'Group Psychology and the Analysis of the Ego,' for 'herd instinct' . . . about which we heard so much during the war." [5]

Treating the relations between psychology and literature, the problem of neurosis in the creative mind, the powers of science and of art, *The Dial* in June, 1925, published the critic who seemed best equipped to compose a schematic theory of life and letters, Paul Valéry. His essay was followed by a study of Valéry where Edmund Wilson, incidentally, touched on the precise problem with which Thayer himself was to confront his physician, Freud. Alyse Gregory later said that Freud told her Thayer was a man of gentle heart, one whose awareness was as sharp as Freud's own. But he feared that Thayer did not at bottom want to heal himself. Returning to America in 1927, Thayer, treated but uncured, retired from the world. Wilson, quite unaware of this interplay between social and literary history, described why Valéry's mind differed from Yeats', why the one survived and the other succumbed. Both men maintained a "chastity and dignity undisturbed by the surrounding medley. But . . . Yeats withdrew completely . . . from a world spoiled for him as much by science as by democratic society" and took "refuge in the . . . obsolete researches of astrology and magic." In contrast, Valéry "has nourished his appetite for abstraction," has hoped to resolve the dilemmas of science and society, to define the magic of art. Distinguishing Valéry from Yeats, Wilson simultaneously isolated some of the reasons why Thayer resigned and why Marianne Moore was appointed to his post.

Miss Moore's appetite for abstraction is of course insatiable, as William Carlos Williams observed in an early essay describing her elusive virtue: "The only help I ever got from Miss Moore

toward the understanding of her verse was that she despised con-
nectives." Williams' essay was one of many appreciations of Miss
Moore which appeared in the magazine during the winter and
spring of 1925 and which were prompted in part by the recent
publication in America of her first book, *Observations,* and in part
by her receipt of *The Dial* Award. Thayer, ceremoniously confer-
ring on Miss Moore a title vacant "since the death of Emily Dickinson," called her "America's most distinguished poetess." He
agreed with Eliot that she must be included among "the half-dozen
most 'exciting' contemporary European and American poets";
indeed, he thought, her work represented the American imagination at its best. Because it reconciled the rewards of experiment
with the comforts of custom, her verse embodied a triumph of
what Thayer called "the informed literary middle-of-the-road."
He was delighted to discover in Miss Moore a poet, homegrown
and loyal, whose genius was shaped by the qualities he valued
most and whose authority might well rival or outdo Eliot's. By
mid-decade Thayer felt himself no longer sympathetic to an editor
who ran a rival magazine which once or twice condescended to say
a word of praise about *The Dial,* a poet whose new manner and
subject he could not follow, a man whose gratitude for *The Dial*'s
cash and honor was, however deep, quiet. Speaking of Miss Moore,
Thayer remarked that the footnotes to "The Waste Land" once
had been "the talk of the town. Yet these now date: They be-
long to the pre-Moore period: They are content pedestrianly
to explain. And in the Demesne of Highe Poesie explanations,
however needful and adroit, are wont to be estimated small
beer."

  Thayer's jeer is gratuitous. There are more subtle, more sensible
reasons why he preferred her verse, reasons which help us to know
why, rebuffed by Brooks, he selected Miss Moore as his successor
on "America's only complete magazine of the creative and the
critical arts." For Miss Moore's method of composition, which
critics have been nonplussed trying to place within any scheme of
letters apart from that imposed by her special genius, is insepa-
rable from *The Dial*'s. As it sought to weld all segments of culture,
all modes of imagination, in an organic journal of art and criticism,
so *Observations* (published in 1924 by *The Dial*'s own press)
comprehends past and present, verse and prose, Europe and

America, popular culture and high art. Each poem, from title to note, draws on all aspects of the national life and the life of the mind. Each performs a criticism of human language and conduct.

Indeed, "Picking and Choosing" can serve as an epigraph for the magazine as a whole during Miss Moore's stint as editor. Adapting the rhythms and idiom of prose, this poem is an exercise in composition, a complete lesson in experiment and decorum. Closing with Kenneth Burke her list of critics who are daring and scrupulous, who fear nothing, neither life nor art, she presents Burke as a "psychologist—of acute, raccoon-/like curiosity. *Summa diligentia.*" This is the point of climax in a poem that realized itself by defining good and bad art, good and bad criticism; that is itself a verse-essay on the connections which link art, criticism, and real life. For if *Observations* discloses some key similarities of method of Miss Moore and *The Dial*, then "Picking and Choosing" displays those segments of the poet's credo which, as we shall see, were to shape the editor's policy.

My argument may sound labored, but in fact I have sought to demonstrate some ways in which certain ideas stirred a few persons to assume particular duties during a germinal but formless time in American letters. Taking over a magazine Thayer had made international in bias, apocalyptic in purpose, synoptic in design, Miss Moore admired her predecessor's bias, respected his purpose, and shared his design. And although no one has associated the art of this poet with the style of that journal, their connection is natural not strange, as Glenway Wescott, almost forty years ago, observed. Celebrating her receipt of the award,* Westcott described Miss Moore's verse as "the product of a novel intelligence, a strange sensibility, a unique scholarship. It is woven . . . with phrases from neglected books and poor magazines. . . . The process by which this miscellany is made to focus about her points of view is fascinating—an object lesson in the exploitation of an environment by a mind." [6] Wescott's analysis of Miss Moore's

---

* Willard Thorp, a scholar of unusual learning and usually strict discipline, has said in print that Miss Moore received the award twice, in 1921 and 1924. *American Writing in the Twentieth Century* (Cambridge, 1960), 212–13. This is one of many pieces of misinformation, both minor and major, transmitted in book after book on the 1920's, works which turn simplest fact into strange and exciting legend.

style applies in almost every detail to the style and purpose of that other miscellany, *The Dial* itself. As editor, therefore, she engaged in an act of the creative process very little different in kind from her former acts of composition, though considerably more expansive and public. From 1925 until 1929 the new editor, on whom Thayer staked all his immortal longings, served as a critic whose poem was *The Dial.*

2

The number for July, 1925, the first for which Miss Moore assumed responsibility, published Kenneth Burke's "Psychology and Form" and thereby introduced Burke as a full-fledged theorist of letters. During the next four and a half years, Burke was to appear often in its pages; indeed, he was to become *The Dial's* representative critic quite as Eliot had been its representative poet. Before we speak further of Burke, however, we must recognize some modifications in tone and purpose which occurred after Thayer's resignation. *The Dial* now represented the tastes of Miss Moore and Dr. Watson who together charted its new course. Although Watson was in Rochester and Miss Moore remained in New York, the magazine each month appeared as a product of their collaboration. "I submitted to [Thayer] and Dr. Watson," Miss Moore says, "my feeling about a manuscript; and when Scofield Thayer was abroad or not actively participating, consulted Dr. Watson; I never . . . independently accepted anything. . . . I relied on my own taste in what I recommended, never disguised my enthusiasm or objections." [7] For a year, Thayer, whose title was "Adviser," sent verse which the editor felt herself constrained to publish. With Watson's preferences she was usually sympathetic even when her own impulse was to reject. Watson, who had long admired Pound's poetry and criticism, and who had praised him in 1920 as the leading American teacher of comparative literature, sent Miss Moore a letter itself auspicious because it shows how their collaboration worked. "I hope you will not feel that I am acting unconscientiously but when I reread this XXII Canto it seemed . . . we really must have it for February or March and in the enthusiasm of the moment I wrote Pound much to that effect without also implying that there had been any doubt in the matter." Miss Moore replied, "It is I who am lacking in conscience, for disapproving of the Canto, and yet being delighted to have it." [8]

Despite a new management, the form of *The Dial* remained unchanged. It continued to show that solicitude for structure which Thayer had imposed as a first rule of editorial tact. It continued to print those works in the plastic arts which so pleased Thayer. He, incidentally, had left behind enough pictures to maintain *The Dial* through 1925, but left Watson and Miss Moore to decide matters in this department on their own after that. During the next years, the editors introduced few new painters or movements. Their art critic McBride, however, maintained his talent for spirited and urbane response to pictures and ideas, as is evident in his remarks on "La Bohémienne Endormie" by Henri Rousseau and on Georgia O'Keeffe. Rousseau left him breathless, but Miss O'Keeffe left him laughing. "She always drew large petunias, but now [in the exhibition for 1927] she makes them the size of pumpkins. . . . Ladies said last year that gazing at Miss O'Keeffe's petunias gave them the strangest imaginable sensations and as the petunias are larger and better this year than ever before, I shall await an account of a ladies' day at this exhibition with real interest." *The Dial* offered both Rousseau and O'Keeffe in reproduction but chose not to print another of McBride's favorites, Miró. Nor did it reprint any work by Peter Arno, in whom this critic saw "something quite our own and something strong." Precisely when that "giddy and prosperous weekly, *The New Yorker,* began using his services I am not sure," but McBride was certain that "the staid historians of [the] . . . future will find us a diverting study—and Mr. Arno's drawings will be a complete source of information for them." Instead of Arno, the editors chose Max Weber and Modigliani, Dufy and Masereel. For in this department where Thayer's crusade was sacred, it offered only the kind of new work which conformed to Thayer's own standard, painting which might move an ordinary intelligent man to a "sincere and acute appreciation of the beautiful."

Watson and Miss Moore preferred to expand *The Dial*'s influence in criticism, that field of inquiry which was to engage all men of letters during the later 1920's. Indeed, precisely because both Watson and Miss Moore were persons whose intelligence was delicate, exact, and cogent, their motives coincided. And this felicity of private accord in turn coincided with certain public events in the dialectic of thought. Watson, announcing in 1926 that the award had been presented to Cummings, feared that it would be "about seventy years" before criticism "would begin to come up with" Cummings' verse; he hoped to speed things along. Miss Moore was wholehearted in assent. Reviewing Wallace Stevens' *Harmonium,* she had remarked that the poet revealed an extraordinary "instinct for words," that this instinct is "determined by the liberties taken with them," and that Stevens takes many liberties. Nevertheless, she said, Stevens set words down "in such a way as to admit of no interpretation . . . but the one intended." Portraying in lawful speech an image of the highest forms of moral life, Stevens is qualified to present imagination as " 'the magnificent cause of being.' " And as editor Miss Moore was determined to discipline those writers whose loose words betrayed slovenly morals and slack minds. "Like a surgeon," Marsden Hartley said in his poem, "Marianne Moore," the editor labored "to find/what ails the sentence, separate fruit/from rind,/the sickness of the hyper-trammeled theme,/or shake the skeleton of a proved factitious/thought." [9]

Her motives were misunderstood, however, by most of her contemporaries who were at first delighted when she was appointed editor. Soon they were outraged. Gorham Munson's *Destinations* in 1928 prayed for a humanist-redeemer "who has lost his illusions . . . a searcher with a vengeance . . . desperate and practical," a person quite different from "the editor of *Dial.* What shall I say about that role? Nothing, but rather ponder on the qualifications of a first order editor, who is so much rarer than a good poet." [10] Hart Crane, who had been paid his "first literary money" by *The Dial,* was "aroused . . . to intense excitement" by Watson's translations of Rimbaud, and decided that Miss Moore was a tyrant. "How much longer [will] our market . . . be in the grip," Crane wrote to Allen Tate, "of two such hysterical virgins as *The Dial* and *Poetry!*" Crane's biographer Philip Horton reports the fate of Crane's poem, "The Wine Menagerie," in illustration of what Horton calls "the incredible editorial presumption for which [Marianne Moore] . . . was notorious." Receiving this work, "she replied that she would accept the poem provided that Crane agreed to certain changes she had made in it. Crane was outraged to find that the changes she insisted on included a new title and wholesale excision of stanzas and lines which left about half the original poem; but his need of money was too desperate to be denied, and in despair he accepted the terms." Immediately, he rushed to Matthew Josephson to tell him about the outrage. Josephson offered to buy back the poem and when Miss Moore asked Crane if Josephson was empowered to act for him, Crane disclaimed responsibility for his friend's behavior. Miss Moore called Josephson an impudent meddler.[11]

This is Mr. Horton's account. Unfortunately, it doesn't mention the correspondence in which the poet wrote his thanks for the editor's suggestions. On November 10, 1925, when changes were completed and negotiations ended, Crane said he agreed with her that the edited version of "The Wine Menagerie," retitled "Again," contained the essential elements of his original poem; he admired the skill and simplicity of her rearrangement.[12] Later, Miss Moore wrote that she "would like to accept your poem 'At Melville's Tomb' if you could allow us to omit the fourth stanza." But, alert after the uproar, she warned Crane that he could "decline to give the poem to *The Dial* if you are unable to make the concession." [13] He chose to publish this poem in *Poetry* but he succeeded in placing it there only after he had explained its meaning to Miss Monroe who published both poem and exegesis.

I have lingered over the Crane affair mainly because Horton's book, a standard work on man and period, has long been a main source of distorted opinion. But it is true that Miss Moore tempered and tinkered and most poets rankled. Although some said nothing, others insisted that she indicate with an ellipsis lines she had recommended for removal. Occasionally alteration was trivial. Sometimes it was devastating. Kreymborg, asked to make "a slight change in the last line," shifted some words; MacLeish told Miss Moore, "I am so happy that you like Nocturne. You may of course drop the four lines you mention and change the title." [14] She made no exceptions though in some instances she did modify her tone.

In 1926, she returned a batch of poems to Yeats and received from him an inquiry: had she sent back the last poems because she disliked that particular poem or because she disliked the school he belonged to. If she had decided to make *The Dial* a literary organ of the school to which she belonged and of that school only then he could not complain.[15] She answered that this was not the case; she had returned the whole group because she was unable to publish all and did not wish to choose among the lot. Corresponding with Mann about "Disorder and Early Sorrow," she proposed that the name Lorlykins be changed to Lorlette. The translator, H. G. Scheffaurer, replied that Mann disagreed but offered Lorli instead. Miss Moore was on a holiday and Burke accepted the change. In the corrected proofs it turned up as Lorlikins and this, she wrote to say, "spelled so . . . is in keeping with the character of young Hergesell." [16]

Miss Moore had, as Watson says, a genius' disdain for the sanctity of genius. Furthermore, she held the same view Eliot has attributed to his editor, Pound: she did not wish to remake a poem in her own image but to enable another poet to fulfill his idea in a language of the sharpest pitch. Like Stevens, who once sent a manuscript to *The Dial* in the morning and that evening dispatched a letter saying "4th line from the end, please changes heavens to the singular: heaven. Otherwise I shall be prostrated!" Miss Moore believed that each letter, each syllable, must count.[17] "As I look over your very careful editing," Robert Hillyer wrote to her in 1926, "I wonder if my work is egregiously trying. . . . if . . . you find each small contribution demanding equal time and care, how do you manage to edit so much material?" [18] She replied that she was "desirous of maintaining the standard and style of writing which Doctor Watson and Mr Thayer regard as essential." Realizing, too, "that they decline contributions rather than request changes, I am exceedingly unhappy in harassing contributors, and in certain instances, close friends of theirs. . . . I have suffered . . . deeply in the dilemma of being compelled either to do this unholy handling, or to see appear in The Dial, that which is inharmonious with the content prescribed by it before I came to the office." But, she concluded, harassment would continue to be her method of dealing with writers whose "work I could not easily relinquish." [19] In a reminiscence written during 1941, Miss Moore recalled those days when "to some contributors . . . The Dial, and I in particular, may have seemed quarrelsome." Now "previous victims of mine have to dread from me . . . nothing more than solicitude that all of us write better." [20]

This was of course Joyce's overriding motive too: as Stephen Dedalus exchanged the word "Repent" for the word "Yes," so Joyce himself sought to find the exact word by which men might live better. Miss Moore, who once admitted that she was surprised "that a field can be a field and still be as narrow as ours is," was unprepared to cultivate Joyce. Nevertheless, knowing of Watson's preferences, aware of his interest in Pound and in Joyce, conscientious in her service as his editor and colleague, she was pleased to receive, on July 12, 1926, a letter from Sylvia Beach. Miss Beach offered *The Dial* 30,000 to 34,000 words of "Joyce's new book, instalments of which have appeared in some of the reviews." The letter continued, "your review occupies the highest place among reviews and is the most appropriate one to bring out Mr. Joyce's work." [21] The segment turned out to be "Anna Livia Plurabelle" which Miss Beach in *Shakespeare and Company* says Joyce was "extremely anxious to introduce . . . to readers in the United States. Aiming high, I sent [it] . . . off to the Dial, hoping its editor, Marianne Moore," would be pleased. "I was glad to get word that the Dial had accepted the work, but it turned out that this was a mistake. It had come in when Miss Moore was away, and she was reluctant to publish it. The Dial didn't back out altogether. I was told, however, that the text would have to be considerably cut down to meet the requirements of the magazine. Now Joyce might have considered the possibility of expanding a work . . . but never, of course, of whittling it down. On the other hand, I couldn't blame the Dial for its prudence in dealing with a piece so full of rivers. . . . I was sorry about A. L. P.'s failure to make the Dial. Joyce, who was still in Belgium, was not surprised." [22]

Miss Beach is kind but her account is not of course the whole story. On July 20, 1926, responding to Miss Beach's offer, Miss Moore wired, "Two cents a word but must see manuscript before deciding." The work arrived almost immediately. And on July 31, Joyce sent the first of three lists of corrections and additions to the typescript. On August 26, the editor wrote to Miss Beach formally accepting the manuscript and requesting a title as well as "some slight biographical data about Mr Joyce." On September 10 and 13 he sent additional lists, each substantial. Then on September 16, Miss Beach wrote to say that Joyce had no title for either book or section: "He says anything will do." As for biography, Miss Moore could consult *Who's Who* or Herbert Gorman's book. But now Miss Moore began to have qualms. In 1958, reminded of the whole incident, she recalled that Joyce had permitted Eliot to publish a short section of *Work in Progress;* that she resented being forced to accept, through an agent, the whole 34,000 words. Also she was fearful, the correspondence shows, that Thayer would be displeased to find this *Work* in his journal. And she wrote her fear to Watson who, on September 16, wired a reply: "Scofield probably not vitally interested either way." He suggested publishing the whole section "using asterisks for omissions of words or short phrases." But Miss Moore was unpersuaded and on September 17, she cabled Miss Beach: "We find that it would not be possible to publish the Joyce manuscript verbatim. We should be obliged if we are to publish it to omit pages and parts of pages, reducing it by one third—perhaps a half. We are very much distressed that this discovery was not made before I had written to you. Do you feel that you must withdraw the manuscript? Or should you be disposed to have us indicate omissions subject to your withdrawal?" On September 19, Miss Beach answered: "Joyce requests return typescript with corrections."

Three days later, Miss Moore wrote to Watson a statement defining her dilemma: "Miss Beach cabled September 19th 'Joyce requests return typescript with corrections.' In going over the chapters, understanding the content as I did not when I first read the manuscript in Maine, I do not see how we could use more than the first section—12 pages—and another section—pages 24–29. You think we might count on Scofield's cooperating more, I fear, than I think we really could. I remember his indignation against the censors of *Ulysses,* but just before he went away he happened to speak to me emphatically of his disbelief in the present Joyce. I suppose you know without my saying it that I am acutely desirous of our having for The Dial, what it is you wish to publish and it is sickeningly ironic to me to refuse the work of one in whose technique I have such delight. I am also distressed to involve us in the disgrace of modifying an affirmative letter. Of course I should . . . concentrate in myself . . . the whole blame and responsibility." [23] Then, during the following week, she wrote again to Miss Beach explaining, sadly, that confusion had occurred because the letter saying that *The Dial* accepted Joyce had not been held "as I had asked that it should be, until a final conference" had been called and a final decision reached.[24] Their last exchange occurred six months later when Miss Beach wrote asking the editor to publish a formal letter of protest on the activity of Samuel Roth, head of the American firm that had pirated *Ulysses*.

For want of a *Dial*, it is tempting to say, *Finnegans Wake* was lost to America; for want of a Joyce, *The Dial* was lost.[25] At a time when the arts grew decorous, when new humanists, promising to import only the most sedulously cultivated foreigners, acquired national support and international fame, *The Dial's* support of Joyce's indecorous, copious, and fluvial work might very well have irrigated a field that had gone dry. On February 3, 1927, Eliot wrote to Miss Moore complimenting her "on the quality and interest of 'The Dial.' It has certainly lost nothing under your direction." But in June, 1927, the effect and prestige of the magazine were seriously diminished; "The Dial seems to have grown a little tired," Eliot's *New Criterion* noted in a review of American journals. The Joyce affair serves as evidence for the diminution of energy that marks *The Dial* during its last years. Miss Moore, admiring Wallace Stevens' instinct for words, was ready to grant Stevens complete freedom to take sheerly linguistic liberty. For she supported innovation when she was certain it involved no betrayals of any sort, of speech or of body or of mind. Doubting that Joyce's instinct was completely reliable, seeing Joyce himself resist her discipline, she preferred to eat her words. Her lapse stems from an excess of virtue and represents a victory of scruple over daring, of picking not choosing, a triumph of what Thayer called the literary middle of the road.

3

Had *The Dial* published "A. L. P.," it would have included among its virtues both flexible wit and intransigent honor. Far more useful than virtue, however, is a most practical matter. *Work in Progress* itself epitomized the thought of those critics whom Miss Moore recommended and Watson approved, of Valéry, I. A. Richards, Aiken, Yvor Winters, Eliot, and Burke. Their speculation occurred in a field Miss Moore was eager to cultivate; their work represented a variety of literary experience on which she imposed no restraint. These are of course the very persons who have hoped to construe and formalize what Malcolm Cowley in *The Dial* for August, 1927, described as the main problems of advanced literary theory: "the relation between poetry and science, the nature of pure poetry, the attitude of the poet to his audience, the proper function of psychology in criticism." All these problems, unresolved still, were introduced into our literature by the critics Miss Moore printed in *The Dial*. I. A. Richards on Gerard Manley Hopkins appeared alongside Valéry on Leonardo. Eliot on Richards was accompanied by Eliot on Baron von Hügel, the Roman Catholic mystic whose "strong blind passionate desire for the unity of Christendom" Eliot much preferred to Richards' arguments for a poetry "detached from all belief." For "if I believe, as I do believe, that the chief distinction of man is to glorify God and enjoy Him for ever, Mr Richards' theory of value is inadequate." Eliot received from Valéry what Valéry had derived from Leonardo, a warrant for faith. The human body, Valéry argued in *The Dial,* "possesses so many functions and resources that it cannot but answer to some transcendental need, sufficiently powerful to have called it into being, yet not sufficiently powerful to dispense with its complexness." That is, the very existence of man, God's work of art, the effect of His creative spirit, Valéry took as proof of God Himself. And the very existence of a poem Valéry treated as evidence of man's capacity to apprehend truth and render it transcendent; close study of literary texts reveals the meaning not only of words but also of the Word.[26] Before long another pioneer New Critic, Ramón Fernández, offered to readers of *The Dial* a theorem designed as a final formulation of Valéry's position: *"Aesthetics must be an imaginative ontology, that is to say that the fundamental problem of aesthetics is no other than the metaphysical problem of being, but transposed on the plane of the imagination."*

From 1925 until 1929, Miss Moore presented nearly all the historic essays in which Eliot and members of his circle, inspired by Valéry, treated problems in the new metaphysics of art. Indeed, *The Dial* seemed to serve as the American echo of Eliot's voice. But today, reading old copies of Miss Moore's magazine, we hear a conversation, formal and fluent, on a wider range of subjects than were offered in *The Criterion*. Unlike Eliot's magazine, *The Dial* was not victimized by what Pound in 1930 called "Criterionism" and defined as a fascination with "dead and moribund writing." Miss Moore kept conversation alive because she included talk by men whose interest in the study of literature was associated with messianic zeal. In 1927, she complimented the spokesman for this other group, William Carlos Williams, for his unremitting defense of her own belief: "In his modestly emphatic respect for America he corroborates Henry James's conviction that young people should 'stick fast and sink up to their necks in everything their own countries and climates can give.'" Yvor Winters, too, discovered in Williams a marvelous candidate for the role of "chief prophet of my own or some future generation." Williams himself, a physician who delivered babies in real life, seemed to be the poet who might very well perform that other kind of obstetrics which Waldo Frank had described in *Salvos*. For only a clinician of criticism and art would "release at last our intellectual youth from the confusion of its larval struggle." [27]

But by 1927, Eliot's group, published in *The Dial* and *The Criterion,* had achieved what Lincoln Kirstein calls a "massive influence." Kirstein, an undergraduate at Harvard, created *Hound & Horn* mainly in response to this influence, chiefly out of "devotion to Eliot at that time; his mind was a great focus for good and bad, but it was focussed and his eye and ear were one person's. . . . I don't any longer feel like this. . . . But at the time, it is inconceivable now to imagine what Eliot meant to all of us. He was Authority, our authority, but he represented the living past, the potential present and the fact of achievement by a living artist as a professional." [28] Not until the mid-1950's, when a new generation rebelled against what Kenneth Patchen calls puerile chalk-talks of the soul, did the prophets begin to shake off some effects of conquest. Among numberless signs of recovery is the journal *Contact*, named for the magazine Williams once edited, which in 1959 dedicated its first number to this poet and published Williams' version of "The Contact Story." His original magazine, he said, had "typified the direct approach to life . . . a concern with . . . The American Idiom." It was well launched when suddenly Eliot's victory "threw us back on our heels for another twenty, maybe nearer forty years. Only today, are we beginning to get our feet under us again, finally rid of the Eliot influence." [29]

From the moment when *The Dial* appeared until it ceased to exist, both kinds of influence, Eliot's and Williams', were admired and nurtured. During its last years, however, early in our modern age of criticism, it was Kenneth Burke who embodied its purpose. His first notable essay, "Psychology and Form," had been designed to resolve "the quarrel between the aesthetes and the geneticists," "the only major tempest now raging in the critical teapot." Submitting this, he imagined it would be "the first of a series of three or four essays in which I hope to round out an attitude toward art." He added that he was "tremendously indebted to The Dial" for having accepted it: "Had you refused it, I should not even have tried to place it elsewhere." [30] These remarks, addressed to Alyse Gregory, occur in letters written during the fall of 1924. Since that time, Burke has sought to round out an abiding attitude. Furthermore, the appearance of "Psychology and Form" marks an association which has continued beyond the life of the journal and led to a lifelong friendship among Miss Moore, Burke, and Watson.

In March, 1924, Burke had replaced Sophia Wittenberg as editorial assistant. Miss Wittenberg had resigned after her marriage to Lewis Mumford. Watson urged his associates to hire Burke. ("Please bind him with hoops if possible.") That summer, Burke served as Thayer's private secretary and lived in Thayer's cottage on Martha's Vineyard. But until 1927 his service was spasmodic. During that year he replaced Paul Rosenfeld as *The Dial*'s music critic and became a regular contributor. By July, 1928, his career and reputation were identified with those of *The Dial*.

During that month, Watson, asking Miss Moore to help him decide who should receive *The Dial* Award, proposed Wallace Stevens as a prime candidate. Miss Moore concurred but reminded Watson, "It is impossible to get anything from Wallace Stevens." Her predecessor too had hoped to elicit verse, but years earlier Stevens had replied, "My spasms are not chronic." [31] In 1927, responding to Miss Moore's importunity, he explained, "The extreme irregularity of my life makes poetry out of the question, for the present, except in momentary instances. But when things grow quieter and I have time to do what I want to do, I shall . . . submit something to you." [32] Replying to Watson, Miss Moore remarked on the range of Burke's performance and the distinction of his genius, on his "faithfulness, discipline and literary susceptibility." Despairing of Stevens, she said Burke was her candidate even though he is "our critic." [33] Watson agreed. In January, 1929, Burke received the last award.

Burke was literally "our critic," but he was *The Dial*'s official critic in ways that Miss Moore may have suspected but did not define. For Burke's thought stems from those Europeans whom *The Dial* had long cherished, from Russell and Mann and Croce, men who never abandoned faith in the efficacies of mind. As Mann wrote of his own aspirations in the German Letter in 1927, so Burke and *The Dial*, "imbued with the social experience of the times," hoped to reconcile "at a stroke" what Mann called "art and conscience," that "phase of contemporary literature . . . which is richest and soundest." Just as Croce, in an essay written for this magazine during the same year, visualized a "new type of philosophical student," so Burke chose to inform himself "in the investigations of history and of science, and in the work and life of his own times." His method was derived from another European, Spengler, who, though "ungainly," Burke wrote to Miss Moore in 1926, was "unquestionably a brilliant writer" and a historian whose "methodology . . . is powerful and imaginative." [34] Later that year, reviewing Spengler's "stupendous piece of work," calling it "formidable, lugubrious, passionate," Burke distinguished between Spengler's method and his conclusion: although men may not be blessed, Burke decided, they are not accursed. Adapting Mann's faith to Spengler's method, then, Burke laid out his task and set his course: he would become what Croce called "a passionately interested observer" who would study all realms of human experience in order to help determine what it is to be "a man in the full sense of the word."

If we regard Miss Moore's familiar tricorn hat as an emblem of its wearer, an emblem symbolic of the motives which thirty years ago animated a woman who planned to fulfill a trio of duties, then we may regard Burke's plan for a trilogy, *The Grammar, Rhetoric and Symbolic of Motives,* as a fulfillment of the whole idea of criticism and of art which animated *The Dial* itself.[35] The goal of this eclectic miscellany, the instruction of its American readers and writers in the highest intensities of the creative and moral life on earth, is Burke's goal too. "Art being a criticism," he said in an essay on William Carlos Williams, also is "in some sense a corrective." He saw in Williams' verse a kind of poetics in which rhyme connoted "the regimentations of contemporary life" and "anti-rhyme" implied moral freedom. "Artistic truth," he noted in "Psychology and Form," the essay with which he launched himself, is the "externalization of taste." And because the end of art is "the conversion, a transcendence, of emotion into eloquence," then "technique and psychology" are one. How shall I write about music, he wondered in 1927 when he assumed Rosenfeld's task. Is it an "orgy" of the spirit, a substitute for religion? Or is it a "mechanism"? Music, he decided, submits "literal representation" —orgy—"to a purely musical destiny"—mechanism. For "music is a vocabulary," a form of human eloquence, and it is *eloquence* which defines "the essence of art."

Since 1925 Burke has sought to reconcile the Eliot influence and the Williams influence in a theory of eloquence, of human language, which is simultaneously a theory of organic life. The humanism of Mann and Croce, the zeal of a whole generation of organicists who inspired and supported Watson and Thayer are at least comprehended in Burke's effort to compose a theory of language which is also a theory of behavior. "All living things are critics," he said in 1935 in *Permanence and Change.* "All organisms are critics in the sense that they interpret the signs about them." Because speech is accessible to reason, it is viable; human beings alone possess speech and can therefore "go beyond the criticism of experience to the criticism of criticism." Proceeding so, arguing that language is the mark of men in action, Burke has used Spengler's method to weave an organic synthesis of history, philosophy, art, and criticism in a unified field theory of human motive as embodied in human speech.

Once we recognize "our own lives as a kind of rough first draft that lends itself at least somewhat to revision," he remarked ten years later in *The Grammar of Motives,* we in America will confront "the global situation with an attitude neither local nor imperialistic." For Burke's system represents the last frontier of the American imagination, the last best abstraction of utopia, the last resort and final stage of a major enterprise in modern letters. Blending Harvard aestheticism and apocalyptic zeal, Watson and Thayer had shaped a program which synthesized ideas drawn from those persons and magazines that had established the new spirit in letters, from Santayana's *Harvard Monthly* and Bourne's *Seven Arts,* Stieglitz's *Camera Work* and Coady's *Soil.* By the time Miss Moore was appointed editor, *The Dial* had become the best available model of its own doctrine. No mere "Miscellany," it was itself a creation of the highest order of intensity, composed as artfully as the most intricate poem.

Then during Miss Moore's tenure, *The Dial* lost zeal but acquired a taste for discrimination, for technical systems which would expand and refine the arts of criticism so that all men would learn to write and live better. The very tone of Miss Moore's art and the style of her mind were embodied in a journal that displayed the virtues of variety and constraint, of picking and choosing, compunction and conviction, experiment and discipline, daring and scruple. But because Miss Moore was after all a person with roots in the Resurgence, with a taste for Whitman, in her turn as editor she achieved one splendid feat.[36] She recognized Kenneth Burke as the critic who might well map a path along a middle road to the heavenly kingdom. Proposing that *The Dial*'s award should go to Burke, she did not celebrate his arrival there. Rather she hoped to dramatize the ways in which Burke exercised the highest care and accuracy and diligence in pursuit of the life of letters.

In her view, he was the one American critic who possessed technique and sensibility enough to reconcile art and culture, science and imagination in a single theory of literary value which is simultaneously a theory of human virtue in a comprehensive but probably not final sense of that bloody word.[37]

In July, 1929, the last number of the Thayer-Moore-Watson *Dial* appeared. In 1929, too, when the last number of Margaret Anderson's review was printed and distributed, the disappearance of both journals seemed to signify the end of an era—"Wanted," *The Little Review* said, "a lost renaissance." Watson, deciding that his magazine had accomplished its ends, thought that the time had come to make way for newer journals. He was uncomfortable, too, about leaving to Miss Moore a greater share of editorial labor than she had bargained for. She, however, was enjoying herself immensely and would have liked to continue. But Watson had convinced himself that her duties as editor were too burdensome; so good a poet, he felt, should write poetry. The question of money was marginal. Although *The Dial*'s list had shrunk to 5,000 subscribers, this in truth made publication easier, not harder: the Dial Publishing Company lost less money in 1928 than it had in 1924 during the time of widest circulation. The economic panic which would occur during the next autumn had no influence at all on Watson's decision. This latter fact must be stressed because everyone, including Miss Herbst writing in 1959, assumed that the "catastrophic crash of 1929" was the last straw.

Unwilling to continue but loathe just to quit, Watson that spring conferred with Thayer's mother, to whom he proposed two plans. Either they should discontinue publication entirely or they should publish *The Dial* as a quarterly, not a monthly. Mrs. Thayer did not wish to stop, but she could not bring herself to agree to any change in her son's original plan. The whole affair ended with the July number, 1929, when Watson wrote a note thanking staff, contributors, and public, and then closed the doors at 152 West 13th Street. Today, comparing *The Dial* in its last year with, say, *The Criterion, The Symposium,* or *The Hound & Horn,* we wonder if Watson did the right thing. Each of these papers isolated, for special study, one or another custom of taste and habit of inquiry. All were concerned, as specialist journals must be, to extend as far as possible one particular line of thought. None cared to carry forward *The Dial*'s policy of sponsorship in all spheres where intelligence and imagination fuse and find most eloquent form.

Eliot's *Criterion,* for example, stressed textual and ontological criticism, and from time to time printed essays of the highest order. But it also printed tiresome argument by English writers who echoed Eliot's tone but lacked his mind. It was not after all Pound, Richards, Benda, and Ramón Fernández who were regular contributors to *The Criterion;* the bulk of work was done by Humbert Wolfe and Montgomery Belgion, T. O. Beachcroft and Orlo Williams, none of whom we recall very clearly today. Verse by Edwin Muir and Spender and Auden is of course commendable, but what can be said for Joseph Gordon Macleod? Fiction by H. E. Bates or Walter de la Mare or T. F. Powys is respectable but not startling. Equally respectable are the reviews of foreign periodicals and the monthly chronicles of art exhibits. Less persuasive are *The Criterion*'s claims to have been the first journal in English to publish Aragon, Cocteau, and Proust. All had appeared in *The Dial* before Eliot's magazine was introduced. Inaccuracy of this kind is neither trivial nor momentous. But the claim itself forty years ago seemed to underscore the vitality and originality of Eliot's magazine, not Thayer's. The point is, of course, not that *The Criterion* was a bad magazine; on the contrary, it was very good. But current high opinion of *The Criterion*'s role in modern thought relies more on the legend of Eliot than on the journal's own worth, more on Eliot's renown than on the particular merit of Eliot's taste.

The Criterion's closest parallel among American journals was not, as Kirstein claimed, *The Hound & Horn.* Rather it was *The Symposium* which took its cue, though not its style, from Eliot's paper. Edited from 1930 until 1934 by James Burnham and Philip E. Wheelright, *The Symposium* specialized in literary and social criticism. It differed from *The Criterion* only insofar as it stressed variety and eclecticism of subject and writer. Herbert Read and Paul Goodman, Sidney Hook and Harold Rosenberg, William Troy and G. Wilson Knight, H. S. Commager and George Boas are the chief contributors to a journal which was striking precisely because it published work by a wide group of persons committed, as Eliot's group was committed, to coherent systems of ideas. Unlike the religionists who wrote for *The Criterion,* however, these men of doctrine in history, psychology, philosophy, and anthropology were encouraged to dispute. So radical were their disputes, indeed, that each mode or discipline of mind had formed, by mid-decade, a competing school of thought or school of criticism. Each had a journal of its own edited by one or another combination of persons initially drawn together by Burnham and Wheelright.

In the end, a single fact remains compelling still: no rival journal at its best outmatched *The Dial* at its worst. In that final year, 1928–29, it attracted and printed materials less portentous than Eliot chose for *The Criterion,* less contentious than Wheelright and Burnham were soon to publish in *The Symposium,* and less prescient than R. P. Blackmur would place in *The Hound & Horn.* But no other journal managed to be both wide and deep, austere and ornamental. In no other magazine could a serious nonspecialist reader find Pound's translations of and commentary on Cavalcanti, Burke's first six "Declamations," or Boris de Schloezer's series of essays on Stravinsky. Paul Claudel's long essay on Japanese art is accompanied by three pieces by Yoné Noguchi. Mann's essay on Tolstoy is fortified by Maxim Gorki's Russian Letter. Joe Gould occurs in company with Eliot. The new Negro writer Jean Toomer and the new writer on Jewish subjects, Albert Halper, are given considerable space; Halper, indeed, was a "discovery." Two poems by Stanley J. Kunitz and four by Louis Zukofsky, new work by as yet undiscovered men, are included with Aiken's "Preludes" and with more customary work by Lawrence, Witter Bynner, Williams, Crane, and Yvor Winters. In addition to dozens of items by unknown writers who seemed worth encouraging, Miss Moore offered single, startling pieces by Lermontov and Valéry. For those whose eye tired of Picasso, Bonnard, Marie Laurencin, Modigliani, and Maillol there was a sketch by Hart Crane of Cummings' legendary friend, Slater Brown. All this was concluded each month with a short essay by Miss Moore herself, referring to some book, idea, person, event, or word which somehow had engaged her mind. Her subjects included an exhibition in the New York Public Library of Dürer's prints, Chief Standing Bear's autobiography, the death of Ellen Terry, and the abuse of circus animals. Such essays furnish an accumulation of materials priceless for students of this poet's imagination and art.

"No, it wasn't the depression at all," Miss Moore said in response to Donald Hall's recent inquiry in *The Paris Review* (Summer-Fall, 1961): "I think it was largely chivalry—the decision to discontinue *The Dial*—because I didn't have time for my own work." A moment earlier in their conversation, Hall had said that he had "been looking at that magazine, the years when you edited it. It's an incredible magazine. . . . It combined George Saintsbury and Ezra Pound in the same issue. How do you account for it? What made it so good?" Miss Moore had replied, "Lack of fear, for one thing. We didn't care what other people said. I never knew a magazine which was so self-propulsive. Everybody liked what he was doing. . . . We certainly didn't have a policy, except I remember hearing the word 'intensity' very often. A thing must have an 'intensity.' That seemed to be the criterion. . . . We didn't care how unhomogeneous they might seem. And didn't Aristotle say that it is the mark of a poet to see resemblances between apparently incongruous things!" [38]

VII. *Advancing on Chaos:*
HENRY MILLER

The Dial made a noise in the world. Ten years after it
ceased publication it was spoken of by young men who
had read it in college. . . . It had its own progeny in
undergraduate quarterlies and in casual little magazines
from Arkansas to Oregon. It was ridiculed by professional literary men and praised by The New York
Times. It directly affected the artistic life of a generation, and indirectly, the life of our whole time.
> GILBERT SELDES, manuscript essay.

Miller is a leading example of a special kind of writer
produced only by our age. I mean the writer who is
essentially seer and prophet.
> WALLACE FOWLIE, in *The Happy Rock,* 1945.

I

IN AUTUMN, 1929, when catastrophe on Wall Street disrupted the
lives of people even in Oyster Bay, young men in Greenwich Village, Westport, Montmartre, and Rapallo agreed that they as-
sisted at the end of an era. Among these was a man as yet unpublished, Henry Miller, Yeats' rough savior whose time had not
come. In 1930 this young man quit his job as personnel manager
at Western Union, left his home in Brooklyn, and went to Europe.
That year another savior, a shade less rough, having left the hills
of North Carolina and arrived in Brooklyn, published *Look
Homeward, Angel.* Thomas Wolfe, described by Herbert J. Muller
as a man "close to native traditions" which, though "suspect
among intellectuals on both the Right and the Left" during the
1920's and 1930's, were "grounded in the national consciousness
over three centuries of history," was a man steeped in the "American myth," and from this vantage point he offered a novel based
in Jack London's perplexities and wants, the *disjecta membra* of
1910.

In 1929, prophets of the center, however opulent, lacked vogue.
During the preceding ten years, led by *The Dial,* they had refur-

bished both the life of letters in America and the role of letters in American life. "The Dial was the first old established magazine in America to adjust its policy and point of view to include newer tendencies in arts and letters. Since The Dial's change of policy, less than three years ago [in 1920], two other well-known, old established magazines have modified their traditional point of view in the direction taken by The Dial. . . . If you like Broom you will like The Dial." [1] And if you had liked either *The Dial* or *Broom,* you would not read *Scribner's,* which continued to publish Brander Matthews and William Crary Brownell. By mid-decade, however, you might have glanced at *Sewanee Review:* in 1919 it had published ordinary work by genteel southern scholars, but by 1924 it had included essays by the first of the new academicians, college teachers who lived at the margins of Bohemia and shared the spirit and purpose of Resurgence. Although *The Yale Review* continued to cultivate Billy Phelps, by March, 1929, it was willing to publish, along with Phelps' "Conversations with George Moore," F. O. Matthiessen's "New Standards in American Criticism." The history of American literature must be rewritten by a new historian, Matthiessen said, who would realize that "great literature is an organic expression of its age and nation," and would "take into account every side of American culture . . . religion . . . education . . . communication and travel, the 'movies' and cartoons, the Ford and the radio, the significance of the fact that the village reads Whittier and Longfellow, and the City, Whitman and James." [2] Matthiessen's writing makes it apparent that *The Dial*'s practice, evident each month during the previous nine years, had assumed an official place in American thought. Today we realize that *The Dial,* at the end of renaissance, had prepared the ground for Matthiessen's *American Renaissance.* In his suicide, a signal event of the 1940's, we recognize the despair of an apostle martyred by the national disease.

By 1929 the "American myth" had been absorbed and refashioned by theorists of reaction and theorists of revolution, the organicists of right and left. *The Dial,* vacating its office, abandoned its position as an organic journal of the center, mediator between the avant-garde and the general reader, between the prophets and the historians of apocalypse. During the 1930's, two new groups emerged: the theorists of literary style and the theorists of social crisis. *The Hound & Horn,* the journal which "has come to take the place of The Dial," started in 1927 by "undergraduates at Harvard University as a college paper based in the London *Criterion,*" maintained one principle only: "Our standard for judging the arts is technical"; the overriding aim is to "wed critic and artist." [3] At first the new magazine seemed, as Francis Fergusson had predicted, "to classify the show according to Mr. Eliot's scheme." [4] But before long the editors received from Ezra Pound a letter called "Criterionism" which they published as an essay. "The danger of the Criterion policy is that one cannot indulge continually in a diet of dead crow without its tainting the breath." Nor can one analyze forever "dead and moribund writing." Pound's comment is characteristically harsh. But these published views are less mordant than his unpublished opinion on similar matters, written in a letter to Marianne Moore during the last days of *The Dial:* if I were a Christian, he said, I would prefer a forthright atheist or deist to some "chap" who adopts Christianity as if it were "a new style of lace cuff" or who went for the communion wafer as if it were "a species of aspirin." [5] In that letter to *Hound & Horn,* too, there are even at this quite late date echoes of the American patriot who years earlier had overwhelmed Ford Madox Ford: "With European civilization going to Hell and America not getting on with the work fast enough to have a bearable civilization ready to take over when Europe collapses, I am against frittering away so much time." [6]

Whether or not Pound's advice influenced Kirstein and Blackmur to shift their policy, in 1930 the editors seemed concerned to wean themselves from Eliot. Announcing that *The Hound & Horn* would offer "Chronicles on Music, Drama and Fine Arts," they dropped the format of a purely critical paper and adopted the form of a "tendenz" magazine. "The Chronicles will receive their sanction if they further the establishment of a technique, a common explored world, and a conscious attitude within a convention of ideas among both the artists and the society to which they appear." "The establishment of a technique, a common world, ideas and a society will supply a national capital or provincial capitals. Without capitals there have been no cultures." Although this reads like a parody of Blackmur's habitual prose, we sense what it is about. Its intricately phrased notions about new ways of national salvation describe a willingness to recreate some capital elements in *The Dial*'s design. As Thayer and Watson had taken their inspiration from *The Seven Arts* in 1919, so now in 1930 Blackmur and Kirstein undertook to systematize *The Dial*'s spirit.

One immediate effect of this decision was *Hound & Horn*'s support of the method and intention of the one new writer whose mind fused technic and prophecy, an ardor for both art and utopia, Louis Zukofsky. In 1931 *Hound & Horn* published his essay in review of William Carlos Williams' *Voyage to Pagany,* an essay which Zukofsky designed as a "postscript to Henry Adams." Earlier he had issued a long personal fierce reading of Adams' *Education.* In order to establish certain links between past and present, to contrast the importance of nineteenth-century Europe on Adams' education with the value for Williams of twentieth-century Europe, Zukofsky wrote his essay in review of Williams' book: "Beginning again with William Carlos Williams . . ." Like Yvor Winters in *The Dial,* he imagined that Williams might serve as a prophet to the new generation because his art penetrates us and enables us to "become clear on all levels." Zukofsky was one of a small group of writers, estranged from the very magazines for which its members wrote, who sensed in the verse of Dr. Williams an antidote to the twin toxins of Eliot and Marx, of textuality and tactlessness.[7]

We cannot tell how far *The Hound & Horn* might have carried its new version of the uses of prophecy. The moment for apocalyptic art and criticism had passed, and once again the time was ripe for revelation through politics. Before Lincoln Kirstein resigned, tired of fighting that drift toward left and right which by the mid-1930's had drawn all journals into one orbit or another, his magazine had circulated good work by Katherine Anne Porter, Allen Tate, and Francis Fergusson. Instead of battling for modern painting, it had tried to cultivate a public for photography and ballet. Instead of attempting, as *The Dial* had done, to become first among equals in an international community of art, *The Hound & Horn* had sought to merge American critics and artists in a single national community where everyone spoke a common tongue.

Both *Hound & Horn* and *The Symposium* were succeeded by two periodicals which, taken together, serve as prototype for virtually all little magazines and grand themes current from the late 1930's until the mid-1950's—*Partisan Review* and *Kenyon Review*. By 1938, *Partisan,* purged of the Stalinists who had shaped its policy in 1934 and reconstituted after a year's suspension (1936–37), had established the boundaries of an empire it continues to tend even now. Both *Partisan,* spokesman for new art in the age of Stalin, and *Kenyon,* sponsor of the New Criticism in the age of Roosevelt, supported only those artists and critics who wrote for each other rather than for that general reader whose soul *The Seven Arts* and *The Dial* had hoped to save. In "the course of its alienation from modern society," William Phillips said in 1941, "modern art has developed a highly organized regime of its own." [8] The entire tradition of *The Dial*—Stieglitz's effort to identify the twin myths of democracy and imagination, Bourne's prophecy, Thayer's search for an intense American art and criticism which would regenerate man, and Burke's idea of eloquence, of Being as an exercise and experiment in linguistics—seemed to wither.

Today old issues of *The Dial* are collectors' items. "Alas," says the art critic of *The New York Times,* Dore Ashton, "nothing has ever appeared to replace *The Dial.*" A few years ago this magazine was recalled as a pioneer but amateurish paper which, because of sheer accident in time, presented the work of some major writers. "In point of creative work—let us admit it here and now—" Phillips and Philip Rahv said in 1944, *"Partisan Review* has been unable to equal the record of some of the little magazines which flourished in the more fertile period that closed with the twenties. We did not have the good fortune of coming across such essentially '*new*' writing as *Ulysses* and *The Waste Land,* or the more significant early fiction of such modern American authors as Anderson, Hemingway, and Faulkner. . . . If we have published poets like Eliot, Stevens, and Marianne Moore, it has been after their merit was generally recognized." [9] Two years later William Barrett, unaware of the reasons which had led *The Dial* to publicize the merit of Anderson, Eliot, Stevens, and Miss Moore, attributed to this journal "the dangerous American tradition" of a purely literary

paper. But the *Partisan Review* "derived its tone and quality,"
Phillips and Rahv said, from a "union of sensibility with a radical
temper," a union which, to my mind, cultivated the arts of social
concern and moral disdain.[10] During the 1930's and 1940's, *Partisan* and *Kenyon* formed what Leslie Fiedler has called a "united
front," a bridge "between the free lance and the University,"
which enabled both journals to stabilize the regime and cultivate
the arts of alienation.[11] In the 1950's, this activity and style of
mind was institutionalized at the School of Letters at Indiana University.

Until 1949, both journals maintained the tone of implacable
pique, a tone which underlay persistent public quarrel, brilliant
and querulous, as well as periodic symposia, both niggling and
moot. The work of a particular kind of writer was favored because
it offered the subtlest flavors of disenchantment and disdain. Paradox furnished the figure most attractive to textual critics, including the new ontologists of *Sewanee Review* and the new academics
of *Hudson Review,* who documented the dogma, prized the por-
trayal, and studied the performance of untranscended anguish.
Then, early in the 1950's, older men of letters became restive.
Irving Howe discovered even in Blackmur's work "an uneasy
abandonment of textual criticism": "Using his own term, *language
as gesture,* we find in his recent essays gestures of . . . preparation for prophecy."

During the last ten years there has been persistent effort to resolve pique and master technique, to recover some of the gestures
of prophecy not to reaffirm but to rephrase the idea of special mission in American letters. The gestures are inherent in a number of
works by familiar contributors but are cogent in Richard Chase's
word "romance," which defines the uniqueness of American fiction.
This word has helped another regular, Hans Meyerhoff, to understand why "the American melting pot has become the cultural
melting pot of the Western world." The "grandeur and pathos of
classic American literature," he says, is its "sense of homelessness." [12] Stirred by advanced thought in Europe, the new geogra-
phers of alienation adopt an old imagery in order to transfigure the
dream. They hope to substitute for old prophecies of organic Amer-

ican rootedness new prophecies of cosmic homelessness. In place of a classic American idealism—the mindless affirmations of 1905, the "Mysticism of the Organic" of 1915, the transnationalization of American letters of 1925—they discover a classic American existentialism. During the last decade, the established avant-garde has reassumed the modes of prophecy in order to say that the American imagination must be honored for its peculiar historic unremitting national instinctive tragic sense of the eternal disparity of things.

2

Their notion is both ingenious and striking enough to interest a large group of writers, critics, and scholars who try to locate abyss and measure fissure in the American mind. This latest manifestation of the Eliot influence in modern letters, tentative at mid-decade, is now in full career. Simultaneously, another series of motives and attitudes, scarcely notable a few years ago, begins to affirm anew some values which contradict these and recall an older image of America. In 1954, when *The Times Literary Supplement* published its first serious inquiry into the American imagination, we learned that "the 'little' or literary magazine, formerly radical, daring, experimental, has become sedate and respectable." Then in 1956, when Van Wyck Brooks wrote a peevish essay in *The New York Times Book Review,* we were offered Melville's injunction: the "time has come . . . that America should 'set, not follow, precedents.' " Our artists must speak "not for the country that is but for the country that promises to be, even if it always breaks its word." A similar view was repeated in the spring of 1959 when Paul Tillich, presenting the Walter Rauschenbusch Lecture at the Colgate-Rochester Divinity School, recalled the religious socialism common among reformers at the time of World War I. That movement, he said, expressed the spirit of utopia in human nature, a spirit which is today "almost eradicated." Tillich ended his remarks, "Between Utopianism and Escape from History," with a call and a lament, an *ubi sunt* of the social gospelers: where are, "we now ask, prophetic spirits among us, spirits of utopia?" [13]

Again in autumn, 1959, C. Wright Mills wrote an article in Williams' old magazine, *Contact,* now revived in California, demanding that we "stop whining about our own alienation long enough to use it to form radical critiques, audacious programs, commanding views of the future. If *we* do not do these things, who will?" And in spring, 1960, in a long essay for the *American Scholar,* Kenneth Keniston combined advanced and modish learning in social science with advanced and modish literature in order to instruct us in the connections which link "Alienation and the Decline of Utopia." Considering the *"gap between aspirations and actualities* as one of the chief sources of alienation" in private and in social life, not only in American society but in all forms of human culture, Mr. Keniston remarks that every "age . . . has its characteristic balance between *positive* . . . hortatory . . . visionary, utopian myths, and *negative* . . . direful, destructive and counter-utopian myths." In our time, conscious, positive "utopia has become counter-utopia"; "what is most unconscious today is the constructive . . . and affirmative part of man." Our task, he concludes, is to translate "alienation" into "reform," "apathy" into "commitment," to acquire courage "to be *for* something despite the perishability and transience of all human endeavors."

Fifty years ago the new social scientists decided to examine the anatomy of government in order to study the cells of destiny. Today, suddenly, there is a new social psychology of American purpose, and this in turn is reinforced by the politics, history, and journalism of utopia. As if in harmony with Keniston's thought, *The New Republic* in September, 1959, announced its "third style change since 1914." "Its editors and writers share Herbert Croly's confidence that American life *has* a 'promise.' " Having learned the lessons of modern history, "it does not assume that truth is easily identified or that the reform of institutions alone assures progress." But the staff is convinced that both Croly's magazine and this nation, having had "one period of glory," must prepare to enter "its second golden age." During the same month, Douglass Cater in the *Times* reported gossip in Washington about "a recent confidential memo" written by Arthur Schlesinger, Jr., and maintaining that "the political epoch lying ahead will more closely resemble

the Progressive period at the turn of this century than it will the
New Deal period. His call to arms for the Democratic Party evokes
the spirit not of Democrat Franklin D. but of Republican Theodore Roosevelt." [14]

His call to arms is echoed in a novel which had a success as
grand and inexplicable as James Gould Cozzens' *By Love Possessed*—Allen Drury's *Advise and Consent*. Both Cozzens' and
Drury's books occur in a new genre which is best described as a
popular fiction of serious Republican ideas. As Mills sought to
reanimate the spirit of "positive utopia" among intellectuals, and
as Schlesinger hopes to evoke this spirit among Democrats, so
Drury, whose sexual, moral, and political sympathies are conservative, hopes to inspire the Republican party to fulfill its task as the
chief steward of our dreams. In a form of rhetoric borrowed from
the Senate itself, Drury writes of the present as if it were a recent
past when "the great promise was being challenged and the great
Republic which embodied it was being desperately threatened. In
his lifetime he had seen America rise and rise and rise, some sort
of golden legend to her own people, some sort of impossible fantasy
to others . . . rise and rise and rise and rise—and then, in the
sudden burst of Soviet science in the later fifties, the golden legend
crumpled, overnight the fall began . . . a too complacent and un-
caring people awoke to find themselves naked with the winds of the
world howling around their ears": "a time of nip and tuck, and a
darkening passageway with only God's good grace, if He cared to
confer it again upon a people who sometimes didn't seem to deserve it any more." Mr. Drury implies, however, in accord with
Henry Luce, that we are lucky to have good men like Richard
Nixon and Everett Dirksen who may see us through.[15]

What used to be called myth, historians now describe as "consensus," a view and attitude of culture which invites national
assent. By 1960, this effort to organize a new "consensus" of "positive utopia" had begun to charm everyone. In Max Lerner's *America as a Civilization,* it is called "dynamism" and characterized as
the central tradition in our lives. Edmund Wilson, whom Schlesinger admires for a "deep-running belief in a national dignity and
national identity," feels himself deracinated and searches out a
sense of continuity more honest than that offered by *Life*.[16] "And

am I . . . I wonder, stranded?" he asked in 1958. Seeking roots, he turned to the American Indian community, hoping to find there a true "consensus" in which he might share. As Schlesinger turns to Edmund Wilson and Edmund Wilson turns to the Iroquois, so H. S. Commager returns to the great man of the Resurgence. Commager, preparing us for the new year, 1960, when in *The New York Times* we crossed a great divide and marched "onto a new world stage," asked us to "recall the appeal of Woodrow Wilson." " 'Men's hearts wait upon us; men's lives hang in the balance; men's hopes call upon us to say what we will do. Who shall live up to the great trust? Who dares fail to try?' " [17] Not President Kennedy, surely, whose New Frontier associates Schlesinger's program with Commager's rhetoric, and whose "brilliant claim to admiration," says the *Manchester Guardian,* is his having "done so much to revive the sense of American mission," to revive "for all our poor sakes . . . a little of the romance of America." [18]

But by far the most startling of all impulses to recover the gestures of prophecy appears in the arts where members of the Beat generation attempt to achieve a balance of positive and negative myth. "To attribute a tradition to . . . the San Francisco jazz-and-poetry movement," two English writers in *The Twentieth Century* remarked, "might be called misleading." [19] But at the end of 1959, Karl Shapiro, issuing a manifesto in support of the idea, said that we have been misled only by the ideas which Beat is designed to controvert, that Beat itself reasserts the most vigorous of all traditions in our literature. Modern verse, a "diseased art," is the work of Dr. Jekyll and Mr. Hyde, Eliot and Pound, who present a poetry of "artificial culture myth and the bleak footnote." Shapiro, formerly one of the most querulous of alienated writers, now a poet-critic whose reputation rests chiefly on *Essay on Rime,* is delighted that a "revolt against Modernism seems to be gaining ground at long last. New poets are turning away from criticism and the dictatorship of the intellectual journals . . . from the sanctimonious evangelists of the Tradition." These new poets are too often illiterate and hysterical, he agrees, but their work is alive and must therefore replace "the poetry of the textbook" which "will shortly find its way to the library stacks where, in fact, its death-wish has always pointed." [20] This is stunning comment in favor of the verse of young men whose wounds are not symbolic but real, who shove at us the very smell of their sickness. For Mr. Shapiro argues that they are well, that their poems present a kind of etiology and prognosis of a disease which is at bottom a form of health. "They are once again seeking that audience which has for so long been outlawed by the aristocrats of the Word. They are seeking to regain spontaneity and the use of the human voice. . . . They are turning to Whitman, the only world-poet America has produced, and to Lawrence and such American contemporaries as William Carlos Williams."

In this fashion Shapiro hoped to establish a "consensus" which is native in origin and transnational in spirit. He confirmed, moreover, the earlier response of another poet whom Van Wyck Brooks might have characterized as a leading victim of Eliot's malaise, Richard Eberhart, who in 1956 traveled to the West Coast and discovered there a "radical group movement of young poets." "Poetry here," Eberhart marveled, has became "a tangible social force, moving and unifying its auditors . . . releasing the energies of the audience through spoken, even shouted verse." These poets rejected the advice Eliot had offered his colleagues in 1928, the recommendation that unless their ear for verse were far better than Whitman's, they absorb their Whitman through Pound. Trained in this school, Eberhart was surprised to learn that "Whitman is the only god worthy of emulation" among poets who "give several poetry readings each week . . . called at the drop of a hat. A card may read 'Celebrated Good Time Poetry Night. Either you go home bugged or completely enlightened. Allen Ginsberg blowing hot; Gary Snyder blowing cool; Philip Whalen puffing the laconic tuba; Mike McClure his hip high notes; Rexroth on the big bass drum. . . . One and only final appearance of this Apocalypse. Admission free.' " [21]

Two years later the new apocalypse was familiar enough to provoke condescension from Herbert Gold, whose dispraise was more strident than Shapiro's support. And during 1959, when Lawrence Lipton published *The Holy Barbarians,* the movement became a main event in the life of the nation, where it was and still is misconceived as the chief form of dissent in our time. Even

Eberhart had been in part mistaken: his professional eye had been startled by the idiom in which these writers worked. But their method was not itself their most impressive accomplishment. For what historians, journalists, and social scientists debated about and plotted over, the Beat movement had already achieved: its work, its language, and its style of life, which by 1956 had existed for nearly a decade, expressed the spirit of utopia among underground men who, emerging to the light of day, undertook to balance dissent and assent, negative and positive "consensus" in a poetry which would penetrate and renew the body and its members. In the later 1940's there was little reason for utopians to remain above ground. When Henry Wallace, for whom Matthiessen had made a seconding speech, was defeated as a candidate for the presidency, Matthiessen killed himself; later, Senator McCarthy destroyed other men of honor. The democratic dogma, in short, suffered forms of outrage all the more terrible because our society had made this world almost insufferable with its latest achievement, the Bomb. As a result, prophets of utopia did indeed go underground.

There, hiding from the community they had planned to serve, bereft of the politics and the Russian Idea, which many artists and intellectuals had hoped would furnish an ideal instrument of service, saviors devised new ways to portray the national disease. Very early they rediscovered Williams, found in him a model of virtue, a poet who "lays down the beat . . . the sound," who "tells it starkly but with energy, energy from the mysterious source of all artistic energy, says it—and stops. . . . From first to last as in Paterson so in Venice West." Williams has become the exemplary American poet in the mind of each new Beat prophet for whom a poem is, Kenneth Rexroth adds, a "ritual act," an "actual social force—something which has always hitherto sounded like a Utopian dream." Williams was the poet on whom "The Waste Land" exploded like an atomic bomb; he was the poet Yvor Winters and Louis Zukofsky foresaw as a prophet to new generations of American writers; he was the poet Watson, the pseudonymous W. C. Blum, cultivated in *The Dial;* he was the poet who, in Watson's journal, approved of Sandburg's verse because it sings "the typical American song, the song of the beaten."

And now Williams, "as a practising family doctor, was already half a shaman from the start," supplied the latest avant-garde with a form of poetic discourse suffused with the dream of utopia. That is, he furnished the materials of positive myth.

No less influential is the writer who furnished this same generation with the discourse and material of negative myth, Henry Miller. Lawrence Lipton, stressing Miller's contribution to the movement, says that he "spans the thirties and forties with a body of work that may yet be seen, in the persepective of the future, as more significant than anyone else's." [22] Whether or not Miller's work is the chief contribution to letters in our time, it does represent an extraordinary effort to turn inside out the ideas of Resurgence. During those years when other American writers organized the regime of art or submitted to the disciplines of politics, Miller refused to join any union whatever. Isolating himself abroad, where he seemed, according to his friend Alfred Perlès, to embody "all the hope, all the glamour and mystery of America," Miller chose to explore those dreams of utopia which lay within the substrata of consciousness.[23] There the dreams flourished untouched by the air-conditioned nightmares of a people no longer interested in saving the world nor even in saving themselves. Years ago Miller decided that the supreme work of an artist in our time is to awaken man "to a consciousness of the Id." His duty is to articulate, as the new social science suggests, our own and our fellows' dimly sensed aspirations. What Mann named the demoniac, that "dementia" which Kierkegaard described as an expression of the divine jealousy, Miller calls an expression of our "lurking" human "divinity" and hopes to evoke in a calculated debauch of prose.

Until 1938 Miller was isolated abroad but, returning home, in 1940 he became a member of an informal group of writers sponsored by Dorothy Norman in a remarkable and, today, anonymous journal, *Twice A Year.* Lewis Mumford is certain that Miss Norman deliberately "gathered around her a new group. . . . She was close to Stieglitz, and had natural affiliations with members of the old Stieglitz circle." [24] Rejecting the arts of alienation, she published a paper from 1938 until 1948 which was orthodox of neither left nor right. Instead, she tried to connect imagination with a specific form of radical politics, civil rights, and to suffuse

both with the modes of prophecy. Inspired by Bourne and dedicated to Stieglitz, Miss Norman remade *Twice A Year* in the twin
images of *The Seven Arts* and *The Dial:* "The voice of the artist is
the prophetic voice of man," the editor said in 1942. The "faith
of the artist is born of his vision of the integration of all aspects
of life into a whole that must be recognized, accepted, affirmed."
"The artist evokes a sense of one-ness between the individual and
all men, between the individual and the universe." Evocations of
this kind, Miss Norman said, define the "synthesis that TWICE A
YEAR attempts to make." [25] This creed is explicit in a segment of
Malraux's *Man's Hope,* published during 1938: " 'Our humble
task, Monsieur Magnin, is to *organize* the apocalypse.' " Adopting
this doctrine, *Twice A Year* became a fulcrum of the 1940's which
links the 1950's with the Resurgence.

In order to accomplish its end, the journal introduced a concern new to magazines of art and letters: it reserved a section for
discussion of civil liberties, a section that began with Hitler and
ended with the Committee on Un-American Activities. This was
composed of reports from the American Civil Liberties Union,
transcriptions of congressional hearings, and reprints of essays in
technical journals among which, despite the claims of *Commentary*
that it was the first general magazine to publish David Riesman,
we discover Riesman along with Max Ascoli, Max Lerner, and
Felix Frankfurter. "Since the need for expression in the ARTS
and the need for CIVIL LIBERTIES spring from the same source, it
seems logical to us to present expressions arising from these needs
together." In accord with this doctrine, *Twice A Year* published
Silone and Bourne, Sartre and Stieglitz, Koestler and Rosenfeld,
Brecht and Patchen. Then in 1946, turning piety into melodrama,
the editor appointed two assistants, Richard Wright and Brom
Weber, and announced their appointment in the same number
which published Camus' "The Human Crisis," a speech given
during his only visit to the United States. Miss Norman remarked
too that "by coincidence, a letter was received from Wright—from
Paris—the very day Stieglitz died. It told of the necessity to send
to France—and to Europe in general—the very kind of synthesis
. . . contained in TWICE A YEAR. This letter arrived like a torch—
as if challenging us to carry on the work begun by a Stieglitz in the

early nineteen hundreds . . . with renewed vitality. Whereas the earlier importations of art from France nourished America at the turn of the century, now, as part of an inevitable cycle it was as if we of a younger generation must take our place more surely among the generative forces of the world of today." [26]

The most forceful and fecund of all the prophets assembled by Miss Norman is Henry Miller who, along with Kenneth Patchen, introduced into this utopian journal the elements of nega-tive myth. Civilization is "drugs, alcohol, engines of war, prostitu-tion, machines and machine slaves . . . bad food, bad taste, prisons, reformatories, lunatic asylums, divorce, perversion, brutal sports, suicides, infanticides, cinema, quackery, demogogy, strikes, lockouts, revolutions . . . condoms, pessaries, syphilis, gonor-rhea, insanity . . . etc., etc." [27] Miller introduced himself and his system in 1940 when his essay on Balzac demonstrated that the French "thinker, visionary, prophet" wrote the novel *Louis Lam-bert* for the same reasons that had impelled Whitman to foretell "in the future of these States," the arrival of poets who " 'will make great poems of death.' " Whitman "saw the democratic idea crystallizing into a vulgar caricature," Miller later remarked in a pamphlet, *Patchen, Man of Anger and Light;* he "saw the great nation, only recently emerged from its blood bath, already grown soft and smug and drifting toward the rocks." And he called for the "sure and prophetic vision of the black poets" who would serve civilization by writing works which, like the "stern fist of the Zen master," would jolt us and cause us to know that "THE WAY MEN LIVE IS A LIE!" [28]

In a world without values, Camus said in 1946, "what did our revolt really signify? It made of us men who said *No*. But we were at the same time men who said *Yes*. We said *No* to this world . . . the civilization of death that was being prepared for us. In saying *No*, we affirmed that things had gone on in this way long enough, that there was a limit to what could be brooked. But at the same time, we . . . affirmed that there was something in us . . . which could not be endlessly humiliated." Uniting "a pessimistic view of the world with a profound optimism about man," he concluded, the freedom we must "finally win is the freedom never to lie." [29] This freedom Miller reserved for the American black poet-prophet-savior who "comes at the darkest hour, rises like a sun, and dispels the gloom and stagnation in which the world was gripped." Led by such poets, "we could inspire such hope, such courage, such enthusiasm that the passion of the French revolutionists would seem like a mere breeze." [30] Balzac's failure, he decided in that 1940 essay, lay in his European blindness to the whole point: "Art is only the stepping-stone to another, larger way of life." [31]

There are those who say "no" to the civilization of death and who, like D. H. Lawrence, teach us how to die in our corruption, "to be reborn, to enjoy a new spirit and a new body and a new life!" But there are still others such as Jasper Deeter who are found only in America and whose life and art display and amplify and realize the Laurentian idea. Returning from Europe, rediscovering America, Miller came to Deeter's Hedgerow Theatre, outside Philadelphia, and discovered there "a vital organism, a little cosmos," the "natural climate of the human family" in which each member enters so "thoroughly and deeply into the life of the theatre that whatever he is called upon to do he will do with his whole being." [32] In Miller's mind Deeter was a man not only of Lawrence's sort but also of Alfred Stieglitz's very special and very American kind: "All his life Stieglitz has been waiting for that public which would celebrate the coming of the artist," Miller wrote in *Twice A Year* in 1942, a public " 'prepared *to experience life as and through Art.*' " [33] This remark is the more striking, too, because it follows some words in homage to Stieglitz written by Carl Zigrosser, an art historian who is both an admirer of Lawrence's and a friend of Bourne's (Zigrosser and Bourne lived together during the latter's early days in New York). A whole modern American history of prophecy is inherent, therefore, in this man's remark describing Lawrence's and Stieglitz's "passionate intensity . . . almost neurotic sensibility. . . . They both longed to found Utopias, Lawrence with a band of equals in Mexico, and Stieglitz with a band of artists at '291.' " [34]

Although Miller could scarcely disagree with Zigrosser, he was convinced that America alone creates a Deeter or a Patchen, a Whitman or a Stieglitz, a "special new type . . . one utterly unlike anything which has preceded us in Europe," a savior whose art enables "the common man" to achieve a "harmony between

inner and outer worlds." [35] In a moment I shall demonstrate how
members of the Beat generation, having taken some cues from
Miller, cast the jazz musician Charlie Parker in the savior's role.
First I must refer to more orthodox occasions in current letters
where Miller's effort enlists accidental as well as deliberate support. It is accidental in Roy Harvey Pearce's study of literary epic
in America from the Federalist poet-patriot Joel Barlow to the un-
reconstructed Ezra Pound. According to Pearce, our epic literature
is conventional in its recreation of national history and its celebration of national triumph, but it is remarkable for its determination
to mold national character. Speaking of Pound's *Cantos,* Pearce
says that the poet decided to "re-create the tribe in order to tell its
tale." "The *Cantos* are that act of creation." Reading Pearce's
statement of Pound's purpose, we realize that this poet, like all his
predecessors, performs a ritual rooted in the cardinal doctrine of
prophetic art: "If it is but done powerfully enough, there will be
no longer a need to tell the tale. For it would be ours—ours in such
a way that we would not have to have it told to us. As in Barlow's
vision, and as in Whitman's practice, the end of poetry is that re-
constitution of man which will entail the withering away of poetry." [36] Supplementing Pearce's comment, we can add Miller to
Pearce's list. For Miller has composed what he calls a *"human
book."* Having created a personal and national song of the blackest
self, having sung of our brotherhood below the belt, Miller has
written an epic self-portrait of the American artist as the eternal
savior of man. This savior, along with all prophets from Barlow to
Pound, from Edward Taylor to Norman Mailer, practices his art
because he would perfect our lives.

What I have called the principle of organic communion Pearce
relates to the history of a single literary form in America. And
what I have called prophetic art another group of scholars, Karl
Shapiro, James E. Miller, and Bernice Slote, have named "cosmic."
Their study of "cosmic poetry," *Start with the Sun,* is written in
part to furnish the enemies of Eliot with a theory and a tradition,
and in part to isolate the reasons why a certain kind of literature
is inexhaustibly deep and grand. Although this special style is not
exclusively an affair of our continent and may boast of Lawrence
and Dylan Thomas as its British spokemen, nevertheless our liter-

ature, mainly because of Whitman, preserves a vested concern in
the key doctrine of cosmic letters: the organic principle. Best
studied in Hart Crane's verse, where "words like *organic* and
dynamic . . . suggest that form is to be found most naturally in
growth and movement," the new organicism propels us into that
spacious and magnetic field in which the cosmic imagination is at
home. There alone, Miss Slote says, we are able to relate the
organic idea to another principle, the concept of fusion. Organic
art is cosmic because it exploits the supreme experience of creation. Cosmic organic art compels its public to "fuse the relation-
ships of the metaphor as it evolves. The poem is not given to the
reader, but the reader helps to create it." [37] In this unnecessarily
intricate and totally antihistorical way, we are forced to double
back and encircle our own minds. Intent on replacing Eliot's authority with Henry Miller's (Miller's "one aim is to give literature
back to life," Shapiro says, for he is one of the last remaining
"celebrants of the soul and of the flesh and of the still-remaining
promise of America"), members of this cosmic circle are unaware
that writers of organic verse do not simply start with the sun and
end with a sort of photosynthesis of the mind. Between the sun
and the organic poem stand the facts of history, to which Pearce
refers, and the quirks of culture, prisms which cause the kind of
refraction I have sought to describe. That "cosmic" art is a mis-
nomer is indisputable, surely, when we realize that the most stunning display of organic philosophy in our time is found not in
letters but in jazz. Its authority in this field dates from 1946, when
Camus and Miller addressed avant-garde audiences in the East
and West, when Stieglitz and Rosenfeld died in New York. During
that spring, 1946, a colored jazz musician called "Bird" Parker,
addicted both to music and to drugs, admitted to a mental hospital
in California, entered American legend. At that moment the prophetic imagination, expressed by jazz, renewed itself in ways both
habitual and extraordinary.

In the early 1940's Parker and others had played a form of
music called "bop," admired by a "fanatically loyal group of intellectuals, artists, and malcontents" who, according to Dave Brubeck, "felt in the tense new music some of their own revolt from
a society that had betrayed them." [38] The most gifted of this group

was Kenneth Rexroth who that year published *The Phoenix and the Tortoise*. In this work he spoke of genocide and the bomb, and described the condition of war not merely as the health of the state: "War is the State," he said, and its health manifests the very disease men must labor to destroy. Like Randolph Bourne, Rexroth sought redemption in art; like Gilbert Seldes, Rexroth found salvation in jazz. Hearing the new music he recognized in its strange sounds the true prophetic note of organic American community. And by the time the 1950's had ended, Rexroth's views on jazz were commonplace among bearded oracles, men of high fashion, jazz critics who urge us to recognize in this music the definitive experience of national culture. It tells us "what's American about America," John A. Kouwenhoven says, because it is "the first art form to give full expression to Emerson's ideal of a union which is perfect only 'when all the uniters are isolated.' " Like Whitman's poetry, *Huckleberry Finn,* the American Constitution itself, jazz exploits the tension between a basic rhythmical pattern and a "restless, sweeping movement." [39] It is also the first art form which satisfies the wants of our men of Resurgence: "the democratic idea of unity through diversity" is expressed in what Daniel G. Hoffman maintains is an aesthetic system new to Western music, an ideal of "integrated communal composition." [40] Brubeck agrees with Hoffman, adds that jazz is quintessentially an event of national life at the instant when "the improviser becomes the articulate voice of the group" and, in an act of "co-creation," unifies the "diverse responses of an audience." In that "inspired moment of unity," the precise effect for which Eliot admired Marie Lloyd and for which Thayer designed *The Dial,* Brubeck recognizes "the reason for jazz and its continued existence." At that instant art, artist, audience, and civilization are one.

As we shall see, it was Henry Miller who led writers and painters to find in prophetic jazz a perfect emblem of negative myth and organic art, to exploit Parker's style in behalf of Emerson's ideal. By the mid-1940's Peggy Guggenheim's Art of This Century Gallery exhibited artists who improvised in paint. Each canvas, "an arena in which to act," not a "space in which to reproduce, redesign, analyze or 'express' an object, actual or imagined," sought not to represent but to "be the world." Like Whit-

man, who "puts together poetry from which the appearance of
poetry has managed to depart," the "new painting has broken
down every distinction between art and life." I have cited Harold
Rosenberg's famed explanation of object and method in action
painting, the style invented by Jackson Pollock and Clyfford Still,
Robert Motherwell and Mark Rothko. These were vanguard
painters who "took to the white expanse of canvas as Melville's
Ishmael took to the sea," Rosenberg says, and as Parker took to
the musical line. The painter met his canvas in an "encounter"
which led to an "event" which was of the same "metaphysical substance as the artist's existence." [41] The final encounter is renewed
daily when painter and viewer enact in concert on the canvas a
pure creative event.*

By 1961 the same mystique, a *Tradition of the New,* as Rosenberg said, had been introduced even in the most downright of
fields, in the crafts where artisans are often housewives seeking a
divorce from Mr. Clean. Turning ancient duties into hip rugs, beat
pots, and cool cloth, they display their accomplishment in a gallery aptly called America House. There a "New Ceramic Presence" begins to show itself, as we learn in *Craft Horizons.* De-
riving its style and ideology less from action painting than from
jazz itself, "American plastic expression" now turns to improvised,
spontaneous shapes in place of the carefully molded piece. Imitating the instrumentalist of jazz who "creates at the same time he
performs," craftsmen labor to "break through expected patterns"
in order to preserve the true American spirit: a sense of "creative
adventure . . . always incomplete, always in process." In this
self-conscious but spirited way, ceramists reproduce the "fearless-
ness, the individuality, the aloneness of each man's search" in
workaday pots, domestic sculpture, which enable creator and wit-
ness to share together "the elation of the creative act." [42]

---

* Reading in *Encounter* a very recent essay by Sir Kenneth Clark, I am
tempted to exploit wordplay in behalf of this play of ideas: the "closest
analogy to action painting," Sir Kenneth says, is indeed "the most popular art
of all—the art of jazz. The trumpeter who rises from his seat as one possessed,
and squirts out his melody like a scarlet scrawl against a background of
plangent dashes and dots, is not as a rule performing for a small body of intellectuals." Sir Kenneth Clark, "The Blot and the Diagram," *Encounter,* XX
(January, 1963), 34.

In our time, therefore, the immediate private and popular life of the nation is shaped in accord with what the seventeenth-century Puritan poet Edward Taylor called "Huswifery." Our craftsmen, our musicians, and our writers assume an office and undertake to perform duties which once were held to be the exclusive rights of our priests alone. Adopting the ineradicable, pivotal dogma of organic art, communion, they dislodge that dream of destiny which this dogma once supported. Today, utopia is a private affair of the hearth. And it is established there because the hipsters of the Beat generation, keening in the wake of man, assumed their vocation in response to the improvised call of Charlie Parker's jazz. To these Howlers, then, whether or not they charm us, the social psychologist Paul Goodman adds, we are in deep debt. For they have "contrived a pattern of culture that . . . costs very little," is "handmade not canned . . . continually improvised." Despite limitation and weakness, "the *fact* of it, of a culture that is communal and . . . creative, is so capital that it must have a future." [43]

3

Whether or not its future is clear, its past is certain. For the poets, painters, and musicians of this generation did not appear out of nowhere to explode a flash of dark in the light. On the contrary, they renew an old American line. Cluttered with the esoterica of Zen, muddled by a silly uniform and bizarre pose, renewal in literature occurred because Henry Miller alone preserved an ancient faith in the powers of prophetic art. Following the demise of *The Dial,* Miller prepared black potions to infuse dead souls. Founder of the new prophetic line, he became high priest of our dark age. In order to demonstrate how his art accomplished these ends, I must refer to the work of a philosopher of history noted for his disdain of fad, Herbert Marcuse, who discerns an "inner link" between dialectical thought and avant-garde literature, between, say, Hegel and Miller. The avant-garde perforce tries "to break the power of facts . . . and to speak a language which is not the language of those who establish, perforce, and benefit from the facts [*i.e.,* power in the world]." Like the drip and splash of paint, like the jargon of hip, such an effort to "speak the language of

contradiction appears increasingly irrational, obscure, artificial."
But at bottom it speaks for an honest search for an "authentic
language," for a form of speech that expresses a "Great Refusal to
accept the rules of a game in which the dice are loaded." The language of negation among members of the avant-garde must therefore be taken as a "positive act." [44]

Inspired by Henry Miller, Beat prophets of organic community
adopted the legendary Parker as the supreme hero of our time. For
Parker seemed to represent the very man, the black poet whose
worth Miller years ago foresaw, a "martyr whether he chooses to be
or not," a maker who does not "generate warmth" but synthesizes a
(cool) "virus with which society must allow itself to be injected or
perish." [45] Miller's startling words, written long before Parker appeared on the scene, are prescient indeed. And as if in conformity
with Miller's injunction, Beat writers seized Parker's martyrdom
as evidence of his sanctity. Equating Parker's heroin and Miller's
"virus," they fancied that his drug-sickness was the source of his
prophetic power. Having learned from Rexroth that jazz is the
paradigm of American art because it portrays an organic community absorbed in the creative process, finding themselves enjoined
by Parker to share his pulsing pizzicatti of pain and joy, to proclaim the catastrophe and affirm the miracle of national life, they
were determined to find a literary language which would perform
in verse the jazz ritual of a communal improvisation.

Because the hipster-poet, "The White Negro" as Mailer described him, was convinced that his jazz-poem must have the
energy, the virtue inherent in Parker's music, he was concerned to
devise a mode of speech suited to the needs of verse and derived
from the language of jazz, the language of negation and liberation.
And this in turn led him to the jargon of drug addiction, a private
argot which has a long public history among primitive American
communities. Among these it is associated with rites designed to
intensify the creative powers of individual persons and to heighten
in each communicant his talent for communality. The ritual use
of peyote, for example, to free the spirit to penetrate chaos and
perceive remote realms of order within the self and in the universe
dates from pre-Columbian times, as we learn from Weston La
Barre's *The Peyote Cult*. Indeed, La Barre describes the theory

of "Mescalero peyotism" in much the fashion used by our addicts of jazz to explain their theory. Led by "the peyote shaman," everyone in the peyote community is helped "to get in rapport with his power(s)" and to feel within the group itself a "multiple 'working together.' " From the earliest record of its use until late in the last century when a "long line of Indian prophet-messiahs" created a Christian form of peyotism called the Native American Church, drugs have been associated with a seer's vision of the heavenly kingdom.[46]

Although there is no direct influence of this church on jazz itself, there is an essay, "peyote," by the Beat scholar Jack Green, which refers to these matters and reinforces, with personal testimony in the idiom of hip, the main line of La Barre's study.[47] Most Beat writers prefer to take their imagery from addiction to heroin as if, in their poems, the bright image of the thing could achieve the black magic of the thing itself. For heroin is a "Faustian drug," Lionel Abel says in his review of *The Connection:* it "adds risk to risk, danger to danger, exhilaration to action." And we, waiting to feel that "all-meaningful 'flash,' " have "already opted for heroin even if we never take it." [48] Those young men of art who do not take the drug are just as eager to produce its effect inside us. Therefore they take their figures of speech from those men of jazz who use heroin to achieve a breakthrough of the sort Mann imagines at the end of *Doctor Faustus,* a heroic triumph of solo improvisation which injects their flash into the audience during that instant of union when note and ear are locked in the act of communal cocreation. Fusing art music and folk music, jazz and poetry, order and chaos, shaman and layman, Beat artists undertake to complete the work of Resurgence, work begun by Stieglitz and Bourne and Brooks.

"I feel that the final purpose of art is to intensify, even, if necessary, to exacerbate the moral consciousness of people," Norman Mailer says.[49] For he is convinced that the Republic is "in real peril," that hipsters are "the cowards who must defend courage, sex, consciousness, the beauty of the body, the search for love, and the capture of what may be, after all, an heroic destiny." [50] If, in pursuit of this lovely old organic American dream, the hipster prefers heroin, Zen, and jazz to primitive recipes for induced vision or Emerson's "Brahma" or German music, we have no reason to complain. Like all his predecessors, the hip artist hopes to " 'destroy our false inorganic connections,' " as Miller says quoting Lawrence, and " 're-establish the living organic connections with the cosmos, the sun and earth, with mankind and nation and family.' " [51] In Ginsberg's language of negation, we are all a Beat generation in "an angry fix" burning for "the ancient heavenly connection to the starry dynamo in the machinery of night." Prophesying our rebirth in a jazz-poem, he sings us to life in a form which "returns poetry to music and to public entertainments," Rexroth believes, as it was in the days of Homer and the troubadors. He stings us and dies, a redeemer redeemed.[52]

Despite grotesque manners and maladroit art, Beat prophets leave their mark on our lives and letters. The actual worth of individual works is doubtless small: Allen Ginsberg, his best friends feel compelled to say, is talented but wanton; Jack Kerouac is slick; Lawrence Ferlinghetti is dull; William Burroughs is brilliant but distraught. Although I have not tried to compose an essay in apology for the Beat generation, I have indeed hoped to relate its motives to certain presiding motifs in classic and modern literature. Among the Beats we recognize an outlandish, perhaps lunatic, but not unintelligent or frivolous materialization of an abiding spirit in our native American church of art.[53] A Beat poem is the instrument with which a hipster-addict-poet-priest-prophet releases his genius in order to fulfill, however meagerly, his mythic American goal. He stabs himself in order to save himself, in order to reveal the organic word which will needle his public and compel it to experience a peyote of the imagination even more vital than that supplied by Whitman's germ, Bourne's and Thayer's and Williams' serum, Henry Miller's virus. In place of the heavenly kingdom, these members of the latest prophetic generation fashion an apocalyptic art that points toward one end only, a single moment of communion. They settle for this. For this is all that is left of utopia in our modern kingdom of transnational hell.

Even as the movement itself disappears, its organicist ritual of negative "consensus" invades even the sternest minds and fussiest journals. "At the heart of Mailer's recent literary and intellectual adventure," Irving Howe permits himself to say in the *Partisan*

Review, "lies a fear which he shares with many reflective people, the fear of stasis" in a period of history when men are "deprived of the hunger for utopia." [54] Not only in *Partisan* but also in the *Sewanee* and *Kenyon* reviews we hear new sounds and a familiar keynote: the "function of poetry in the modern world is revelation." [55] But when Wright Morris invokes the shade of early Pound, relates this to jazz in order to define once and for all the mystique of America, then surely we have come the whole distance from Bourne to Beat. Morris says flatly that the key to American genius is a genius for improvisation. "And what is new in jazz is that improvisation . . . has been raised to the level of art. The man who . . . achieves more than a form of musical doodling, creatively produces something new out of something that was old. . . . *Make it new* is precisely this challenge. Often he muffs it. Even in jazz such talent is rare. But today he knows what he is about, and the American mania to tamper is slowly emerging into an American form of art. . . . In the harmonious sounds of jazz blend the discords of our nature." [56]

A cultivated taste for improvisation in art is therefore organic to persons of prophetic imagination in our time, when sophisticated men continue to preserve a mystic faith in the authority of sheer utterance, in the ineffable Word. Connecting psyche and symbol, poet and public, soul and society in the experience of total communion, this Word evokes centuries of human longing for order in the world. Indeed, the entire history of myth itself is subsumed in the myth of organicism to which our prophets devote their lives and which they turn into the chief attraction of our literature, as Simone de Beauvoir testifies. This mystique keeps America new, fresh, a place "still in transcendence, its history . . . is the history of the creation of the whole world." [57]

In the first decade of our century, organicists of every persuasion decided that myth and history would be reconciled only when their prophetic arts had managed somehow to utter the fabled Word. Twentieth-century American painting and drama—from the Provincetown Players to the Group Theatre, from the Hedgerow Theatre to the Actor's Studio—poetry, social criticism, and literary theory come into being in response to this congeries of ideas. But the most ambitious and influential of all such programs appeared during the time of *The Dial.* For that remarkable miscellany sought to blend disparate materials in a form calculated to suffuse national culture with organic art.

Although Thayer's program could not succeed, *The Dial*'s example did establish a model imitated by all avant-garde magazines in our time. Achieving this effect, it fulfilled its own unique history. For in the history of American literary journalism this magazine has staked out a distinctive role: since 1840 it has served as the leading vehicle for the thought of each new generation. In 1941, twelve years after Watson decided to quit, St. John Perse urged Gilbert Seldes to drop whatever he was doing and start the magazine again. Within the last few years it has appeared in double recrudescence as a quarterly magazine of fiction, a synthesis of the hip and the square, and as a magazine of verse.[58]

Each journal disputes the other's right to the name but in fact neither has clear title. Both are drawn to a figure of speech which holds within itself the fame of an American magazine of the 1920's and connotes the entire modern history of prophetic art. Doctrine, legend, and figure appear first in that series of lectures, *On Heroes, Hero-Worship, and the Heroic in History,* which Carlyle gave during the very year when Emerson's new journal was introduced. Proclaiming in public those views which doubtless he and Emerson seven years earlier had exchanged in private, Carlyle defined intensity as the force which enables a poet to get "into the essence of all." To penetrate and portray "the sacred mystery of the Universe" is the goal of men marked by genius of this order, men who speak for their nation "what the heart of it means!" Such a man, "Vates, whether Prophet or poet," possesses both an "articulate voice" and "the seeing eye! It is this that discloses the inner harmony of things."

Carlyle's way of describing nature's gift to intense artists who serve as heroes of culture, the gift Emerson called a transparency of eyeball and Henry Miller calls a cosmology of eye, is taken from no less a personage than Goethe. Carlyle says that Goethe himself had been led to this formulation by a study of Shakespeare in which he realized that Shakespeare's characters, " 'like watches with dial-plates of transparent crystal,' " show the hour and simultaneously make visible its " 'inward mechanism' " too. We realize, therefore, that Emerson's *Dial* displays Carlyle's prophetic vision of order in the heart of things, Goethe's image of harmony between men and culture, and Shakespeare's timeless, ceaseless yearning to advance on chaos and the dark.[59]

In that day and in this American journal, as we are told in a very recent study of the transcendentalist *Dial,* poetry was substituted "for religion and the poet for the priest." And although its effort was "quixotic," Emerson's *Dial* "produced a trend of thought that, however submerged from time to time," has been of abiding influence in American letters.* Our men of prophetic imagination, having decided that "every man [is] . . . a poet," [60] struggle not only to make poetry but also, as Miller maintains, to make "life a poem." "Art is Living," we read today in an advertisement for *Art in America,* a magazine which draws its doctrine straight out of Thayer's *Dial* and folio, *Living Art.* Said one way or another, Thayer's way or Thoreau's ("My life has been the poem I would have writ"), called dream or consensus or myth, this is the supreme fiction which makes America a "dedication as well as a country," a place where "the literary discipline is pursued" not as a "hobby for amateurs but . . . a special form of psychic structure," Malcolm Bradbury says, "an architecture for the soul." [61]

Although Bradbury caught the spirit of our letters, he missed those unique turns of phrase which the soul selects as its special idiom. For even now, today, as we begin to recover from the national disease, we reformulate the legend of mission and realize that "our national objective must not be an unattainable millennium." America will honor its past, as Senator Fulbright argues,

---

* "The real Beat Generation consists of four seer-prophets-poets: Allen Ginsberg, Jack Kerouac, William Burroughs and myself . . . heralding both dark and light, and making a poetry destined in its time to advance the consciousness of man." During the winter of 1962, in the *New York Herald-Tribune,* Paris, there was a controversy in "Letters from the Mailbag" which provoked this statement of credo from Gregory Corso, "Man of Letters." Another critic who, incidentally, discerns in the Beat school of letters some historic moods of a kind distinct from yet linked to those I have stressed is Ihab Hassan. "The improvised theology of Mailer, the inept prosody of Kerouac, the Jazzy flapdoodle of the San Francisco cellars do not exhaust the meaning of Beat" or its "utopian" ideal. Its "gospel, when it makes itself heard," is a "gospel of wonder and love"; its "hero stands at the end of the line of American 'innocents' who consume their vision in rebellion and are themselves consummated in affliction." Engaged in "a compulsive quest for salvation," they seem to represent an atavism, a "throwback to pieties long honored by the American conscience." *Radical Innocence* (Princeton, 1961), 89, 93, 94.

if it succeeds in establishing a "system of permanent processes for the gradual improvement of the human condition on earth." To-day, the latest revisions of politics are recorded in the old dis-course of prophecy.[62] And as if in translation of Fulbright's thought, Kenneth Rexroth says the historic role of living art is to fashion an "organic community of men," an organic "community of love." [63]

He is exultant thinking that the latest literary generation, hav-ing overcome the influence of Eliot, has restored American speech to American poetry and thereby returned verse itself "to society as a whole." For on "the day that Robert Frost read at the Presi-dential Inauguration," Rexroth introduced Carl Sandburg to a packed house in San Francisco. When Sandburg finished, "the audience rose spontaneously and stood applauding until he left the platform." Members of that audience, celebrating what I have called the sacred rite of secular art, experienced for a second the mystique of organic community. For that "great mass of people" understood "that they were paying tribute to a man who was an essential part, and a better part of American life—of their own lives." It "was a moving ovation." [64]

I think we can assume that neither Frost's reading nor Sand-burg's ovation would have occurred had not Thayer and Watson, in celebration of service to American letters, conferred *The Dial* Award, from 1921 until 1929, on the most daring and durable of our writers: Sherwood Anderson, Eliot, Brooks, Marianne Moore, Cummings, Williams, Pound, and Kenneth Burke. During the time between President Wilson's inauguration and President Kennedy's, it was this journal, its editors and contributors, that transmuted the thought, crystallized the form, and embodied the style of an ideal of culture to which all of us, artists and audiences, now re-spond with instinctive assent. What had begun in 1919 as a *Seven Arts* without politics, in the end, in 1929, had emerged as a form of revelation. Although *The Dial* may offer us an illusion; al-though we may be deluded believing that poets can save us, surely it would be a grave disorder of the spirit—I paraphrase the proph-ecy of Freud—to suppose that we can find anywhere else what they cannot give us.

Notes to Chapters

I. *The National Disease:* EZRA POUND

1. Arthur M. Schlesinger, Jr., "Portrait of America, Warts and All," *The New York Times Book Review,* December 20, 1959, 14.
2. Vladimir Nabokov, *Pnin* (New York, 1957), 84.
3. Alfred Kazin, *On Native Grounds* (New York, 1942), 115.
4. Hamilton Basso, *Mainstream* (New York, 1943), 144.
5. Paul Radin, "Boas and 'The Mind of Primitive Man,'" *Books That Changed Our Minds,* edited by Malcolm Cowley and Bernard Smith (New York, 1938), 129–42.
6. Members of the Eight painted urban subjects with "an enthusiasm and a sense of pioneering which had its literary parallel in the writings of Jack London and Frank Norris, and with whom indeed they are occasionally compared." John I. H. Bauer, *Revolution and Tradition in Modern American Art* (Cambridge, 1958), 15. The comparison is inapt. Their mood is not retrospective but anticipatory; it does not recall the 1890's but foreshadows the time of Resurgence when painters and poets who, as John Macy said, "vibrate with a tremendous sense of life," joined in a revolt against the view that art is "a refuge from life." See Lloyd Morris, *The Young Idea* (New York, 1917), 207.
7. Max Lerner, "Beard's 'Economic Interpretation of the Constitution,'" *Books That Change Our Minds,* edited by Malcolm Cowley and Bernard Smith (New York, 1938), 145–60.
8. H. J. Laski, *The American Democracy* (New York, 1948), 423.
9. Richard Chase, "The Fate of the Avant Garde," *Partisan Review,* XXIV (Summer, 1957), 363–72.
10. Granville Hicks, *John Reed* (New York, 1936), 93.
11. William Phillips, "The Intellectuals' Tradition," *The Partisan Reader,* edited by William Phillips and Philip Rahv (New York, 1946), 491.
12. Eric Goldman, *Rendezvous with Destiny* (New York, 1952), 224.
13. Allen Churchill, *The Improper Bohemians* (New York, 1959), 216.
14. A. Lawrence Lowell, "The Physiology of Politics," *The American Political Science Review,* IV (February, 1910), 1–14. Cf. Robert E. Cushman, "Voting Organic Laws," *Political Science Quarterly,* XXVIII (June, 1913), 207–29; Jesse Macy, "The Scientific Spirit in Politics," *The American Political Science Review,* XI (February, 1917), 4–6.
15. Woodrow Wilson, "The Law and the Facts," *The American Political Science Review,* V (February, 1911), 1–11.
16. Murray Krieger, *The New Apologists for Poetry* (Minnesota, 1956), 198.

17. J. E. Spingarn, *Creative Criticism and Other Essays* (New York, 1931), 3–38. "Criticism at last can free itself of its age-long self-contempt, now that it may realise that aesthetic judgment and artistic creation are instinct with the same vital life." (37) Although I anticipate my own argument, I must insert now some remarks published in *The Dial* twelve years after Spingarn's initial statement of credo. "The arts . . . are as old as life itself, but it is only recently that their real place and function in the life of man have been clearly understood." The "true critic distinguishes clearly between art, religion, morals, and philosophy . . . for the purpose of . . . establishing their essential unity in the life of the spirit." J. E. Spingarn, "Foreword to Tsang-Lang Discourse on Poetry," *The Dial*, LXXIII (September, 1922) 271–73. During the preceding June, *The Freeman* had printed Spingarn's "New Manifesto" which Scofield Thayer chose for special comment—and approval—in the July number of *The Dial:* "The whole essay reasserts the dignity of the creative life." A few weeks later Spingarn wrote a note to the editor saying that he was both amused and amazed by the response to his manifesto: Except for that comment in The Dial, all of the discussion seemed wide of the mark. Letter, Spingarn to Gilbert Seldes, July 24, 1922.

18. Llewellyn Jones, *First Impressions* (New York, 1925), 208.

19. Spingarn, *Creative Criticism*, 142.

20. Herbert Hoover, *The Ordeal of Woodrow Wilson* (New York, 1958), viii.

21. Carl L. Becker, *Beginnings of the American People* (Cambridge, 1915), 199.

22. Carl L. Becker, *The United States: An Experiment in Democracy* (New York, 1920), 1–2, 50. Becker was remarkably well suited to serve as a propagandist for Resurgence because, despite his respect for historic detail, his proper métier was myth. David W. Noble characterizes Becker as a man equipped to "live in a world without permanent values" because he maintained "faith in the possibility of social regeneration." *The Paradox of Progressive Thought* (Minneapolis, 1959), 32, 33.

23. Everett Webber, *Escape to Utopia: The Communal Movement in America* (New York, 1959), 27–28. Flight to utopia includes not only the mystics of our nineteenth century and rationalists in eighteenth-century France and England, but also random groups of Spaniards whose "belief in a universal utopia" made "possible their common action. . . . Some came to the New World to find gold; others to find order; still others to save souls." Eric R. Wolfe, "Conquest of Utopia," *Midway Number 3* (1960), 95–115.

24. *The Intellectuals*, edited by George B. de Huszar (Glencoe, Illinois, 1960), 27, 59.

25. Royal Meeker, "The Promise of American Life," *Political Science Quarterly*, XXV (December, 1910), 688–99. Although in *Vanity Fair* Frank Crowninshield tried to rid the nation of all kinds of stupefaction, nevertheless at the outset he too invoked what I have called the "prophetic imagination." "In March, 1914, he announced *Vanity Fair*'s creed: 'First, to believe in the

progress and promise of American life, and second, to chronicle that progress cheerfully, truthfully, and entertainingly.'" Elizabeth Janeway, "How We Lived Then—or Wanted to," *The New York Times Book Review,* October 30, 1960, 1.

26. *The Letters of Ezra Pound 1907–1941,* edited by D. D. Paige (New York, 1950), 157, 256.

27. Ezra Pound, *Patria Mia* (Chicago, 1950), 64–65. Pound, who imposes heresy, exacts orthodoxy, and invites slander, perplexes us all. Cf. *Florence Ayscough and Amy Lowell,* edited by H. F. McNain (Chicago, 1945), 253. Harry Levin believes that his alienation is especially ironic in that "it started from art-for-art's-sake and culminated in the very grossest propaganda." "Literature and Exile," *The Listener,* LXII (October 15, 1959), 613–17. But in fact it starts and ends with a vision of millennium in which Pound alone is qualified to serve as prophet and poet and priest.

28. Paige (ed.), *The Letters of Ezra Pound,* 257.

29. Ford Madox Ford, *New York Essays* (New York, 1927), 35, 36.

30. Letter, Pound to Marianne Moore, July 25, 1928.

31. Paige (ed.), *The Letters of Ezra Pound,* 244.

32. Harold Loeb, *The Way It Was* (New York, 1959), 123, 81.

33. H. L. Mencken, *Prejudices: First Series* (New York, 1929), 16. Mencken's phrase is flip but apt, cleverer than Mencken himself knew. For it refers to a brand of disorder common among men of his generation, men both noted and unknown, whose idea of mission was at best distorted and at worst mad. Harry Crosby, whom Malcolm Cowley considers the representative figure of that time, is one of these. Less familiar is Edward J. O'Brien, who undertook to promote a revival among laymen of the Franciscan idea. During the later 1920's, O'Brien was to acquire authority as the editor of a volume of best short stories of the year; his judgment was cited whenever little magazines advertised their successes in order to enlarge their subscription lists. But power over lists of subscribers was far more modest than powers announced in 1921 when O'Brien claimed to have seen twice a vision of Christ from which he learned that the world would be redeemed if he led a movement of "holy fools" to Florence, to the place of Savonarola's martyrdom, and there announced a new Franciscan creed. O'Brien's "vast and messianic mission to redeem humanity," says his most sympathetic friend, fizzled in the spring of 1922. John Gould Fletcher, *Life Is My Song* (New York, 1937), 297.

34. Randolph Bourne, *The History of a Literary Radical* (New York, 1920), xi–xii.

II. *Lost, Right and Left:* ALFRED STIEGLITZ

1. Richard P. Adams, "Emerson and the Organic Metaphor," *Interpretations of American Literature,* edited by Charles Feidelson, Jr. and Paul Brodtkorb, Jr. (New York, 1959), 137–52.

2. Raymond Williams, *Culture and Society* (Garden City, 1960), 281.

3. Van Wyck Brooks, *Scenes and Portraits* (New York, 1954), 117.

4. Letter, Mumford to Wasserstrom, June 16, 1959.

5. Edmund Wilson, *The American Earthquake* (Garden City, 1958), 149.

6. Brooks, *Scenes and Portraits,* 114.

7. Van Wyck Brooks, *Days of the Phoenix* (New York, 1957), 75–76.

8. Van Wyck Brooks, *The Dream of Arcadia* (New York, 1958), 45.

9. T. M. Brown, "Greenough, Paine, Emerson and the Organic Aesthetic," *Journal of Aesthetics and Art Criticism,* XIV (March, 1956), 304–17.

10. Williams, *Culture and Society,* 140, 149.

11. Louis P. Simpson, "Federalism and the Crisis of Literary Order," *American Literature,* XXXII (November, 1960), 253–66.

12. Rollo May, "The Significance of Symbols," *Symbolism in Religion and Literature,* edited by Rollo May (New York, 1960), 33.

13. Erich Kahler, "The Nature of the Symbol," *Symbolism in Religion and Literature,* 63.

14. Charles Feidelson, Jr., *Symbolism and American Literature* (Chicago, 1953), 90–91.

15. *The Poems of Edward Taylor,* edited by Donald E. Sanford (New Haven, 1960), li.

16. Sanford, *The Poems of Edward Taylor,* xxxvii.

17. R. W. B. Lewis, *The American Adam* (Chicago, 1955), 23, 186, 188.

18. John Stafford, *The Literary Criticism of "Young America"* (Berkeley, 1952), 17, 19, 126.

19. F. W. Dupee, "The Americanism of Van Wyck Brooks," *The Partisan Reader,* edited by William Phillips and Philip Rahv (New York, 1946), 368–72.

20. *America and Alfred Stieglitz,* edited by Waldo Frank, Lewis Mumford, Dorothy Norman, Paul Rosenfeld, and Harold Rugg (New York, 1934), 4, 43, 186, 220–21, 222, 274. These encomia stem from each man's admiration not only of Stieglitz's doctrine but of his example, too, his courage in setting himself against the drift and power of orthodox taste in America. He provided an "ambience," Mabel Dodge Luhan said, "where the frightened artist dared to be himself." *Movers and Shakers* (New York, 1936), 72. Aside from the volume written in Stieglitz's honor and apart from random comment in one autobiography or another, Stieglitz's effect on modern letters is as yet unnoticed. Neglect is unconscionable indeed, inexplicable too, when we realize that Gorham Munson, thirty-five years ago, noted that an "outstanding feature of the last decade in American letters has been . . . a nationalistic impulse" expressed by "the group that animated *The Seven Arts* and . . . Alfred Stieglitz." *Destinations* (New York, 1928), 116–17. See also Robert Doty, *Photo-Secession: Photography as a Fine Art* (Rochester, 1960); Dorothy Norman, *Alfred Stieglitz* (New York, 1960).

21. Cleveland Rodgers, "Highways and Parkways," *The Studio,* 127 (June 1944), 204–08.

22. Mr. Karolik, an amateur, is an evangel not of art itself but of the American mission; the "old slogan, 'Art for Art's Sake,' is gone forever. The new slogan 'Art for Life's Sake,' is here to stay," he writes in the catalogue. "It is obvious . . . that the fine arts and music are . . . interwoven more and more with the daily life of the people of this nation. I am convinced that . . . we shall have in years to come a much finer type of citizen . . . capable of building the Democracy we all long for." *American Paintings 1815–1865* (Boston, 1956), 7–9.

23. Harriet Monroe, *A Poet's Life* (New York, 1938), 270.

24. Margaret Anderson, *My Thirty Years' War* (New York, 1930), 28, 108.

25. Margaret Anderson, *The Fiery Fountains* (New York, 1951), 124.

26. A few years later, on the occasion of Coady's death, the man who succeeded James Huneker as art critic on *The Sun* and served simultaneously as art critic on *The Dial*, Henry McBride, wrote a notice in obituary and reminiscence. See Rudi Blesh, *Modern Art USA* (New York, 1956), 51, for a description of McBride's role in art criticism. McBride's view of Coady, however, attests the viability of the latter's thought and demonstrates its effect not only on McBride's taste but on *The Dial* as well. "Coady, who died last month in Brooklyn, was a great might-have-been. . . . He at once saw, for Paris had opened his eyes, immense possibilities for art in America, and lavished serious praise upon the distinctively native artists. . . . He catalogued lists of desirable motives for artists that were as lengthy and as impressive as certain similarly intentioned poems of Walt Whitman. But the sluggish public . . . laughed outright at the idea that America could develop an art of its own. Coady died without much recognition from the public. He did not die, however, without vividly impressing his ideas upon a few of his own contemporaries and ideas as potent as his were to have a vitality of their own." "Modern Art," *The Dial*, LXX (March, 1921), 357. McBride brought to *The Dial* the aims and fervor of Robert Coady; Paul Rosenfeld, the music critic, preserved Stieglitz's faith and doctrine; and Scofield Thayer, the editor—as I demonstrate in the third chapter—took his inspiration from Randolph Bourne. *The Dial* came into existence, therefore, not to debate the efficacy but to manifest the power of organic art in America.

27. Brooks, *Days of the Phoenix*, 17, 20, 22.

28. James Oppenheim, "The Story of the *Seven Arts*," *American Mercury*, XX (June, 1930), 156–64.

29. Louis Filler, *Randolph Bourne* (Washington, D.C., 1943), 136.

30. Randolph Bourne, *History of a Literary Radical* (New York, 1920), 288.

31. *The European Caravan: An Anthology of the New Spirit in European Literature*, edited by Samuel Putnam, M. C. Danton, G. Reavy, and J. Bronowski (New York, 1931), 85–86.

32. What Rolland's message represents is not a forlornness of the European mind but a responsiveness, five years late, to the new spirit, to the idiom of prophecy, to the resurgence of organic philosophy in America. "Behind you,

alone, the elemental Voice of a great pioneer, in whose message you may well find an almost legendary omen of your task to come,—your Homer: Walt Whitman." Romain Rolland, "America and the Arts," *The Seven Arts,* I (November, 1916), 47–51.

33. *The Freeman Book* (New York, 1924), 19.

34. Waldo Frank, *Our America* (New York, 1919), 10, 169, 230.

35. Donald Davidson, "The Thankless Muse and Her Fugitive Poets," *The Sewanee Review,* LXVI (Spring, 1958), 201–28.

36. *Paul Rosenfeld Voyager in the Arts,* edited by J. Mellquist and L. Wiese (New York, 1948), 142. Cf. John M. Bradbury, *The Fugitives* (Chapel Hill, 1958), 12.

37. Van Wyck Brooks, *Letters and Leadership* (New York, 1918), 122, 22.

38. *The Letters of Hart Crane 1916–1932,* edited by Brom Weber (New York, 1952), 124, 138. Crane's career—its disasters and triumphs—reproduces as if in parody the style of a whole generation. "The age and I don't seem to be on very intimate speaking terms," in 1927 Edward Sapir wrote to Ruth Benedict. Sapir preferred even a mindless primitivism to "all this nervous excitement of Hart Crane's." *An Anthropologist at Work,* edited by Margaret Mead (Boston, 1959), 185.

39. *Humanism and America,* edited by Norman Foerster (New York, 1930), 233, x, xii, 203, 49.

40. *The Freeman Book,* 355.

41. John Gould Fletcher, "Dewey's Latest Disciple," *The American Review,* III (Summer, 1934), 392–98.

42. Glenway Wescott, *Fear and Trembling* (New York, 1932), 177, 192.

43. T. S. Eliot, *Notes Toward the Definition of Culture* (London, 1948), 119. Eliot's final essay in this volume, "The Unity of European Culture," reflects on the program his *Criterion* had sponsored during its seventeen years of publication. What turns up is *The Dial*'s policy, Bourne's organic trans-nationality, and American myth. "In starting this review, I had the aim of bringing together the best in new thinking . . . from all the countries of Europe." (115) "I tried to establish relations with those literary periodicals abroad" whose aims "corresponded most nearly to my own . . . the Nouvelle Revue Française . . . the Neue Rundschau, the Neue Schweizer Rundschau, the Revista de Occidente . . . Il Convegno. . . . And through such co-operation" Eliot planned to bring "into public view those works of literature which are not only of local, but of European significance." (115–16) Determined to maintain "European intellectual activity at the highest level," (118) *The Criterion* hoped, too, to discover what was the "common element in European culture." (119) "For the health of the culture of Europe two conditions are required: that the culture of each country should be unique, and that the different cultures should recognize their relationship to each other." (119) What enables Europeans to share both a sense of uniqueness and a sense of community, says this self-styled "student of social biology," (122) is a "common patrimony" of which the nations of Europe are chosen

trustees: Christianity. Eliot's ideas are charming, his motives kind, his aims sweet. In point of fact and of history, however, Europeans, like Mazzini, stirred by the example of America and the glamor of its experiment, earlier had fashioned similar programs for a United States of Europe. Eliot offers a chic piety as the binding thing, itself alien to a continent bound together neither by piety nor politics, but only by the pressure, today economic, to survive. Europe is a "pesthouse" full of "humiliated bodies and lost souls." To believe in the spirit of Europe today is "an act of faith," faith not in unity, for "Europe does not lend itself to political unity," but faith in the "need for justice and dignity in the soul of everyone." This alone, we learn from a volume printed in 1945, all "the terror camps in the world will not alter"; this alone is inexpungable among an "old people with old things to look at and a beautiful rhythm to listen to and proud thoughts to think." *New Road*, edited by Fred Marnau (London, 1945), 9–10. "American culture is basically different from all this," Daniel Boorstin observes, because "we started our culture with some semblance of wholeness and homogeneity." *America and the Image of Europe* (New York, 1960), 46.

44. *Proletarian Literature in the United States,* edited by Granville Hicks, Michael Gold, Isidor Schneider, Joseph North, Paul Peters, Alan Culver (New York, 1935), 25.

45. V. F. Calverton, *The Liberation of American Literature* (New York, 1932), 413, 480. Cf. *The Newer Spirit* (New York, 1925), 145. Cf. "American Stuff," *Direction,* I (1938), 1.

46. Letter, Mumford to Wasserstrom, December 4, 1959.

47. Joseph Freeman, *An American Testament* (New York, 1936), 634, 639.

48. Lee Simonson, *The Art of Scenic Design* (New York, 1950), 19.

49. *The Theatre of Robert Edmond Jones,* edited by Ralph Pendleton (Middletown, 1958), 16.

50. Harold Clurman, *Lies Like Truth* (New York, 1958), 250, 253.

III. *Beacon of Light: THE DIAL*

1. Letter, Mumford to Wasserstrom, June 5, 1959.

2. *Saturday Papers,* edited by H. S. Canby, W. R. Benét, Amy Loveman (New York, 1921), 53. I cite this remark in order to illustrate how quickly this metaphor invaded the speech even of the businessmen and faddists of letters. Benét and his wife, Elinor Wylie, "skimmed the surfaces of New York literary Bohemia in Greenwich Village, and found their true level several layers above it: Benét in literary journalism on *The Saturday Review of Literature;* Wylie in the editorial offices of Condé Nast's *Vanity Fair,* a place where smartly dressed young women from Vassar, Smith or Bryn Mawr and young men from Princeton or Yale . . . played at knowing the latest fashions in dress, painting and literature." Horace Gregory, *Amy Lowell* (New York, 1958), 183.

3. Merle Armitage, *George Gershwin: Man and Legend* (New York, 1958), 33. Lamenting Paul Rosenfeld's low opinion of Gershwin's work, Armitage recalls the power Rosenfeld "once exerted in the aesthetic world." Because he "wrote regularly for The Dial, an extraordinary publication with unrivalled influence in the world of art, literature and music," his "misunderstanding" was "so important, and so discouraging." Armitage, *Gershwin,* 109. This question of *The Dial*'s value and power has long been a confusing matter: "I think there is no publication in England that has the artistic and literary importance of *The Dial,*" Burton Rascoe said flatly. *A Bookman's Daybook* (New York, 1929), 7. "From . . . a conservative worshiper of the elder gods it changed overnight to a leader of radical opinion in the arts; and retained its prestige until, after a brilliant career of nine and a half years, its history ended in silence." Harriet Monroe, *A Poet's Life* (New York, 1938), 315. It is Ezra Pound, however, predictably acerb, who summarized the views of those in dissent. Pound admired this or that issue but found the journal as a whole, its policy and its achievement, disappointing. In 1940 Pound dismissed the whole enterprise in three sentences. *"The Dial* might fool the casual observer; but its policy was *not* to get the best work or best writers. It got some. But Thayer aimed at names, wanted European celebrities and spent vast sums getting their left-overs." *The Letters of Ezra Pound,* edited by D. D. Paige (New York, 1950), 346. When Pound was notified of *The Dial*'s demise he wrote a postcard (June 2, 1929) saying, Ladies, it's regrettable that The Dial is to be discontinued and that Miss Moore's mother is ill. Among contributors themselves, only E. E. Cummings, whom Pound calls *The Dial*'s white-haired boy, is wholehearted in his respect for the journal and his affection for its editors: "Through Harvard I met Scofield Thayer; and at Harvard, Sibley Watson— two men who subsequently transformed a dogooding periodical called The Dial into a first rate magazine of the fine arts; and together fought the eternal battle of selfhood against mobism; the immortal battle of beauty against ugliness." *Six Nonlectures* (Cambridge, 1953), 50.

4. Stanley T. Williams, "Carl Van Doren's *A Roving Critic,*" *The Yale Review,* XIII (July, 1924), 823–27. I ought to add that *The Yale Review* selected William Rose Benét to write its review of *The Waste Land.* In this connection, Henri Peyre's recent comment is apt: "Future authors of dissertations will one day stand aghast at the distorted view of American literature at its liveliest (1919–1939) which will emerge from the criticism in our quarterlies during these two decades." Henri Peyre, "American Book-Reviewing," *Daedalus* (Winter, 1963), 141.

5. Harold Loeb, *The Way It Was* (New York, 1959), 155.

6. Percy H. Boynton, *More Contemporary Americans* (Chicago, 1927), 123.

7. At the University of Wisconsin, where Kenneth Fearing arrived in the early 1920's, "undergraduate literary circles were divided between those who read *The Dial* (under Scofield Thayer's editorship) and those who read *The Smart Set;* Fearing read *The Smart Set,* but his best friends . . . read *The*

Dial." Horace Gregory and Marya Zaturenska, *History of American Poetry 1900–1940* (New York, 1946), 464, 317.

8. Alyse Gregory, *The Day Is Gone* (New York, 1948), 178, 179.

9. Llewelyn Powys, *The Verdict of Bridlegoose* (New York, 1926), 164–66.

10. I am grateful to Miss Betty W. Gash, librarian at the Groton school, whose letter of October 16, 1959 says the *Grotonian* for March, 1913 does in fact report a speech by Chapman " 'at the Lenten Service in the Chapel on February 27.' " Miss Gash remarks that she is unable to find either a copy of his talk or a record of his subject on that occasion.

11. To information drawn from informal talk with Dr. Watson, I must add appropriate comment by Kenneth Burke. "As for the good Doctor (J. S. W.): Duns Scotus would say that each of us is *sui generis* (as per the steps from *animalitas* through *humanitas* to *Socratitas*). But certainly the good Doctor is *primus inter pares*. . . . And sometimes, as you suggest, simply *primus."* Letter, Burke to Wasserstrom, October 16, 1959. Simply *primus* hits the mark, as even Margaret Anderson had special reason to know. "At tea time a tall blond man arrived, introduced himself as J. S. Watson of the *Dial,* said he wanted to buy a copy of Eliot's 'Prufrock.' . . . As I put the dollar away I chanced to look at it. It was a hundred-dollar bill. I ran after Mr. Watson to tell him he had made a mistake." Watson said it was no mistake, that he wanted *The Little Review* to have it. "I made him come back and talk. We became friends and so remained during all our attacks on the *Dial* as a de-alcoholized version of *The Little Review.* Watson came several times with his salutary hundred-dollar bill which kept the magazine alive when otherwise it would have succumbed. As Jane [Heap] said, he knew a good magazine when he saw one." *My Thirty Years' War* (New York, 1930), 188–89. Watson did in fact envy *The Little Review* its spirit but his motive in this matter is consistent with his own character (and the character of his journal) which, as Marianne Moore remarks, was Lincolnesque in its desire "to lift 'artificial weights from all shoulders . . . and afford all an unfettered start.' " Marianne Moore, "The Dial (Part 2)," *Life and Letters Today,* XXVIII (January, 1941), 3–9.

12. Letter, Wilson to Wasserstrom, November 4, 1958.

13. Letter, Miss Moore to Wasserstrom, July 12, 1957.

14. Van Wyck Brooks, *Scenes and Portraits* (New York, 1954), 103. Aestheticism nourished passions strong enough to draw together as editors of the *Monthly* both Robert Herrick and Bernard Berenson. See Kenneth S. Lynn, *The Dream of Success* (Boston, 1955), 219.

15. Mary Colum, *Life and the Dream* (Garden City, 1947), 384. "On June 12, J. S. Watson, Jr. . . . sent three hundred more." Richard Ellmann, *James Joyce* (New York, 1959), 471.

16. Margaret Anderson, *My Thirty Years' War* (New York, 1930), 28.

17. Harriet Monroe, *A Poet's Life* (New York, 1938), 314–15.

18. John Chamberlain, *Farewell to Reform* (New York, 1932), 295. These remarks are supposed to have been off the record, addressed to Frank Cobb, editor of the *New York World*.

19. Floyd Dell, *Homecoming* (New York, 1933), 311.

20. Gregory, *The Day Is Gone*, 177.

21. Robert Morss Lovett, *All Our Years* (New York, 1948), 46. Lovett describes how he tried "to make it possible for both John Dewey and Randoph Bourne to remain with the magazine." Bourne's essay " 'The Intellectuals and the War' in *The Seven Arts* had been the death of that brilliant journal in 1917." And in spite of Thayer's support, "Dewey's opposition" caused Johnson not to list Bourne's name among the editors. Lewis Mumford, a member of the board of editors, confirms Lovett's recollection, adds that he was himself surprised to discover in Dewey a particular taste for infighting. See James Oppenheim, "Editorial," *The Seven Arts,* II (August, 1917), 489–92.

22. I rely here on Waldo Frank's chronology of events, related in F. J. Hoffman, C. Allen, C. F. Ulrich, *The Little Magazine* (Princeton, 1946), 92.

23. "Scofield Thayer and his cousin, Dr. J. S. Watson, with Gilbert Seldes, Kenneth Burke, and Marianne Moore successively as assistant editors, made the Dial for several years the most distinguished organ of art and letters that America has produced." Lovett, *All Our Years*, 156. Lovett's memory of events and facts is not entirely accurate—Watson and Thayer were not cousins, and Seldes, Burke, and Miss Moore were not assistant editors—but in general his memory is reliable. Doubtless he did suggest that Thayer buy out Johnson, but it was on Watson's proposal that the two men decided to act. Cf. Charles Norman, *The Magic-Maker* (New York, 1958), 150.

24. Randolph Bourne, "Traps for the Unwary," *The Dial,* LXIV (March 28, 1918), 277–79.

25. W. C. Blum (J. S. Watson), "American Letter," *The Dial,* LXX (April, 1921), 563–68.

26. A. F. Beringause, "The Double Martyrdom of Randolph Bourne," *The Journal of the History of Ideas,* XVIII (October, 1957), 594–603.

27. Randolph Bourne, *The History of a Literary Radical* (New York, 1920), 43. Although it is generally recognized, as Howard Mumford Jones has observed, that "Bourne helped to create a program of ideas" for the pursuits of prophecy in his time, Bourne's role in shaping *The Dial* is either little known or mistaken. *The Bright Medusa* (Illinois, 1952), 94. See M. D. Zabel, *Literary Opinion in America* (New York, 1937), 625, where we are told that *The Seven Arts* "merged with *The Dial*."

28. S. Foster Damon, *Amy Lowell* (Boston and New York, 1935), 519.

IV. *Liberating Dangerous Words:* WILLIAM CARLOS WILLIAMS

1. Alfred Kazin, *On Native Grounds* (New York, 1942), 195.

2. *The Dial,* LXXII (January, 1922), iv.

3. Josephine Herbst, " 'The Dial' and Modern Art," *Arts*, XXX (September, 1959), 27–33.

4. Oliver Larkin, *Art and Life in America* (New York, 1949), 374.

5. Letter, Pound to Marianne Moore, July 27, 1928.

6. *Paul Rosenfeld Voyager in the Arts,* edited by J. Mellquist and L. Wiese (New York, 1948), 93.

7. "Mr Thayer sometime ago . . . tried to secure [Maxim] Gorky in this capacity, but was unsuccessful," Alyse Gregory wrote to Gorky's agent on October 10, 1924.

8. Letter, Smith to Marianne Moore, February 7, 1927.

9. Letter, Ortega to *The Dial,* May 28, 1925.

10. Letter, Von Hofmannsthal to Marianne Moore, April 18, 1928.

11. Letter, Stieglitz to *The Dial,* August 15, 1925. On August 24, 1922, Stieglitz had written to offer his "most enthusiastic congratulations:—the September number of The Dial has arrived. The Color Reproduction of Franz Marc's horses is a beautiful achievement. . . . The whole number looks like a real feast."

12. Letter, Gould to *The Dial,* February 26, 1926. Other stanzas of this kind made the rounds too:

> If your verse is vile
> You might send it to The Dial.
> If your verse is viler still
> Send, oh, send it to The Quill.

Irene and Allen Cleaton, *Books and Battles* (Boston, 1937), 161. *The Dial*'s solemnity invited both sneer and, as in a poem by Hemingway, scurrility:

> They say Ezra is the shit
> But Ezra is nice.
> Come let us build a monument to Ezra.
> Good a very nice monument
>
> . . . .
>
> You have all been successful Children
> Now let us clean the mess up.
> The Dial does a monument to Proust.
> We have done a monument to Ezra.

Called "The Soul of Spain (In the Manner of Gertrude Stein)," it appeared in the autumn number, *Der Querschnitt,* 1924. For this reference I must thank George Ford, former colleague at the University of Rochester.

13. Letter, Cowley to Marianne Moore, April 16, 1926.

14. Miss Moore's opinion, dated March 7, 1925, was given in response to a request from Thayer, transmitted by his assistant: "Since you and Mr Thayer have discussed Hemingway, Mr Thayer thought you might be willing to give your judgement of this manuscript which Mr Thayer and Dr Watson and Miss Gregory disagree upon." Letter, D. E. de Pollier to Marianne Moore, March

6, 1925. (It is incidental but not uninteresting to note that Hemingway's covering letter, January 21, 1925, had congratulated the editor for having chosen Miss Moore to receive *The Dial* Award.) But no one seems to know who started the rumor about *The Dial*'s opinion of Hemingway's verse. "Ezra Pound . . . sent six of Hemingway's poems to Scofield Thayer," Charles Fenton says. *The Apprenticeship of Ernest Hemingway* (New York, 1954), 146.

15. *The Letters of Hart Crane*, edited by Brom Weber (New York, 1952), 124.

16. Letter, Seldes to Williams, November 17, 1922.

17. Letter, George Moore to Marianne Moore, March 1, 1926.

18. Letter, Thayer to Mann, February 13, 1924.

19. Letter, Thayer to Murry, January 24, 1924.

20. Kenneth Burke, *The Grammar of Motives* (New York, 1945), 492.

21. Letter, Wescott to Marianne Moore, August 20, 1926.

22. "A young poet of my acquaintance told me . . . that the only people who knew Kunitz was a poet were poets themselves, and that among them, he and Yvor Winters exerted the strongest 'subterranean influence.'" Ralph J. Mills, Jr., "The Art of Stanley Kunitz," *Chicago Review*, XIV (Summer, 1960), 103–12. Kunitz says that *The Dial* was the first paper to accept his work.

23. R. P. Blackmur, *Anni Mirabiles* (Washington, 1956), 10–13.

24. Letter, Stevens to Marianne Moore, November 19, 1925.

25. Malcolm Cowley, *Exile's Return* (New York, 1951), 79.

26. Their exchange is undated but occurs during October, 1922.

27. These remarks appear in letters written on November 18 and November 16, 1922, the time when Williams sent a string of notes to Seldes.

28. Letter, Williams to Marianne Moore, November 29, 1926.

29. Letter, Williams to Marianne Moore, December 16, 1926.

30. Letter, Williams to Wasserstrom, November 13, 1958.

31. Daniel Catton Rich, "Dial M for Modern," *The Dial and the Dial Collection* (Worcester, 1959), 7–24.

32. Scofield Thayer, "General Instructions for Editorial Department," office memorandum, no date, 3.

33. A. R. Orage, *Readers and Writers* (New York, 1922), 111, 165.

V. *"Living Art"*: T. S. ELIOT

1. Scofield Thayer, "Comment," *The Dial*, LXXIII (December, 1922), 685.

2. Letter, Cummings to Wasserstrom, October 26, 1959.

3. M. H. Abrams, *The Mirror and the Lamp* (New York, 1953), 132–38.

4. Bernard Berenson, *Aesthetics and History* (Garden City, 1953), 150. Reading Brooks' appraisal of Berenson's effect, we come on the very group of terms which inspired a whole generation of utopians to transform the gen-

teel pursuit of art into an aesthetics of salvation: "The art that is life-intensifying, life-expanding, life-enhancing tends to refine, he thought, and perfect us as instruments" honed to shape utopia. Van Wyck Brooks, *The Dream of Arcadia* (New York, 1958), 254.

5. Letter, Marianne Moore to Wasserstrom, October 13, 1959.

6. "The Art of Poetry: T. S. Eliot," *The Paris Review*, XXI (Spring–Summer, 1959), 49–70. "So far, Eliot's poetry has not been directly challenged. But it is being 'placed,' and . . . the placing consists of the discovery that Eliot is an American before he is an English poet." Walter Allen, "The Time and Place of T. S. Eliot," *The New York Times Book Review*, April 9, 1961, 1, 40–41.

7. Conrad Aiken, *Ushant* (New York and Boston, 1952), 276–77. Cf. Joseph Freeman, *An American Testament* (New York, 1936), 209: "In Chelsea . . . I lost some of my romantic notions about the literary life. The secret of literary success sometimes lies in pretending that the ideas of other people are your own. After a conversation which would last till dawn, an author would sometimes say to me: 'Do you mind if I use that idea of yours in my next essay?' . . . Soon I came to realize that there were economic and social reasons for plagiarism."

8. "Ambition drove Eliot . . . the honorable, desperate and irremediable ambition to pursue and cry a conviction, to be a preacher, a Savonarola (his mother's hero), and to change the world." Herbert Howart, "T. S. Eliot's Criterion: The Editor and His Contributors," *Comparative Literature*, XI (Spring, 1959), 97–110.

9. By December, 1922, when Eliot resigned his post as London correspondent, Thayer and Watson had published ten separate items (including "The Possibility of a Poetic Drama," "Ulysses, Order and Myth," and "The Waste Land"), given him *The Dial* Award, printed reviews of his work by Miss Moore, Cummings, and Edmund Wilson, and in space reserved for the editor's own comment, pronounced him the exemplary modern poet and critic. Then during its remaining years, even as Eliot's own *Criterion* enlarged its sphere of interest, *The Dial* printed six additional pieces. Among these is a version of "The Hollow Men" which, so far as I know, has not been studied by a specialist. In *A Reader's Guide to T. S. Eliot,* George Williamson's standard work on problems of analysis and text, this poem is described as the first to illustrate what Williamson calls Eliot's habit of piecemeal composition and publication. Williamson notes that Part III appeared as the third item in another group called "Doris's Dream Songs," and that only Part V was not published separately. But he does not specify another fact: the poem Eliot published in *The Dial* appears without parts IV and V. This draft, which serves as a kind of worksheet for the final poem, swallows lines later reserved for rhetorical effect, makes no reference to the prickly pear, and ends without bang or whimper.

10. Letter, Seldes to Watson, August 31, 1922. The last act in preparation was a special announcement printed on the page usually held for advertise-

ment: "The Editors of The Dial take exceptional pleasure in announcing for
their November issue the publication of . . . The Waste Land by T. S. Eliot.
. . . The Waste Land is a long poem, the first by Mr. Eliot in several years
. . . a work of profound significance . . . its publication an event of capital
importance. It is not improbable that the appearance of The Waste Land will
rank with that of Ulysses in the degree of interest it will call forth."

11. Letter, Seldes to Saintsbury, October 10, 1922.

12. Echoes of the great event continue to return from remote places even
in 1960 when, in Enid Starkie's study of French influences on English writing,
we hear that Eliot, "awarded by *The Dial* . . . their poetry prize for his
Waste Land . . . became the most significant poet in the English language of
his day." *From Gautier to Eliot* (London, 1960), 167. See Lionel Trilling's
description of its effect on him: "Somewhere in my university office is a copy
of *The Dial* for November, 1922. . . . I can remember how I read it—with
some resentment, in a fever of incomprehension, having only the sense that
it was important and very moving, that it was about my own life and the
unhappy epoch that I, as a Columbia College sophomore, was condemned to
live in." *The Columbia University Forum*, II (Fall, 1958), 11.

13. "Eliot's aim in drama is the participation of the whole audience in a
religious ritual." Howart, "T. S. Eliot's Criterion," 105. Today the phrase
Eliot uses to describe verse drama—"applied poetry"—connotes social efficacy
not sacred prophecy. For the prevailing mood of Eliot's drama is now a kind
of nondirective therapy of the social organism. See John Lehmann, "T. S. Eliot
Talks about Himself and the Drive to Create," *The New York Times Book
Review*, November 29, 1953, 5; Gerald Weales, "The Latest Eliot," *The
Kenyon Review*, XXI (Summer, 1959), 473–78.

VI. *The Mark of a Poet:* MARIANNE MOORE

1. Letter, Brooks to Wasserstrom, November 22, 1958. Gilbert Seldes recalls that Thayer's admiration for Freud was exceeded only by his pride in his
own mind. Speculating on the reasons for Thayer's breakdown, Seldes wonders
if his madness were not in some degree a willful but unconscious act designed
to demonstrate the inefficacy of Freud's system. Thayer's old friend Hermann
Riccius holds other views, as do Miss Colum and Miss Gregory. There is, however, some confirmation of Seldes' thought in Thayer's boyhood essay on Mar-
lowe. "As in Aeschylus and Sophocles and Racine, the core of the grandeur
of this tragedy is in the victory of fate over man. . . . Dr. Faustus is given
a mighty soul, not to glorify himself, but rather that his conqueror may add to
itself the strength of his vanquished soul." "Dr. Faustus and Greek Tragedy,"
The Harvard Monthly, LI (December, 1912), 69–77. Like Seldes, an amateur
of the mind is tempted to imagine that Thayer, the Faustian editor, impelled
to achieve the highest grandeur, composed his own tragedy in which Freud,
Thayer's physician, is cast in the role of Fate. Rejecting sanity, Thayer dis-

dained to glorify Freud and instead, with awesome irrationality, preferred madness in order that his "conqueror" might not add to himself the strength of Thayer's "vanquished"—redeemed, sane—soul. I should add that my guesses are drawn from scanty materials but that Seldes was with Thayer in Vienna.

2. *The European Caravan,* edited by S. Putnam, M. C. Danton, G. Reavey, J. Bronowski (New York, 1931), 17.

3. Gorham Munson, "Van Wyck Brooks," *The Dial,* LXXVIII (January, 1925), 28–42.

4. Clive Bell, "Dr Freud on Art," *The Dial,* LXXVIII (April, 1925), 280–84.

5. W. C. Blum, "Improbable Purity," *The Dial,* LXXVIII (April, 1925), 318–23.

6. Glenway Wescott, "Concerning Miss Moore's Observations," *The Dial,* LXXVIII (January, 1925), 1–4.

7. Letter, Miss Moore to Wasserstrom, October 13, 1959. Thayer's "General Instructions" had prescribed a different system of duties: "If Miss Moore so prefers, or if Dr Watson is absent, Miss Moore decides alone."

8. Letter, Watson to Miss Moore, November 11, 1927; letter, Miss Moore to Watson, November 14, 1927.

9. *Selected Poems of Marsden Hartley,* edited by Henry W. Wells (New York, 1945), 107.

10. Gorham Munson, *Destinations* (New York, 1928), 88, 209.

11. Philip Horton, *Hart Crane* (New York, 1937), 115, 228.

12. Letter, Crane to Marianne Moore, November 10, 1925. Because these matters troubled many writers, certain details ought to be mentioned too. Miss Moore was both a severe editor and a loving critic; her letters of rejection and acceptance are often small essays in appreciation or disapproval. Although she admired Crane's verse—indeed, as Crane's good friend Munson remarks, "No markets opened for this prodigy . . . with the exception of The Dial on a few occasions"—she tried in letters of rejection to say why his work sometimes lacked "simplicity and cumulative force." Letter, Miss Moore to Crane, October 13, 1925. Grateful for Miss Moore's interest in his verse, happy for solicitude from persons in high places, Crane wrote to thank her again for her criticism and interest. Letter, Crane to Miss Moore, October 21, 1925.

13. Thereafter Miss Moore took what pleased her, returned without much comment what she disliked, and in the end printed only Crane's best things: "Repose of Rivers," "To Brooklyn Bridge," and "Powhatan's Daughter," which Malcolm Cowley, on October 12, 1927, said "swept me off my feet."

14. Letter, MacLeish to Marianne Moore, October 22, 1925. A year later (February 27, 1926) MacLeish wrote to tell her that *The Criterion* too had taken one of his poems, and that her approval and Eliot's had helped to give him the beginnings of confidence because she and Eliot were the two poets he strove to please, the two critics whose approval he sought.

15. Letter, Yeats to Marianne Moore, April 23, 1926.

16. Scheffaurer, like many contributors, was amazed by her concern for exactitude and clarity, and he wrote saying that almost all her "suggestions are good, and in the nature of improvements, and I gladly accept them and thank you for the great trouble you have taken." September 22, 1926.

17. Letter, Stevens to Alyse Gregory, March 24, 1924.

18. Letter, Hillyer to Marianne Moore, February 19, 1926.

19. Letter, Miss Moore to Hillyer, June 7, 1926.

20. She added that everyone at the magazine felt that Thayer and Watson "could do better than we what we were trying to do." Their effect on the staff, she went on, was to furnish it with "strength of purpose toward straightness, crispness, and usefulness." Marianne Moore, "The Dial (Part 2)," *Life and Letters Today*, XXVIII (January, 1941), 3–9.

21. Letter, Sylvia Beach to Marianne Moore, July 12, 1926.

22. Sylvia Beach, *Shakespeare and Company* (New York, 1959), 170.

23. Letter, Miss Moore to Watson, September 22, 1926.

24. Letter, Miss Moore to Sylvia Beach, September 17, 1926. "You will share our great disappointment I know," she added. "Our Joyce, I suppose, will be more philosophical than either you or we, for an author—at whatever cost—writes what he wishes above all else to write."

25. "A. L. P." was not completed to Joyce's satisfaction until October 27, 1927. It then appeared in a de luxe edition of eight hundred and fifty copies, the Gaige edition, on October 29, 1928. See Fred Higgenson, *Anna Livia Plurabelle: The Making of a Chapter* (Minneapolis, 1959). But this was not the way Joyce had planned to publish a section which cost him twelve hundred hours of work and on which he had been prepared " 'to stake everything.' " Richard Ellmann, *James Joyce* (New York, 1959), 610.

26. Valéry's thought, as is well known, helped to crystallize the method and aims of New Critics everywhere. On September 29, 1927, Julien Monod, writing in Valéry's behalf, told Miss Moore that Valéry was well aware that this review had done much to make his name and works known in the United States.

27. Waldo Frank, *Salvos* (New York, 1924), 14.

28. Letter, Kirstein to Wasserstrom, November 20, 1958.

29. William Carlos Williams, "The Contact Story," *Contact*, I (1958), 75–77.

30. Letters, Burke to Alyse Gregory, November 20 and December 23, 1924.

31. Letter, Stevens to Seldes, February 9, 1922. In response to Seldes' request for autobiography, Stevens (May 5, 1922) said, "I am a lawyer and live in Hartford. But such facts are neither gay nor instructive."

32. Letter, Stevens to Marianne Moore, September 3, 1927.

33. Letter, Miss Moore to Watson, July 18, 1928.

34. Letter, Burke to Marianne Moore, April 26, 1926.

35. "A member of *The Dial* circle since the 1920's, Mr. Burke" has undertaken to "explore human motives in life and literature, and to relate the two."

But "if we feel anything for literature at all we cannot read Mr. Burke without distrust, and, very often, nausea. . . . And yet we cannot help being impressed by the vast, if shapeless and uncoordinated, labours of this mind which, for the past thirty years, has been labouring at what is no less than an attempt to explore and to order the whole of human nature. If only Mr. Burke had never heard of Freud, or better still of literature!" This mishmash of accurate history and muddled opinion appeared in the section called "Literary Criticism," *The Times Literary Supplement*, September 17, 1954, viii–ix. As Thayer chose Miss Moore, so Watson and Miss Moore selected Burke as a guardian of their purposes in *The Dial*. And Burke is not simply exploring motives but is instead, as Blackmur says of I. A. Richards, intent on "saving man by poetry." R. P. Blackmur, "San Giovanni in Venere," *Sewanee Review*, LXVII (Winter, 1959), 618.

36. Miss Moore lives in Brooklyn, on the very street where Whitman "worked as a journeyman carpenter and probably helped build the family house." Malcolm Cowley, "Walt Whitman, Champion of America," *The New York Times Book Review*, February 6, 1955, 1.

37. "Miss Moore was too exceptional a poet to make the ideal editor; and high among her faults was the fact that she was so exceptionally conscientious. Another of her notable faults was that she was quite kind to me." Letter, Burke to Wasserstrom, May 6, 1959.

38. Donald Hall, "Marianne Moore." *The Paris Review*, Number 26 (Summer–Fall, 1961), 41–66.

VII. *Advancing on Chaos:* HENRY MILLER

1. Advertisement, *Broom*, IV (January, 1923).

2. F. O. Matthiessen, "New Standards in American Criticism," *The Yale Review*, XVIII (March, 1929), 603–05.

3. *Hound & Horn*, VII (July–September, 1934), 563–65.

4. Francis Fergusson, "T. S. Eliot and His Impersonal Theory of Art," *American Caravan*, edited by V. W. Brooks, A. Kreymborg, L. Mumford, P. Rosenfeld (New York, 1927), 446–53.

5. Letter, Pound to Marianne Moore, July 25, 1928.

6. Ezra Pound, "Criterionism," *Hound & Horn*, IV (Fall, 1930), 113–16.

7. The age of Marx and Eliot imposed hard times on all prophets of the center. Williams survived by composing his visionary epic, *Paterson;* Zukofsky went underground. And Edmund Wilson established peace between old terminology and new politics by tracing Lenin's course *To the Finland Station.* This book begins in 1725 when "an imaginative genius of remarkable power and scope," Vico in *Scienza Nuova*, conceived "the organic character of human society." It ends in 1940 when Marxism seemed to represent what, in my view, served as the chief ideal of American Resurgence: the desire to establish a society "which will be homogeneous and cooperative . . . directed . . .

by the conscious creative minds of its members." *To the Finland Station* (Garden City, 1953), 3, 484. Unlike Wilson, Paul Rosenfeld was utterly lost when *The Dial* suspended publication. In its place there were "second-rate academic papers and the commentaries of Talmudic Marxists," as Wilson himself remarks, trying to explain why Rosenfeld's career seemed to end in 1929. Thereafter, Rosenfeld remained inflexible, a "being organically moral on whom one could always rely, with a passion for creative art extinguishable only with life." Edmund Wilson, "Paul Rosenfeld: Three Phases," *Paul Rosenfeld Voyager in the Arts,* edited by J. Mellquist and L. Wiese (New York, 1948), 3–19.

8. William Phillips, "The Intellectuals' Tradition," *The Partisan Reader,* edited by W. Phillips and Philip Rahv (New York, 1946), 484–93. The tradition does indeed eddy and flow but seems constantly to draw on a common pool, a reservoir of persons who channel the general fund of ideas. It was Lincoln Kirstein's friend George L. K. Morris—the man whom Kirstein, influenced by Thayer's *Living Art,* persuaded to sit for the sculptor Lachaise, himself the man who had memorialized *The Dial* group in bronzes now held in The Dial Collection—who supported *Partisan* from 1937 until 1943.

9. William Barrett, "The Little Magazine," *Partisan Review,* XIII (September–October, 1946), 478–88.

10. Phillips and Rahv, "In Retrospect," *The Partisan Reader,* 679–88.

11. Leslie A. Fiedler, " '*Partisan Review*'; Phoenix or Dodo," *Perspectives USA 15,* (Spring, 1956), 82–97.

12. Hans Meyerhoff, "An American Odyssey," *Partisan Review,* XXV (Summer, 1958), 443–53.

13. Paul Tillich, "Between Utopianism and Escape from History," *Colgate-Rochester Divinity School Bulletin,* XXXI (May, 1959), 32–40.

14. Douglass Cater, "How to Tell a Democrat from a Republican," *The New York Times Magazine,* September 20, 1959, 37.

15. Allen Drury, *Advise and Consent* (Garden City, 1959), 36, 37. When Mr. Drury's novel appeared in the form of a play, Howard Taubman said: "Analyze the play thoughtfully and it is deficient as human drama, meretricious as a conflict of political ideas and ignobly distorted as a commentary on our times." *The New York Times,* November 27, 1960, Section 2, 1. Alfred Knopf wrote to congratulate Taubman "for the very desirable mayhem which he performed on 'Advise and Consent,' " one of the "most disgusting, pernicious, unpatriotic affairs of our time." His note was one of a batch in which by far the most stunning response is Drury's: "In seventeen years in Washington I have never seen a more savage and shocking attack upon the liberal position," he said of Taubman's review, "than that put forward . . . by this incompetent little man in his ill-conceived, ill-grounded, ill-starred and illogical review of the play 'Advise and Consent.' " *The New York Times,* December 11, 1960, Section 2, 8. My own remarks about Drury's novel were written before this debate appeared in print.

16. "One feels in him above all a sense of old-fashioned American rootedness, an organic relationship with the American past." Arthur M. Schlesinger,

Jr., "From the Golden Days of Boom to the Desperation of Bust," *The New York Times Book Review,* February 9, 1958, 3.

17. Henry Steele Commager, "Brave New World of the Year 2000," *The New York Times Magazine,* November 1, 1959, 24–32.

18. James Morris, "Mr. Kennedy's New Frontiers," *Manchester Guardian Weekly,* March 16, 1961, 3.

19. Christopher Logue and Charles Fox, "Jazz and Poetry," *The Twentieth Century,* XLVVI (August, 1959), 84–94. Logue and Fox have an ally in Dwight Macdonald who believes that the "avant-garde has passed and left no successors." "The two currently most prominent groups, the 'action painters' and the beatnik academy of letters, differ from the old avant-garde in two interesting ways. They are cut off from tradition. . . . And they have had too much publicity too soon." "Masscult and Midcult: II," *Partisan Review,* XXVII (Winter, 1960), 589–631. Macdonald's views are the more remarkable because he alone among current students of ideas and movements recalls Randolph Bourne's vision of a transnational America, Bourne's arguments for a pluralistic not a melting-pot culture. But Macdonald sees no continuity of tradition linking the Beats, hierophants of that form of art which incarnates pluralism—jazz—and the men of Resurgence.

20. Karl Shapiro, "What's the Matter with Poetry?" *The New York Times Book Review,* December 13, 1959, 1, 22.

21. Richard Eberhart, "West Coast Rhythms," *The New York Times Book Review,* September 2, 1956, 7.

22. Lawrence Lipton, *The Holy Barbarians* (New York, 1959), 234–37, 252.

23. Alfred Perlès, *My Friend Henry Miller* (New York, 1956), 214.

24. Letter, Mumford to Wasserstrom, December 4, 1959.

25. Dorothy Norman, "Introductory Note for Double Number VIII–IX," *Twice A Year* (New York, 1942), 11–23.

26. Dorothy Norman, "Introductory Statement," *Twice A Year* (New York, 1946), 11–18.

27. Henry Miller, *The Cosmological Eye* (Norfolk, Connecticut, 1939), 177–78.

28. Henry Miller, *Patchen Man of Anger and Light* (New York, 1946), 12.

29. Albert Camus, "The Human Crisis," *Twice A Year* (New York, 1946), 19–33.

30. Henry Miller, *Remember to Remember* (London, 1952), 32, 17.

31. Henry Miller, "Balzac and His Double," *Twice A Year* (New York, 1940), 247–69.

32. Miller, *Remember to Remember,* 130.

33. Henry Miller, "Stieglitz and Marin," *Twice A Year* (New York, 1942), 146–55. Three years later these remarks were included in *The Air-Conditioned Nightmare.*

34. Carl Zigrosser, "Alfred Stieglitz," *Twice A Year* (New York, 1942), 137–45.

35. Miller, *Remember to Remember,* 129, 141.

36. Roy Harvey Pearce, "Towards an American Epic," *The Hudson Review,* XII (Autumn, 1959), 362–77.

37. James E. Miller, Jr., Karl Shapiro, Bernice Slote, *Start with the Sun* (Lincoln, 1960), 164, 205.

38. Dave Brubeck, "Jazz Perspective," *Perspectives USA 15* (Spring, 1956), 21–29.

39. John A. Kouwenhoven, "What's American about America," *Essays Today 3,* edited by Richard M. Ludwig (New York, 1958), 121–33.

40. Daniel G. Hoffman, "Jazz: The Survival of a Folk Art," *Perspectives USA 15* (Spring, 1956), 29–42.

41. Harold Rosenberg, *The Tradition of the New* (New York, 1959), 23, 28, 31. In 1946 Mark Rothko wrote an "admiring foreword to Still's show, saying that Still belonged to 'the small band of Myth Makers who emerged here during the war.' " This "messianic fervor," says Dore Ashton, was transmitted to "students and disciples in San Francisco from 1946 to 1950." *The New York Times,* November 15, 1959, Section 2, 19.

42. Rose Slivka, "The New Ceramic Presence," *Craft Horizons,* XXI (July–August, 1961), 30–37.

43. Paul Goodman, *Growing Up Absurd* (New York, 1960), 65–66.

44. Herbert Marcuse, "Actuality of Dialectic," *Diogenes 31* (Fall, 1960), 80–88. That Marcuse's theory encompasses the meaning of Miller's career is incontrovertible when we recall, in *The Cosmological Eye,* two sentences which epitomize Miller's subject and style. "The religious leader, like the analyst, awakens men to a consciousness of the Id, the great unknown reservoir and fundament of humanity. In making men conscious of this identity of substratum, this brotherhood below the belt, this lurking humanity so to speak, he sets in motion an oppositional force, divinity." (175) Perhaps even more striking, however, is the identity of Marcuse's thought with that of Scofield Thayer at a time when that savior, prototypical man of Resurgence, was still an undergraduate writing for the *Monthly.* "We are all revolutionists at bottom," Thayer said, "and the more disillusioned we have become, the more ready we are to rebel against the monstrous tyranny of fact." "Shelley: or the Poetic Value of Revolutionary Principles," *The Harvard Monthly,* LVI (April, 1913) 62–67.

45. Miller, *Patchen,* 19.

46. Weston La Barre, *The Peyote Cult* (Hamden, Connecticut, 1959), 42, 8. See also Humphrey Osmond, "That Night in the Tepi," *Twentieth Century,* CLXX (Autumn, 1961), 38–50.

47. Jack Green, "peyote," *The Beats,* edited by Seymour Krim (New York, 1960), 94–107.

48. Lionel Abel, "Not Everyone Is in the Fix," *Partisan Review,* XXVII (Winter, 1960), 131–36. The argot of jazz and of narcotics came together during the 1920's. "A key word like 'hip' . . . derives from the opium smoker's repeatedly lying on the same hip while he balanced his opium-smoking equipment on the other hip, so that he developed a hip callous."

Jive was a "synonym for marijuana as long ago as 1925." Furthermore, there is a "relationship between the effects of a drug and the nature of the jazz played at the time the drug is popular." These observations are taken from an essay by the Director of a clinic established to treat addict-musicians. Charles Winick, "How High the Moon—Jazz and Drugs," *Antioch Review,* XXI (Spring, 1961), 53–68. When we recall, too, William Carlos Williams' lifelong effort to fashion an American idiom, a modern language calculated to unify art and culture, we realize why the jargon of jazz, a language that stems from public and historic as well as private and unconscious experience, may seem to offer poets a proper idiom in which to compose apocalyptic verse.

49. Richard G. Stern, "Hip, Hell and the Navigator," *Western Review,* XXIII (Winter, 1959), 101–09.

50. Norman Mailer, *Advertisements for Myself* (New York, 1959), 23–24.

51. Henry Miller, "Shadowy Monomania," *New Road,* edited by Fred Marnau (London, 1945), 113–45.

52. Kenneth Rexroth, *The Nation,* March 29, 1958, 282–83. Cf. Constantin Brailoiu, "The Case for Collective Musical Creation," *Diogenes 25* (Spring, 1959), 74–83.

53. "They represent mythmaking in process as surely as Hemingway's characters did in their time, Scott Fitzgerald's in theirs." Jerome S. Bruner, "Myth and Identity," *Daedalus,* 88 (Spring, 1958), 348–58.

54. Irving Howe, "The Quest for Peril," *Partisan Review,* XXVII (Winter, 1960), 143–48.

55. Robert Jordan, "Poetry and Philosophy: Two Modes of Revelation," *Sewanee Review,* LXVII (Winter, 1959), 1–27.

56. Wright Morris, "Made in USA," *The American Scholar,* XXIX (Autumn, 1960), 483–94. Whether or not Parker's music justifies the Parker legend there is no doubt that the legend, even among musicians themselves, supports Morris' thought. "A little group of jazzmen clustered around a hilltop grave in Lincoln Cemetery Tuesday. They were there to serenade one of the great alto saxophonists of jazz, Charlie (Bird) Parker. Leading the combo was trumpeter Dizzy Gillespie, another musician who has won a measure of immortality as a jazz innovator. . . . 'I once asked a friend what he wanted to amount to in life,' " Gillespie remarked at graveside. " 'He said he wanted to leave something behind, like ideas, so he would be hard to get rid of— hard to forget. Bird is going to be hard to get rid of.' " "Jazzmen Didn't Have to Play; They Remembered the Bird," *Syracuse Herald-Journal,* October 4, 1961, 28.

57. Simone de Beauvoir, *America Day by Day* (New York, 1953), 328.

58. "Just to add to the general confusion of life, there now are two . . . magazines with the 'Dial' in the title. One is The Dial, a magazine of fiction which is published by the Dial Press. The other is called Poetry Dial [and] . . . claims spiritual kinship with The Dial of the Twenties, when Marianne Moore was editor." Lewis Nichols, "In and Out of Books," *The New York Times Book Review,* February 12, 1961, 8. But Mr. Nichols' comment is mis-

leading, for J. Wm. Myers, editor of *Poetry Dial,* claims that his magazine continues a tradition which begins in 1840, comes to fruition in the 1920's and now, after a time of dormancy, is renewed once more: "POETRY DIAL is a magazine of new verse bearing a distinguished old name—one that from 1840 to the present has been synonymous with works of unique literary significance. It was founded as THE DIAL in New England by Ralph Waldo Emerson and Margaret Fuller but was to reach its poetic summit during the 1920's under the editorship of Marianne Moore. This DIAL published the best in contemporary poetry. Conrad Aiken, Maxwell Bodenheim, Alfred Kreymborg, Marianne Moore, E. E. Cummings, Ezra Pound, T. S. Eliot, Hart Crane, Witter Bynner, William Carlos Williams, W. B. Yeats and Carl Sandburg were among its poets. Both Ezra Pound and T. S. Eliot printed much of their early criticism here, and "The Wasteland" had its first American publication.

"It is in this tradition of 'the father of the American little magazine' that POETRY DIAL continues publishing the work of the new poets. Therefore, the editorial attitude once expressed by Miss Moore shall be our touchstone, 'If a magazine isn't to be simply a waste of good white paper, it ought to print with some regularity, either such work as would otherwise have to wait years for publication, or such as would not be acceptable elsewhere.'" J. Wm. Myers, undated brochure.

59. Shakespeare is the "man of men," Emerson says in *Representative Men,* because he "planted the standard of humanity some furlongs forward into chaos."

60. Helen Hennessy, *"The Dial:* Its Poetry and Poetic Criticism," *The New England Quarterly,* XXXI (March, 1958), 66–87.

61. Malcolm Bradbury, "The American Imagination: Its Strength and Scope," *The London Magazine,* VII (February, 1960), 67–70.

62. E. W. Kenworthy, "Fulbright becomes a National Issue," *The New York Times Magazine,* October 1, 1961, 92.

63. *Lipton,* Holy Barbarians, 7, 295.

64. Kenneth Rexroth, "Bearded Barbarians or Real Bards," *The New York Times Book Review,* February 12, 1961, 1, 44, 45.

Index